ROBERTSON DAVIES, PLAYWRIGHT

Robertson Davies, Playwright

A SEARCH FOR THE SELF ON THE CANADIAN STAGE

Susan Stone-Blackburn

University of British Columbia Press
Vancouver
1985

ROBERTSON DAVIES, PLAYWRIGHT
A Search for the Self on the Canadian Stage

This book has been published with the help of a grant from the
Canadian Federation for the Humanities, using funds provided by the
Social Sciences and Humanities Research Council of Canada, and a
grant from the Endowment Fund of The University of Calgary.

Canadian Cataloguing in Publication Data

Stone-Blackburn, Susan, 1941-
   Robertson Davies, playwright

Includes index.
Bibliography: p. 242
ISBN 0-7748-0211-1

1. Davies, Robertson, 1913-   - Criticism and
interpretation. I. Title.
PS8507.A94Z88 1985   C812'.54   C84-091443-1
PR9199.3.D3Z88 1985

International Standard Book Number 0-7748-0211-1
Printed in Canada

To my parents

CONTENTS

Acknowledgments   ix

1. A Passion for the Theatre   3
2. The One-Act Plays   11
3. Theatre of Wholeness and Canadian Little Theatre: *King Phoenix* 32
4. Cultural Poverty in Modern Canada: *Fortune, My Foe*   51
5. Cultural Poverty in Colonial Canada: *At My Heart's Core*   71
6. A Masque for U.C.C. and *A Jig* for the Crest   92
7. The Magic of Self-Discovery in *Hunting Stuart*   115
8. Jung and Casanova: The Artist in Search of Himself
   in *General Confession*   132
9. A Novel for Broadway: *Leaven of Malice*   153
10. *Punch*, Demonic Humour, and *The Black Art*   172
11. The Politician in Search of Himself in *Question Time*   188
12. The Innermost Heart: Theatre in the Courtroom in *Pontiac*   205
13. Conclusions   221

Notes   229
Bibliographical Note   242
Index   244

ACKNOWLEDGMENTS

I am especially grateful to Robertson Davies for patiently and graciously answering in both interviews and letters my many questions and for permitting me to use a number of his manuscripts. His secretary, Moira Whalon, was also helpful. I benefitted from correspondence with scholars Judith Skelton Grant and Gordon Roper, and I particularly appreciate helpful comments from Judith Skelton Grant, who read the book in manuscript.

For the time they gave to interviews and for the interest they showed in my work, I thank Ronald Bryden, Barbara Chilcott, Donald Davis, Martin Hunter, Leon Major, Herbert Whittaker and Tony Van Bridge. Richard Howard, Headmaster of Upper Canada College, Cindy Murrell, Drama Librarian at The University of Calgary, and Judith Roberts-Moore, Archivist at the Public Archives of Canada, also responded helpfully to my requests for assistance.

I appreciate resources shared and helpful hints contributed by colleagues William Blackburn, Catherine McLay and Charles Steele and assistance from Carol Fullerton. Freda Adams, Joyce Kee, Barbara MacLeod and Betty O'Keeffe contributed their secretarial skills, and for the later stages of the project my son, Blake Stone, introduced me to the joys of word processing.

Much of Chapter 9 appeared in *Canadian Literature*, which published an earlier version, "The Novelist as Dramatist" in No. 86 (Autumn 1980), pp. 71-86.

ROBERTSON DAVIES, PLAYWRIGHT

1

A Passion for the Theatre

ROBERTSON DAVIES has been an actor, a journalist, an educator, and a prolific writer of practically everything from newspaper fillers to award-winning fiction. But throughout his life, whatever his occupation, his passion for the theatre has been manifest. His first appearance on stage came even before he began school; when his formal education ended, his first choice of career was acting; when he turned to journalism, he used his spare time to write and direct plays. His first novel was about amateur theatre, and when his fame as a novelist surpassed his reputation as a playwright, he continued to write plays and hoped that the success of his novels would attract more attention to his plays.

The story of Robertson Davies, playwright, is part of the larger story of the growth of Canadian drama. Of the environment in which Canadian drama had to grow he wrote in the persona of Samuel Marchbanks in 1950 giving advice to an aspiring playwright:

> The first thing you had better acquaint yourself with is the physical conditions of the Canadian theatre. Every great drama, as you know, has been shaped by its playhouse. The Greek drama gained grandeur from its marble outdoor theatres; the Elizabethan drama was given fluidity by the extreme adaptability of the Elizabethan playhouse stage; French classical drama took its formal tone from its exquisite candle-lit theatres. You see what I mean.

Now what is the Canadian playhouse? Nine times out of ten ... it is a school hall, smelling of chalk and kids, and decorated in the Early Concrete style. The stage is a small raised room at one end. And I mean room. If you step into the wings suddenly you will fracture your nose against the wall. There is no place for storing scenery, no place for the actors to dress, and the lighting is designed to warm the stage but not to illuminate it.

Write your plays, then, for such a stage. Do not demand any processions of elephants, or dances by the maidens of the Caliph's harem. Keep away from sunsets and storms at sea. Place as many scenes as you can in cellars and kindred spots. And don't have more than three characters on the stage at one time, or the weakest of them is sure to be nudged into the audience.[1]

Humorists tend to exaggerate, but the description in the second paragraph seems quite straightforward; it is the implications developed in the first and third paragraphs that account for the humour, and a wry sort of humour it is. Not only the characteristics of playhouses but also the capacities of the actors and directors who are available to produce plays and the taste of the people who patronize the theatre can influence what the playwright writes. The Canadian environment for theatre and other arts, if not altogether hostile, not precisely nourishing either, is a subject which concerned Davies greatly, particularly at mid-century. He worked not only to promote favourable conditions for his own plays but to educate the public taste, to improve working conditions and opportunities for artists, and in whatever way he could to improve the Canadian cultural climate. Several of his early plays feature the theme of Canadian cultural poverty, and although he naturally considers his plays his most important contribution to Canadian theatre, he found other ways to promote the cause of theatre in Canada: serving as governor of the Dominion Drama Festival and the Stratford Shakespeare Festival, writing articles about Canadian theatre, providing information and recommendations towards formulating government policy on theatre, teaching theatre students at the University of Toronto.

Davies's playwriting career spans a period of rapid change in Canadian theatre, from the 1940s, when a good amateur production of his play and a prize at the Dominion Drama Festival was the most a playwright could hope for, to the present, when a Canadian play has a fair chance of a lavish professional production. Even conservative academics are ready now to acknowledge that some Canadian plays merit critical acclaim, that Canadian drama has earned a place among Canada's commendable cultural accomplishments. Still, the drama is the youngest and least widely recognized of Canada's literary arts. Writing in his Marchbanks guise at mid-century, Davies spoke wryly of the uphill battle for any Canadian play-wright who hoped to win acclaim, giving his award for Most Tactless Remark to the lady who approached the only Canadian playwright to have a full-length play in the Dominion Drama Festival with the query, "Well, and when are you going to write a novel?"[2] Even such success as it was possible for a Canadian playwright to attain failed to impress the representative Canadian. Davies began his first novel immediately afterward,[3] and many novels and plays later, the tactless lady is as representative of the public in the eighties as she was in the forties — Davies the novelist still wins more acclaim than Davies the playwright. Ironically, now that Canadian play-wrights have won their battle for a place in professional theatre, Davies's plays are rarely among the many Canadian plays receiving professional productions. Most of his creative energy goes into novels now, and most Canadians think of him as a novelist, not as a playwright.

Robertson Davies is a fine playwright. Some of his plays have been very popular. Some of his best have not. The reasons for this and for the fact that a writer who was always devoted to theatre has apparently stopped writing for it are to be found in the interplay between the ideals of the playwright and the theatrical conditions of his time and place. His plays are the children of a sporadically fruitful, not always blissful, union between Robertson Davies and Canadian theatrical conditions. As long as one partner finds ways to accommodate the other without violating anything essential in himself, new plays result. When the two partners find no common ground, the union fails, and no plays are conceived. This book about Davies's plays is in part a study of the way his playwriting has been influenced by the dominant taste of the time and by the conditions under which his plays have been performed. But primarily it is a study of the way that the tastes and concerns of one of Canada's leading writers have been given dramatic expression. His fondness for theatricality as opposed to realism, for mythic flavour and archetypal character, his romanticism, and his irrepressible humour are important factors in the style and tone of his plays. His most prominent themes relate to an ideal of wholeness that prompts him to combat many forms of narrowness and repression in both the individual and the national character.

William Robertson Davies was born 28 August 1913 in Thamesville, a small town in southwestern Ontario. His father, William Rupert Davies, had left his native Wales at fifteen to find work, and he began his journalistic career as a printer's devil for the *Brantford Expositor*. In Brantford, he met and married Florence Sheppard McKay, whose ancestry was Dutch and Scottish. Rob was their third son, and by the time of his birth, his father had worked his way up in the newspaper business to the position of owner and editor of the weekly *Thamesville Herald*. Tyrone Guthrie wrote of

Davies's parents with admiration that "both made an instantaneous impression of quite extraordinary force — forces that must either make or break a sensitive child. That they did not break this child is a great tribute to all parties." In his introduction to Davies's one-act plays, Guthrie reflects that "the grapple, largely but not wholly unconscious, with The Family patently underlies many of the ideas that emerge in these plays — notably it governs the concept of 'Canada,' dear and formidable."[4]

His parents were both great readers and there were many good books around the house.[5] They were also theatre-goers, and they frequently took part in musicals, being "really more singers than actors," Davies recalls. "My mother had stopped by the time I was born, but my father was acting in amateur drama group productions until he was sixty." Young Rob was drawn into the action before he began school, as a member of a children's chorus in the opera *Queen Esther*. Among his earliest memorable experiences was a performance by the Marks family during World War I when he was about four years old. He absorbed his parents' enthusiasm for Shakespeare, and before he could read, he pored over the pictures in the family volume of Shakespeare, which was illustrated with portraits of famous actors in their most celebrated roles.[6] He remembers seeing many plays in Renfrew, north of Ottawa, where the family lived from 1919 until 1926. *The Renfrew Mercury*, which his father owned and edited, was a family business. Davies was writing fillers for it by the age of eleven, and his mother rewrote correspondents' copy and set type.

Davies's education he describes amusingly as his alter-ego, Marchbanks, in "The Double Life of Robertson Davies." He enjoyed reading, and he was always close to the top of his class, though never first as he also enjoyed playing. The family fortune was made in Kingston, where Rupert Davies bought the foundering *British Whig* and combined it with another paper to create the *Whig-Standard*. There, at thirteen or fourteen, young Davies demonstrated his potential as a playwright by dramatizing the scenes from Dickens's *Great Expectations* in which Pip meets Mr. Jaggers and goes to dinner with him for performance by his schoolmates at the Kingston Collegiate Institute.[7] Davies does not think of his school days as particularly remarkable, though students today might be surprised to hear the offhand remark, "We never studied a play of Shakespeare's without reading it all aloud; sometimes we put on parts of it on special occasions." He knew, though, that the school texts were expurgated, and he found formal education in Shakespeare less than inspiring: "The Ontario Department of Education was hard at its impossible task of trying to educate the masses without in any permanent way inflaming their minds."[8]

Success enabled the elder Davies to send his youngest son at fifteen to Upper Canada College in Toronto, where, Marchbanks comments with wicked glee, "he achieved distinction as the stupidest boy in mathematics ever to cross those historic portals .... As he continued to be quite good in his other studies this gave his educational career a lop-sided air, like a cake which has not been well mixed." Lacking matriculation in mathematics, Davies had to attend Queen's University as a special student, for, March-banks sneers (whether at Canadian universities or at Davies's deficiency is not altogether clear), "It was plain that such a donkey could never be awarded a degree by a Canadian university, all of which demanded some proficiency in mathematics of their freshmen." Though he never conquered mathematics, his seven years at U.C.C. and Queen's had other rewards. His interest in music was encouraged and broadened at U.C.C., he was active in school dramatics, chiefly performances of Gilbert and Sullivan and Shakespeare, and in his last year he edited the school paper. At Queen's he pursued his interest in music and journalism and continued his theatrical activities with the Queen's Drama Guild, which was successfully producing comedies but was criticized because so few people could partici-pate. Davies reacted to the problem by directing a production of *Oedipus Rex* in which over 100 people took part. These school years were a time not only of active participation in theatre but of frequent, enthusiastic attendance in both Kingston and Toronto at productions of touring and stock companies. Davies kept a diary in which he often commented on his visits to the theatre. In February 1929 he saw a Hart House production of *Midsummer Night's Dream* directed by Dora Mavor Moore which toured the schools, and in March a Stratford tour brought him *The Merchant of Venice*, *Hamlet*, *The Merry Wives of Windsor*, and *The Taming of the Shrew*. He saw Maurice Colburne's company perform Shaw's *Man and Superman* and *The Apple Cart*. Everything from "such theatrical fossils as John Martin-Harvey's productions of *The Lyons Mail* and *The Corsican Brothers*" to Pirandello and the new drama of Eugene O'Neill was available, and young Davies took it all in.[9]

To complete his formal education, his parents sent him in 1935 to Balliol College in Oxford, which did not have the Canadian prejudice against inept mathematicians and did not balk at awarding him a B.Litt. degree in 1938 for his accomplishments, notably a thesis directed by Nevill Coghill on the boy actors in Shakespeare's theatre. He also worked with Sir Edmund Chambers, Percy Simpson, and the Reverend Roy Ridley, assisting in Ridley's work on the New Temple edition of Shakespeare, and "the gusto which these men brought to their work" liberated Davies from the effects of Ontario pedantry.[10] He was active in the Oxford University Dramatic Society, which produced Shakespeare, engaging professional directors and actresses because women at Oxford were not permitted to act. Davies played Malvolio in *Twelfth Night* and Christopher Sly in *The Taming of the Shrew*, and he was stage-manager for *Macbeth*, directed by Hugh Hunt,[11] for *As you Like It*, and for *Richard II*, which Vivien Leigh acted in and John Gielgud directed. During his last year at Oxford, Davies wrote his first play, *Three Gypsies*, a modern comedy about a love affair set in a Welsh country house.[12] The year after his studies at Oxford were completed, Davies's thesis was published, the first of his many books.[13] The study of the effects of boy actors on the way Shakespeare wrote women's roles and the implications for modern interpretations of the roles is well-researched, thoughtful, and purposeful, and it is enlivened by hints of humour, a quality sadly rare in serious scholarly study.

Davies wanted to act, and after leaving Oxford, he joined a provincial tour of a play about Sir Thomas More, *Traitor's Gate*. He played the Duke of Norfolk,[14] but judged to be lacking in "weight and distinction," he was removed from his role and given the position of assistant stage manager. Marchbanks notes that "he also played the virginals (an inexperienced and feeble-voiced ancestor of the piano) offstage during the sentimental scenes." Looking to better things, he moved on to the prestigious Old Vic Repertory Theatre, where Tyrone Guthrie was resident producer, in December 1938. He was hired as an actor and as a lecturer in the history of the theatre in the Old Vic's school. His acting was confined to small parts, "chiefly," Marchbanks claims, "drunks, idiots, and fathers to the more interesting characters." He played the innkeeper in *She Stoops to Conquer*, Romeo's father in *Romeo and Juliet*,[15] and though his roles were minor, the work could still be demanding: he had five parts in *The Taming of the Shrew*. He understudied major roles such as Dr. Stockman in *Enemy of the People* and Squire Hardcastle in *She Stoops to Conquer*, but the chance to perform such roles never came. Much as he loved acting, Davies was probably not cut out to be a first-rate actor. "It is hard to tell with beginners," Guthrie ventured cautiously, "but I had the impression that he had not outstanding gifts as an actor. Almost anyone can, with practice and enthusiasm, act adequately; but clever and well-educated people rarely find that acting is their medium of expression."[16] Guthrie knew how to make good use of Davies's cleverness and education, however, and he became a literary assistant, working to prepare versions of plays for production: cutting *Romeo and Juliet* to the desired length, giving *Taming of the Shrew* a *commedia dell'arte* style, writing a new prologue for Goldsmith's *The Good-Natured Man*.[17]

The war clamped down on theatre in London, and Davies, rejected for military service, decided to return to Canada. Though his time at the Old Vic had been brief, that year gave him not only some invaluable experience in the theatre and a lifelong friendship with one of the twentieth century's foremost directors, but a wife as well. Brenda Mathews from Melbourne,

Australia, a stage manager at the Old Vic, married Robertson Davies in London on 2 February 1940, "thus," chortles Marchbanks, "giving a crowning touch to his long preoccupation with stage management." Tyrone Guthrie gave the bride away and later became godfather to two of the Davieses' daughters.

After a trip to Wales, the couple sailed for Canada on 1 March. A job hunt in Toronto, which included dashed hopes for a position as *The Globe and Mail* drama critic,[18] ended in November, when B. K. Sandwell, editor of *Saturday Night*, accepted Davies's application to fill the vacancy of book editor. He wrote a weekly column, "The Bookshelf," as well as articles on ballet, opera, theatre, and other subjects. Davies, who had begun a few months earlier to write for the *Peterborough Examiner*, one of the papers his father owned, settled into writing quite naturally once he had had his fling at acting. "I was born a writer the way the son of a chimney sweeper is born to be a chimney sweeper. My father was a writer. Both my brothers wrote things. I had a great uncle who was quite a remarkable writer. I had another great uncle who was a quite eminent medical writer, and writing just ran in the family."[19] In 1942 Davies took on the job of editing the *Peterborough Examiner*, and in 1946 he became publisher as well. Among other things, he wrote the humorous Marchbanks column, selections from which were reprinted in three books, *The Diary of Samuel Marchbanks* (1947), *The Table Talk of Samuel Marchbanks* (1949), and *Samuel Marchbanks' Almanack* (1967). The frustrations and demands of his work as a newspaper editor are clearly reflected in his novel *Leaven of Malice* (1954), which features a small-town newspaper and its editor.

Davies's life in the early forties was filled with his new career and his young family. The Davieses' first daughter, Miranda, was born at the end of 1940, and their second, Jennifer, in 1942. Rosamond completed the family in 1947. During the war years, theatrical activity was minimal. The Dominion Drama Festival, the centre of Canada's vigorous amateur theatre, was discontinued between 1939 and 1947. The British were more concerned with survival than with culture. While the war and his career and his family absorbed him, Davies's love of theatre was temporarily submerged, though it found a kind of expression in his textbook, *Shakespeare for Young Players*, published in 1942. By 1944[20] Davies was writing for the London stage, anticipating the time when the many theatre people who had been caught up in the war effort would be free to turn their energies back to theatre. Despite the demands of his job (for which he was writing 14,000 words per week)[21] and family, he made time in the evenings and on weekends to write two plays, *The King Who Could Not Dream* and *Benoni*, which later became *A Jig for the Gypsy*.

A new era in Davies's life was beginning. For the next decade, he would be deeply involved in Canadian theatre. This decade, from the mid-forties to the mid-fifties, saw the heart of Canadian drama shift from the amateur to the professional stage. The end of the war brought the rebirth of the Dominion Drama Festival, which had encouraged and rewarded the efforts of amateur theatre groups and Canadian playwrights such as Merrill Denison and John Coulter in the thirties. Davies was very much a part of this theatrical activity, both as director of Peterborough Little Theatre productions and as a playwright whose plays were performed by a variety of little theatre groups. He was a governor of the Dominion Drama Festival from 1948 to 1958, a vice-president in 1952 and 1953.[22] Active and proficient as amateur theatre groups were, however, a true theatre enthusiast naturally longed for a professional theatre which featured Canadian work to replace the reigning combination of amateur theatre which performed some Canadian plays and professional theatre which featured plays and players from England and the United States. The decade following the war saw the rise of professional Canadian theatre, in which Davies figured as Governor of the Stratford Shakespeare Festival and as playwright for the Crest Theatre in Toronto. Canadian drama and Robertson Davies, playwright, came of age together.

2

The One-Act Plays

DAVIES'S efforts to get London productions for *The King Who Could Not Dream* and *Benoni* were unsuccessful. *The King Who Could Not Dream*, about Ethelred the Unready, his Queen, and a Caliph who is Ethelred's opposite, the man he might have been, Davies sent to John Gielgud.[1] Gielgud had directed the production of *Richard II* for which Davies had been stage manager at Oxford, and he had liked Davies's *Shakespeare's Boy Actors*. Davies hoped he would be interested in the roles of the King and Caliph, which were intended for one actor, but no production materialized. Tyrone Guthrie, who spent Christmas of 1945 with the Davieses in Peterborough, sent *Benoni* to Dame Sybil Thorndike in London,[2] but again hopes for a prestigious production were disappointed.

Meanwhile, Canadian amateur theatre was infused with post-war vigour. Little theatre groups that had kept going during the war were given new impetus by the resurrection of the Dominion Drama Festival, and new groups were coming to life, among them the Peterborough Little Theatre which Rob and Brenda Davies helped to organize in 1947. Some amateur groups performed Canadian plays occasionally, usually one-acts such as Marjorie Pickthall's *The Woodcarver's Wife*, George A. Palmer's *Madame Vérité at Bath*, A. M. D. Fairbairn's *Ebbtide*, Gwen Pharis Ringwood's *Still Stands the House*, and Merrill Denison's *Brothers in Arms*,[3] and the Dominion Drama Festival showed a desire to foster Canadian drama by offering a prize for the best production of a Canadian play. Davies was writing one-act plays about Canadians, taking about a week to write each during his spare time.[4]

The first of the one-acts was *Hope Deferred*.[5] Davies's imagination was aroused by an account of a production of Molière's *Tartuffe* planned by the Governor of New France, Count Frontenac, but abandoned after the intervention of the bishop. In *Count Frontenac*, William D. Le Sueur told of Frontenac's attempt to bring some of the culture of the French court to his court at Quebec with performances of *Nicomède* and *Mithridate* by officers and ladies during the 1693-94 holiday season. The plays were "wholly unobjectionable" and enthusiastically received, Le Sueur relates.

> Everybody was happy except the clergy, who saw in such mundanities the most serious danger to the spiritual welfare of the community.... *Tartuffe*, although his majesty had listened to it on more than one occasion, and entertained a particular friendship for its author, was to the ecclesiastical world a terror. The bishop had heard a report that it was to be put upon the boards next, and fearing that his mandate alone might not have sufficient effect, he took occasion of a chance meeting with Frontenac to offer him a thousand francs if he would not produce it. Frontenac's friends say that he never had any intention of producing it; but he took the bishop's money all the same, and, it is stated, gave it next day to the hospitals.[6]

Davies made no effort to ensure factual accuracy in his dramatization of the episode. Though the three men of his play are historical, dates and relationships have been altered for the sake of dramatic compression and effect. The bishop in Le Sueur's account was Saint-Vallier, who had succeeded Laval several years before the date when Davies's play is set, 1693. Davies brings Laval into his play to give added weight to the forces which oppose Frontenac. Although Davies's sympathies are with Frontenac, his opponents must have strength to make Frontenac's capitulation dramatically acceptable. Laval had no part in this episode historically, but he is a more familiar figure than Saint-Vallier, and he provides effective contrast in character with Saint-Vallier. Without Laval, Frontenac's opposition would consist solely of a hot-headed, narrow-minded fanatic. Davies's willingness to rewrite history is also evident in his portrayal of Frontenac as a more attractive character than history records. A concise description is offered by Gustave Lanctot in *A History of Canada*: Frontenac was "energetic and imperious to the point of violence, infatuated with his position, unhampered by scruples, very much given to ostentation and endowed with a gift for the written and spoken word."[7] Le Sueur too acknowledges something in Frontenac's character that "clashed with his finer and more distinguished qualities."[8] Davies gives us the man of culture and minimizes or ignores the rest in his characterization. The character of Chimène, the Huron orphan just returned from Paris, where Frontenac sent her to be educated and trained as an actress, is Davies's invention, and a delightful if historically incredible invention she is. Nowhere is Davies's preference for dramatic interest and development of his theme, rather than historical accuracy, more evident than in his portrayal of Chimène. That five years could transform an Indian girl into this educated, sophisticated, and accomplished charmer is incredible, particularly when her outstanding attribute as an actress is supposedly her skill as a speaker of French dialogue. Her values are those of a Parisian sophisticate; there is no trace in her of the Huron, despite Frontenac's amused assertion that her taste for "Corneille in the morning" shows "the gross sensibilities of an Indian."[9] Davies does not attempt to persuade us that Chimène is really possible; she is a delightful concoction dressed in *"a 17th century compromise between Indian dress and Parisian fashion,"* who dances *"a French dancing master's notion of an Indian war dance"* (57).

Chimène adds humour and charm, especially to the opening of the play, she strengthens our impression of Frontenac's devotion to the art of the theatre, she adds her weight to Frontenac's arguments in favour of culture, and she permits the introduction in an historical context of the modern theme of Canada's exportation of its artistic talent. These add up to more than sufficient justification for violating historical probability, though Chimène's declaration of her intention to take her artistic talents to Paris weakens the ending by too obviously introducing a contemporary note: "My own land does not want me: I shall go where I am wanted" (76). Davies thought of his heroine, named for the heroine of *Le Cid*, as "Canada, imbued with a cosmopolitan civilization but retaining all that is vital in her native endowment."[10] *Hope Deferred* is not dramatized history; rather, an historical incident provides the setting and some of the characters for Davies's exploration of a conflict in values which contributed to Canada's cultural poverty and its emotional effect on the champions of art, the losers in the conflict.

The play develops in three stages of increasing emotional intensity. The first introduces Frontenac's struggle "to keep the wilderness at bay" by showing in Chimène to what lengths he has gone to secure for Quebec an actress with professional training. The chagrin of Laval and Saint-Vallier at this revelation introduces the second stage of development, revealing the purpose of their visit: to persuade Frontenac to give up the proposed production of *Tartuffe* "for the sake of the humble people of New France and particularly for the Indians," who will not be able to grasp the subtlety that the piety which is mocked in *Tartuffe* is false piety. This second stage concludes with the bishops' demand for an end to all plays; since they have Frontenac over a political barrel, it is clear that they will have their way. The last part of the play is an exploration of the implications of the bishops' demand. Their plan is that this new land shall be made good first of all, and greatness will follow. Art is of no concern; it will take care of itself in time. The strongest argument against this position is voiced by Chimène: "Goodness without the arts demands a simplicity bordering on the idiotic. A simple man without the arts is a clod, or a saint, or a bigot: saints are very rare: clods and bigots are many. Are you trying to put my country into their hands?" (74). Chimène's question is left unanswered at the end of the play, as is Frontenac's earlier question: "Are you asking me to reduce the intellectual tone of this whole country to what is fit for Indians and shop-keepers?" (70). These questions reflect Davies's concern for the Canada of his own time.

Although *Hope Deferred* is set early in Canada's history, Davies does not allow us to forget that he is questioning the values of mid-twentieth-century Canada as well. Statements such as "we are always twenty years or so behind the old world in our thinking, and I dare say we always will be" (68) and "it will be a thousand years before this country has such a quantity of brains that it can export them without causing a famine at home" (76) point from the past to the present without seeming flagrantly anachronistic. This defeat for the forces of culture suffered early in Canada's history appears to be an ill omen of things to come rather than a temporary loss on the way to victory. Although the closing speeches emphasize "espérance," the "hope" of the title, the emotions displayed are anger and sorrow, reminding us of the proverb from which the play takes it title: "hope deferred maketh the heart sick." Tyrone Guthrie asserts in his introduction to the five one-act plays that "all these plays are comedies,"[11] but *Hope Deferred* does not fit easily into that category. The strength of *Hope Deferred* lies in the emotional struggle between the lovers of piety, one a bigot and the other a saint, and the lovers of art. The sincerity of all is essential to the play, and the pain of the defeat suffered by the lovers of art is in no way mitigated for the sake of a happy ending. The emotional effect is not wholly satisfactory, since the play is comic in tone until the ending, and the defeat of Frontenac and Chimène is a disappointment.

The very dissatisfaction that the play's ending arouses is appropriate to Davies's theme about the unsatisfactory state of Canadian culture. His country's inclination to sacrifice the beautiful to the good or the comforta-ble, to look after religion and trade and leave art to look after itself, is the most prominent theme in his early plays about Canada. The fact that initially he wanted to write for London theatre suggests that the Canadian theatrical scene was not particularly inviting. Once he did decide to write plays for Canadians, he wrote about the very conditions that caused him initially to look away from the Canadian stage. He was writing not just about historical reasons why Canada's cultural life was unsatisfactory, but about conditions which he felt were essentially the same in the twentieth century as in the seventeenth. The aesthetic distance created by the period setting meant that Davies could show clearly that the high priority given to profit and piety was detrimental to New France's cultural development and at the same time he could portray the poignancy of the loss felt by Chimène and Frontenac without making the emotion seem like a grandstand play by members of that Canadian minority to which he belongs, those who value intellectual and cultural pursuits. Writing of *Hope Deferred* in 1980, Davies suggests its relation to his later work in which he clearly values wholeness in life as opposed to restrictive virtue. He observes: "The arts are at odds with official virtue because the arts insist on looking at both sides of life, the good and the bad, in a way that understandably makes the determinedly good feel nervous." [12] Though the arts are not the only means by which Davies's characters learn to look fearlessly at the whole of life, the conviction that one had better do so is apparent in all his writing.

By the spring of 1946, Davies completed *Overlaid*, a second one-act play on the theme of Canada's cultural poverty. Again there is the conflict between different values; Ethel in *Overlaid* is the modern lay equivalent of the bishops in *Hope Deferred* (though she is neither as attractive as Laval nor as repugnant as Saint-Vallier), and Pop is the modern but rural and uneducated proponent of values shared by Frontenac and Chimène. *Overlaid* was Tyrone Guthrie's favourite among Davies's five short plays, [13] and Michael Tait in *The Literary History of Canada* calls it "perhaps the most entertaining short play ever written in this country." [14] Davies says that it "has been performed scores of times ... attaining a popularity that I could not have foreseen." [15] Its success is largely attributable to the characterization of Pop and Ethel, who are depicted with a depth and subtlety remarkable in a one-act comedy.

Ethel seems at first to be just a middle-aged, domineering, no-nonsense housewife, a familiar enough subject for caricature. She bosses, demands, complains. She is self-assertively industrious, *"ironing as though she were punishing the clothes, sprinkling and thumping ill-naturedly"* (83), and her excessively Puritanical notions are indeed a source of laughter. Pop's sage observation, "You're emotionally understimulated," elicits a response of bristling moral indignation: "Listen, Poppa. I've stood a good deal from you, but I won't have that kind of talk .... Emotion and that. Suppose little Jimmy was to hear?" (83-84). From the beginning, however, there are hints which add up to an Ethel who is something more than a comic butt. Her sick headaches and the affection she lavishes on her teenaged son support Pop's contention that she is sorely in need of emotional stimulation. While the conventionally comic Ethel is most in evidence at the beginning of the play and in the middle, when George Bailey is on the scene, the last part of the play exposes the depth of her spiritual poverty, winning our pity as well as Pop's. Ethel's deepest yearning is the more poignant for her earnest effort to keep it hidden and for being entirely in character:

> We ought to have a proper family plot, with a chain fence round it, and a headstone with the family name on it. A headstone! Oh, a big family headstone! We could get that plot surrounding Mother, right on the crest of the hill, and it'd be seen from every place in the cemetery. A headstone! Not a broken pillar, or a draped urn, or anything flashy and cheap, but a great big block of granite — the gray, not the red — smooth-finished on the faces, but rough on the sides and top, and the name on the base, cut deep! Dignified! Quiet! But the best quality — the finest in the cemetery (98).

This speech sums up the emptiness of her life. Death is the ultimate reward for a life of conventional respectability; death is the epitome of quiet dignity. Ethel, who finds any colour or flair in life lacking in respectability, naturally rejects a pillar or an urn as "flashy and cheap," preferring "a great big block of granite" — her self-image — not red, but gray. Ethel at the end of the play is no less the middle-aged, domineering, no-nonsense housewife, though Pop's indulgence inspires reciprocal indulgence from her, but now we feel for her; our laughter is tinged with sympathy, not contempt.

Pop is perhaps even more difficult to make convincing; Ethels are many, but Pops are few. An old man with little formal education who had worked on the farm all his life, his aspirations to culture are surprising and often comic, as when he asserts that Mrs. August Belmont, a New York socialite who is President of the Opera Radio Guild, is "my kind" (83), or when he explains the white work gloves he is wearing while listening to the opera by announcing loftily: "In New York white gloves for the op'ry are *dee rigger*. That's French for you can't get in without 'em" (86). Bailey's uproarious incredulity may be our initial response as well, yet Davies's explanation of Pop's comic excesses is a perfectly reasonable one:

> Pop has need of something that the circumstances of his life have provided in stingy quantity and poor quality. The larger world of imagination, romance and transporting emotions exists for him only as a Saturday afternoon radio programme. The people with whom he lives, and his neighbours, cannot understand what it means to him, and

it takes courage to hold out against their mockery and disapproval. Like many people who have had to defend what is dear to them in the face of incomprehension, Pop has become a little strident, a little self-assertive in his opinions.[16]

The uncomprehending opposition Pop faces is abundantly indicated by Ethel and George Bailey, the only other characters of the play. But Pop's resilience, his persistence and toughness, his ability to outlast and outface the others, are indicated by his buoyancy and his longevity — he has outlived his statistical allotment by ten years and looks good for another ten. His wife was driven to "the bughouse" by the life Pop takes in stride, and Ethel with her sick headaches is a candidate for the same fate. Pop, Davies observes, "is a lover of Life and a conqueror, whereas poor Ethel is wedded to Death and dissolution."[17]

Pop is in earnest about his desire to buy a greater share of life with his $1,200 windfall, but his account of how he would spend the money in New York is exaggerated "*with a full sense of the effect of what he says on Ethel and Bailey*":

> I'd get some stylish clothes, and I'd go into one o' these restrunts, and I'd order vittles you never heard of — better'n the burnt truck Ethel calls food — and I'd get a bottle o' wine — cost a dollar, maybe two — and drink it all, and then I'd mosey along to the Metropolitan Opera House and I'd buy me a seat right down beside the trap-drummer, and there I'd sit an' listen, and holler and hoot and raise hell whenever I liked the music, an' throw bookies to the gals, an' wink at the chorus, and when it was over I'd go to one o' these here nightclubs an' eat some more, an' drink whisky, and watch the gals that take off their clothes — every last dud, kinda slow an' devilish till they're bare-naked — an' maybe I'd give one of 'em fifty bucks for her brazeer — (90).

For once, he has the upper hand, because it is his money they are arguing about. Though part of what he says comes from the heart, his phrasing is calculated to outrage his listeners. He enjoys their scandalized protests. The experience must be sweet, for as the sole defender of the full life against the defenders of the virtuous life, he must have been always at the mercy of that "special kind o' power" (100) that comes from his opponents' belief in their own goodness. This power is again a factor in Pop's decision to turn his money over to Ethel, to grant her wish instead of his own, but his understanding and pity for her wasted life, her "starved an' tormented" soul (91) is at least equal in importance.

While the theme of *Overlaid* is clearly related to that of *Hope Deferred*, and while the conclusions appear similar in the triumph of defenders of piety over the more appealingly depicted defenders of richer life, *Overlaid* is the more complex play. *Hope Deferred* begins with theatre in particular and expands to include the arts in general in an exploration of cultural poverty. *Overlaid* begins with radio opera but expands much further than what is ordinarily considered "culture" or the arts in its exploration of the spiritual poverty of life in rural Canada. Pop yearns for stylish clothes, good food and wine, opera, strippers, and even "high-toned conversation — all the things a man can't get here because everybody's too damn dumb to know they're alive" (91). Pop is insufficiently articulate to generalize his desires, but his creator has no such difficulty: "the larger world of imagination, romance and transporting emotions" is what beckons Pop. The primary function of George Bailey, who comes to announce that Pop is due $1,200 from his life insurance, is to add the weight of numbers to Ethel's viewpoint; he and Ethel represent those who either reject this larger world or fail to recognize its existence. The minority Pop represents is a very small one: "I'm the bohemian set of Smith township, all in one man" (84), he asserts proudly. In *The Table Talk of Samuel Marchbanks*, Davies perceives Ontario, and presumably Canada, as a vast collection of Baileys and Ethels, remarking on the wonder of seeing at a performance of *The Importance of Being Earnest* "those stony, disapproving, thin-lipped faces, eloquent of our bitter winters, our bitter politics, and our bitter religion, melt into unaccustomed merriment."[18] Enrichment of the Puritanically narrow life is Pop's goal — and Davies's.

The conclusion to *Overlaid* is not the unmitigated defeat to the forces of enrichment which is suffered in *Hope Deferred*. Pop no doubt recognizes the truth in Ethel's contention that he does not belong in New York, where he will "just be a lost old man, and everybody will laugh at you and rob you" (94). His concession is voluntary, unlike Frontenac's, made as a gesture of sympathy in the knowledge that he is in fact better off than Ethel. Pop's life-long deprivation is sad, but he is no worse off at the end of the play than at the beginning; he has allowed Ethel to win over him, but he "ain't overlaid for good" (101). The comedy of *Hope Deferred* is lost in the development of its theme, and there is no attempt to develop character fully, but in *Overlaid* the development of theme and of character, the poignancy and the laughter are kept in perfect balance.

Overlaid brought to Davies his first taste of success as a playwright. The Ottawa Drama League, among the country's oldest and best equipped amateur theatre groups, held an annual playwriting competition, and Davies submitted *Overlaid* in 1946. It won in a field of nearly fifty plays, and Charles B. Rittenhouse, the adjudicator, said that it was undoubtedly one of the best plays written in Canada.[19] The Drama League production of *Overlaid* was well received, and it was entered in the Eastern Ontario Drama Festival, the regional "play-offs" for the Dominion Drama Festival held in Kingston early in 1947. Happy with praise of his play, Davies was nevertheless somewhat bewildered to be informed that it was "fit to stand beside the best of E. P. Conkle." Who, he wondered, was Conkle? Rather taken aback when he discovered that Conkle wrote plays especially for Boy Scouts, Davies decided to write an altogether different sort of play for the 1947 competition.[20]

He submitted *Eros at Breakfast* under the pseudonym of "Phelim," convinced that the sophisticates of Ottawa amateur theatre thought that anyone from Peterborough probably had chicken feathers in his hair[21] and recognizing that the style and characters of *Overlaid* did little to counteract that impression. Charles Rittenhouse, adjudicating the playwriting contest for the third time, commented in his report on the increase in both quantity (seventy-six plays) and quality of the submissions, but he had little difficulty in choosing *Eros*, "an extraordinarily clever and original satiric fantasy," for first prize. Davies evidently achieved his goal of establishing himself as a playwright without chicken feathers in his hair, because Rittenhouse found *Eros* "the smartest work for the Canadian stage yet written." Not realizing that they were written by the same playwright, he exulted that "this and last year's winner, the folk comedy, *Overlaid*, should prove that the drama is at last coming of age in Canada." "*Overlaid*," he reflected, "is, perhaps, a more nearly perfect work, since *Eros at Breakfast* loses momentum for a few pages, once in a while favouring a rather academic type of humour, and needs a bit of pruning; but still it is a most sparkling, novel, and exhilarating piece of 'psychosomatic' foolery by a very gifted playwright."[22] The Ottawa Drama League's production of *Eros* won the 1948 Dominion Drama Festival's Sir Barry Jackson Trophy for the best production of a Canadian play, and Davies was awarded the $100 cash prize for the author of the best Canadian play in the Festival. And the following year when the Dominion Drama Festival was invited to present a one-act play at the Edinburgh Festival in Scotland, *Eros* was the play chosen.[23]

Davies is generally reluctant to probe consciously the sources for his work, apparently fearing that the magic which operates to transform the raw material into literature will desert him if he attempts to turn it into science.[24] He is uncharacteristically informative about the origins of *Eros at Breakfast*, however:

I was impressed as a child by a health dialogue the scene of which was laid in a human stomach. Various characters appeared there, of which some were quarrelsome and harmful like Piece of Pie and Slice of Cake, and others were of a noble and uplifting nature like Fresh Vegetables and Wholewheat Bread. The hero and heroine were handsome young Mr. Apple and Miss Glass of Milk. But it was not the message of the play that impressed me; it was the setting. How delightful, I thought, to have a play going on *inside* somebody. And, half consciously, I felt that the author had not made much of his opportunity.[25]

Years later Davies used that intriguing setting in *Eros at Breakfast*, subtitled "A Psychosomatic Interlude." While hardly a health dialogue, it might be regarded as a sort of "mental health dialogue," Davies suggests, "for it is rooted in the idea that intellectual disturbances can bring about painful physical consequences."[26] Thus a young man's first experience of love is presented through characters representing his intelligence (the sensible response), his heart (the sentimental, romantic response), his solar plexus (the instinctive, "gut-level" response), and his liver (the exhilarated response prompted by surging adrenalin). The characters interact with disagreements, doubts, and celebrations as the young man's first love affair develops.

The setting, suggesting "*a superior departmental office*" (3), depicts "one of the departmental bureaux of the soul" of a young man, explains the head of the department in his opening address to the audience. He greets them as "distinguished psychologists," because "human nature is the principal stock-in-trade" of theatre, so every play-goer is necessarily a student of human nature. He offers to show them "something of the human soul at work," asserting that the soul, at least in part, is the result of the working of the bodily organs" (4-5). The conflict between the Intelligence Department and the Departments of Feeling and Intuition, the Solar Plexus, is most effectively developed. It comes to the fore early in an argument between the two over the mother of Mr. P. S. (Psyche Soma, the young man whose internal workings are dramatized):

CHREMES: ... A boring woman.
ARISTOPHONTES: Oh, come. I can't admit that.
CHREMES: Precisely. You fellows in the Intelligence Department can't, or won't, admit that Mr. P. S.'s mother is a bore. But we in the Departments of Feeling and Intuition have known it for years. When Feeling is more accurate in summing up a situation than Intelligence, there is bound to be some uneasiness.
ARISTOPHONTES: *sententiously, as though repeating something he has said for years*: Mr. P. S.'s mother is a Good, Kind, Woman. She would do anything in the world for him. Remember how ill she was

when she bore him. She is completely wrapped up in him —
CRITO [also of the Solar Plexus Department], *languidly*: I wish she
were dead (13).

The quarrel spoils Mr. P. S.'s breakfast; he is reported to be grumbling
about his food and experiencing hints of heartburn. Davies extends this
sketch of a son's feelings for his mother later in Solly Bridgetower's mixed
feelings for his mother in the Salterton novels. In *Eros* it functions primarily
as the groundwork for the larger disagreement between Intellect and
Instinct over romantic love.

The play moves through four basic segments. The first introduces the
Solar Plexus characters Crito and Chremes to explain the central artifice of
the play. The second brings in the Intelligence character Aristophontes and
the conflict between intellect and instinct, as the first effects of Eros are felt
and the dramatic problem is introduced: how should the prospect of love be
dealt with? The third adds the Heart representative Parmeno, develops a
bureaucratic squabble over who runs what, and explores the different
effects love is likely to have on various departments. The fourth adds
Hepatica, the "dash of woman in every proper man" (21), who represents
the "liver and lights." Her brisk and hoydenish enthusiasm for the salutary
effects love is likely to have on the system quicken the pace as the play larks
towards its inevitable conclusion. All but Aristophontes decide in favour of
love for reasons of eroticism, romance, or physical well-being, and finally
the sceptical Intellect is plied with liquor until he concedes, so love conquers all.

The situation presented in *Eros*, a young man's first love affair, is a
universal one, but Davies includes a few specific jibes at Canadians. The
play's central subject, Mr. P. S., is described as having "no doubts about
religion; no doubts about politics — except for the week when he thought
he was a socialist — no tiresome intellectual curiosity of any sort; a
thoroughly solid young Canadian, in fact" (9). And the subject of poetry,
introduced in connection with the young man's efforts at versification,
inspires the observation that "in Canada ... damned little poetry is written
from the Solar Plexus. It is squeezed out painfully by the Intelligence
Department" (10). Davies's characteristic satiric thrusts at Canadian dullness are present even in a play about universal human experience when he
writes for the Canadian stage.

Most of the humour, however, arises from the conflicting viewpoints of
the different "departments" of the personality. Characterization is simple,
largely allegorical in nature. Guthrie complained of the Greek names and
the medical terminology in the play but concluded, "Much that in reading is
sicklied o'er with the pale cast of allegory and the mumbo-jumbo of the

consulting room, would come quickly to life in the hands of actors."[27] Though the Greek names do seem distracting, the "medical terminology" is integral to the basic conception of the play; brain, heart, liver, and solar plexus relate to various elements of the personality, and the role of *soma* is as essential here as that of *psyche*. Costuming, makeup, and style of acting eradicate the confusion which may exist among characters on the printed page. Davies directs that the representative of the heart, for instance, *"is magnificently dressed in a hussar's uniform, with a pelisse, sabretache and every possible redundancy of military grandeur; his whole being speaks of romance; he wears no hat and appears to be dressed for a ball. His hair and short sidewhiskers are perfect; he might be Byron or Pushkin .... When he speaks his manner and voice bear out his impression of romantic grandeur"*(15). Dialogue elaborates the distinctions among characters in even the simplest matters: spring means male conquest to Crito and Chremes of the Solar Plexus, housecleaning to Hepatica of the Liver, romance to Parmeno of the Heart, and university examinations to Aristophontes of the Intelligence. Messages to the Intelligence Department keep the characters (and the audience) informed of external events, such as the letter "Mr. P. S." receives from the object of his affections, so there is just enough development to give a sense of plot to the short play.

Guthrie is surely right in his estimation of the play's liveliness on stage. The skirmishes between characters and the mounting urgency of their need to respond to the call of love give the play life, and its successful depiction of our diverse internal impulses gives it interest. In Davies's hands, the unpromising subject of an undistinguished young man's unremarkable first love becomes a very inventive, lively, and amusing play.

Davies wrote two more one-act plays in 1948, *The Voice of the People* and *At the Gates of the Righteous*.[28] *The Voice of the People* resembles *Overlaid* in its simple modern domestic setting and its unsophisticated characters, though it is set in town, not in the country. *The Voice of the People* however, lacks the depth and poignancy of *Overlaid*; it is the slightest of the one-acts, "intended only to amuse," Davies says.[29] Obviously, the play springs from his experience as editor of the *Peterborough Examiner*. "During that time I read thousands of Letters to the Editor," he remembers. "Quite a lot of them were on the level of Shorty's outburst in *The Voice of the People*."[30] In his 1954 novel, *Leaven of Malice*, Gloster Ridley wades through a day's assortment of letters to the editor, noting among the ten one that is clearly libellous, two that are badly written, three whose writers want to remain anonymous. (One calls himself "Fair Play," as Shorty does in *The Voice of the People*.) Four Ridley regards as inappropriate in content for various reasons. He concludes his labours over the letters wearily: "The voice of the people, no editor is ever permitted to forget, is the voice of God. It was a pity, he reflected, that God's utterances needed such a lot of editorial revision."[31] The play, written earlier, approaches the subject from a different angle, showing the genesis of a libellous, badly written, anonymous, and inappropriate letter and characterizing its writer, Shorty Morton.

Shorty is a loud-mouthed, cocksure barber whose opinions are noteworthy for the frequency and belligerency with which he utters them, rather than for their inherent value. His propensity for criticism is quickly established upon his entrance, when he criticizes in rapid succession his wife, Aggie, Sam North, who is there repairing the stove, the paperboy, children in general, the newspaper, and a public official who allegedly approves of newspapers. Since he appears to be in a good mood, one deduces that indiscriminate criticism is simply a feature of his character, from which his ludicrously ill-informed, belligerent letter to the editor follows naturally.

The play revolves around Shorty and Sam. Shorty's wife and their daughter, Myrtle, function as targets and "straight men" for Shorty, and they fill the time while Shorty writes his letter with mother-and-daughter prattle along standard domestic comedy lines. Sam, however, is more important as a foil to Shorty. Without him, the play might appear to be a rather ill-natured attack on the stupidity of the working man. Davies has never pretended to embrace the mediocrity of "the people." *The Diary of Samuel Marchbanks* contains the observation that the modern enthusiasm for the Common Man "is popular cant; in order to get anywhere or be anything a man must still possess some qualities above the ordinary. But talk about the Common Man gives the yahoo element in the population a mighty conceit of itself, which may or may not be a good thing for democracy which, by the way, was the result of some uncommon thinking by some very uncommon men."[32] Certainly Shorty is the Yahoo element embodying mighty conceit. That Davies is not satirizing any group definable by job or income or small-town habitation, however, is made clear by Shorty's foil, Sam. A repairman, Sam is not Shorty's social or economic superior. Still, he is undeniably superior. He is well informed, displaying interest in world affairs, some acquaintance with Latin, and a thorough knowledge of the Bible (to which Shorty indiscriminately attributes every familiar quotation). He is thoughtful, thorough, and restrained, as admirable as Shorty is ridiculous. He saves Davies from any conceivable charge of bigotry, but his perfect urbanity, contrasted with Shorty's perfect idiocy, contributes to the superficiality of the play.

The Voice of the People works well enough on its own terms, as simple entertainment, up to the climax at which Shorty's letter is read. The dénouement is a disappointment. The successive revelations that Shorty has not read the letter upon which his own letter is meant as a counterattack but is going entirely on hearsay, that the letter did not say what he assumed it did, and that it was not written by the man he is lambasting in his "reply" are precisely what we expect and so not very interesting dramatically. That Sam is the writer is a surprise, but for the purpose of the play it does not really matter who wrote the original letter; the too-pat contrivance of having Sam turn out to be the author undercuts the value of the surprise. The blatant moral tag of Sam's curtain line, "he that answereth a matter before he heareth it, it is folly and shame unto him" (54), is inconsistent with the tone of the rest of the play; its effect is simply to make Sam unbearably supercilious. Though this is a play which undoubtedly does better on the stage than on the page because it is lively and funny, and it has been quite popular, it is the least impressive of the short plays.

Considerably more complex and interesting is *At the Gates of the Righteous*. Quite different from any of the other one-acts, it is the most Shavian in dramatic technique of Davies's plays. The "Canadian Shaw" label is one with which Davies is uncomfortable, though it is often well meant by admirers who are proud to find a Canadian playwright who merits comparison with the greatest English playwright of the twentieth century. It is evident, however, that because of the many facets of G. B. Shaw, the comparison means different things to different people. Epigrammatic wit, self-exploration, didactic fervour, characters who all talk like their creator, "novelistic" drama, dramatic inventiveness, scintillating dialogue, and good sense — each has been at one time or another the meaning of the term "Shavian" as applied to Davies's drama.[33] Like Shaw's, Davies's dialogue is sprightly and polished; like Shaw's, Davies's plays convey humorously the perceptions of a thoughtful man. But Davies objects to being labelled "Shavian" on a number of counts, ranging from modesty to valid critical distinctions. "Not to be drawn toward the limpidity, the elegance and the sprightliness of his dialogue suggests insensitivity in a playwright. But imitation — the conscious desire to write *like* Shaw and produce a reflection of a Shavian play — never occurred to me. So many of my ideas about life are unlike Shaw's, and my conception of human character and the main-springs of human action are so utterly un-Shavian, that this criticism [of imitation] always surprised me."[34] Davies dismisses comparisons between himself and Shaw with the claim that they are based on the assumption that all bearded playwrights are alike, which suggests that such comparisons are excessively superficial. Most important, he wants to avoid being identified with Shaw, the "playwright of ideas," because he sees emotions rather than ideas as the basic stuff of drama.[35]

Nonetheless, this one early play, *At the Gates of the Righteous*, is Shavian in conception, both in the central idea that outlaws are likely to be as morally conventional as anyone's maiden aunt and in the beautifully executed technique of the reversal of audience expectation. Response to this play too is reminiscent of responses to Shaw's early plays, and Davies's explanation, though it contains no reference to Shaw, reinforces the connection. He admits that it "has not often been performed, and when I have seen it on the stage the audience has found it amusing but puzzling. It suggests that roguery flourishes more readily when it co-operates with the law than when it openly defies it and that the youthful notion of revolution as a path to freedom is mistaken. Audiences do not greatly care for inversions of popular opinions, and when they are combined with mockery of our hallowed, pioneer past the mixture may prove disturbing."[36] Certainly Shaw's audiences found his inversions of popular opinions puzzling and his mockery of hallowed institutions disturbing; Davies is in good company.

At the Gates of the Righteous, set in 1860, opens on a cosy domestic scene. Effie is practising "The Maiden's Prayer" on the parlour organ, instructed by Ronnie Fitzalan, who wears clerical garb. Bill Balmer, sitting in an armchair with his feet up, reads *The Globe*, periodically commenting on choice bits and clipping them, while Angus dozes in another armchair. Their conversation is trivial. The apparently innocent situation is left ambiguous for a short time after Jessie and Fingal leap in through the window, because Fingal is more poetic than straightforward. But Fingal's declaration, "You're Bad Bill Balmer" and the shot Angus fires at him immediately afterwards transform the scene like a bolt of lightning and a clap of thunder. Our perception of the characters is abruptly and dramatically altered; at a stroke, the cosy domestic group is revealed as a gang of highwaymen. The rest of the play gradually reveals, however, that our first perception was not inaccurate; this gang is in most ways no worse than the ordinary citizens they appeared to be — or, more to the point, ordinary citizens are no better than these highwaymen. The reversal offers a multitude of comic possibilities, and Davies makes the most of them. To the great disappointment of Fingal, who had hoped to join up with noble-hearted defenders of freedom, the gang's attitudes towards law, trade, medicine, marriage, religion, and motherhood are revealed as the most commonplace conventional moralizing; they think Fingal, quoting Keats and declaiming about fulfillment of the soul and the glory of Power in Action, is simply mad. Effie's speech in defence of the ideal of motherhood is a marvel of comic irony: "The Dear knows I never got along with my Maw, but that was because she was kind of ignorant and lowdown and never properly sympathized with my wish to better myself in the world. But in spite of it all, I honour her, and now that she's gone to her long rest and I'll never hear her voice again I honour her more than ever" (122). Bill's speech on the same subject initiates the next stage of development of the play's theme, as it evokes Ronnie's admiring observation: "You are wasted in the holdup game, Bill; your obvious field is politics'' (123). On the theory that "the best pickings are always inside the law" (125), the gang prepares for a new life of conventional respectability. Ronnie, Bill figures, "can't fail as a high-grade evangelist... a business that makes highway robbery look like nothing at all" (124). Thus a double reversal is accomplished as the gang is again transformed, this time back into what they appeared to be at the opening of the play. Jessie and Fingal are left trussed up to await rescue, with Fingal, who is utterly disgusted by the gang's "maudlin display of self-delusion, hypocrisy, cant and shoddy thinking" (125), chafing at the gang's failure to live up to his romantic ideals.

Davies's mastery of dialogue is particularly evident in this play. The speech of each character is clearly differentiated from that of the others. Angus does not speak and Jessie speaks but little, the timid, "nice" and naive dialogue of the well-brought-up schoolgirl. Fingal's every line expresses his Byronic posture of romantic rebellion. His speech is exaggeratedly, comically poetic and idealistic. Bill Balmer and Effie are uneducated "salt of the earth" types, but while Effie's speech is always simple, Bill is capable of rising to forensic flights, larding his speech with high-flown clichés which contrast amusingly with his own grammar and diction: "Ma, I am rich beyond the dreams of avarice, and I done it all for you" (123). Ronnie's speech is unfailingly cultured and elegant — dandified more than refined. Of the gang members, he is the only one with sufficient intelligence and education to explain to Fingal why he should not be surprised at the sentiments of Balmer's gang: the ancient wisdom of the Bible avows that "the evil bow before the good, and the wicked at the gates of the righteous" (128).

At the Gates of the Righteous is nine-tenths sheer delight, with plot, theme, characterization, and dialogue all contributing neatly to the comedy. Even the death of Angus, adroitly handled as it is, does not detract from the hilarity. Only the conclusion of the play, when the gang has left and the spotlight is on Fingal, is less than successful. Davies wanted to close on the bitter lesson the aspiring revolutionary learns, expressed by Ronnie in the title line and in his observation that rebellions against social codes do not begin in the lower ranks, which are ill equipped for the purpose. Fingal is doubly disillusioned, with the gang and with Jessie, his comrade in the search for Freedom and Destiny, who is reduced by her experience to a whining baby. The curtain line is his response to her complaint, "I'm hungry." "So am I, and sick, too, for I have swallowed a bitter pill this day" (129). The conclusion seems flat; because the comedy of Bad Bill Balmer's gang is so successful, it is impossible to switch the focus effectively to Fingal at the end. Depending too much on a single speech to round out and sum up a play tends to produce weak endings; this seems to be the difficulty with both *At the Gates of the Righteous* and *The Voice of the People*. *Overlaid* concludes more effectively, for Pop's speech, which ends with "I ain't overlaid for good, Ethel, an' that stone'll rest lighter on me than it will on you" (101), is conclusive and thematically appropriate and still entirely characteristic of Pop, and the postures of Pop and Ethel combined with the sounds of Ethel's eggbeater and Pop's whistled operatic air as the curtain falls reinforce the character contrast which is the key to the play. *Hope Deferred* also employs action as well as speech, though the contrast between the hope expressed in words and the despair implied in action may be puzzling. The conclusion to *Eros at Breakfast* is as successful in its way as the one to *Overlaid*; a thoroughly theatrical combination of speeches commenting on the advisability of exposing the audience to such a close-up view of love, postures characterizing the participants' reactions to love, and the business of closing the curtain, bring the play to a close in a style entirely in keeping with what has gone before. Davies admits to the difficulty of concluding a play: "Nothing is ever really ended. You have to chop it off and bring the curtain down somehow. It's a technical difficulty that I've never really been completely happy about."[37] In his one-acts he tries an assortment of solutions to the problem, with varying results.

Variety is evident no matter what aspect of the one-acts is considered. Relationships in theme and style can be found among some of the plays, though neither *Eros* nor *Righteous* is easily grouped with any of the other plays. Attempts to generalize about the five plays meet with no more profound observations than Tyrone Guthrie's statement that they are all comedies (though they range from farce to tragicomedy) and that "in each of them there runs a strong vein of satire," the object of which is "stupidity, dullness, unsophisticated dullness."[38] Davies's inventiveness and range are apparent even at this early stage of his playwriting, even when he restricts himself to writing for Canadian audiences and amateur theatre groups, and even when he is working within the confines of the one-act form. In style, the allegorical fantasy of *Eros* is at the non-representational extreme of theatre. Its setting inside a person's digestive tract, its allegorical characters, and their direct acknowledgments of the audience's presence are all at the farthest remove from realistic drama. At the other end of his stylistic range are *The Voice of the People* and *Overlaid*, which might be considered close to realism. Davies, however, firmly rejects the suggestion that any of his plays are realistic, and even in a "real-life" play like *Overlaid*, comic exaggeration is freely employed. Pop's "get-up," for instance, the battered top hat and white cotton workman's gloves, could hardly be considered realistic dress for even the most enthusiastic and unsophisticated radio opera buff. The style of setting Davies prefers for the play is an indicator of the distance between his conception of theatre and

realism, which he thinks is better suited to film. He describes with enthusiasm the effect created by Peterborough Little Theatre designer Earla
MacVannel who used a backdrop that looked like the country in winter —

> nothingness, and sitting in the middle of it was a little kitchen, about the
> size of a small farm kitchen. It was open to the sky and there was a stove
> on one side and a few chairs and things. It was all painted in a sort of
> cartoon technique, and it gave the impression immediately that you
> were not looking at a reproduction of reality. It was a sort of compres-
> sion, a suggestion. The actors played in a rather high, foreign style too:
> they really let go and talked rhetorically instead of attempting to imitate
> daily speech.[39]

Even in these early plays, Davies shows remarkable facility in comic
characterization; he can create successfully both those characters with one
outstanding comic trait which are most appropriate for satire and those who
are complete enough to be psychologically convincing as well as amusing.
Pop and Ethel belong in the latter category; Bad Bill Balmer is another
candidate, though such a character is almost impossible to create in a
one-act play which splits the focus among several characters. Shorty
Morton is a triumph of satiric characterization, but other characters show
that Davies can sketch in skilfully even a fairly minor character who is
distinctive and memorable: Laval, the wise and humane bishop of *Hope
Deferred*, is one example; the vivacious Hepatica in *Eros* is another.

A skill that is obviously related to success in comic characterization and
that Davies evidently possessed from the start of his playwriting is the
ability to write dialogue that is both amusing and true to character. The
economy necessary for effective stage dialogue dictates some refinement of
practically all natural speech, but beyond that, the diction and rhythm of
his characters' speeches seem appropriate to the character who speaks and
are yet contrived to maximize comic effect. In one instance, a single speech
carries the entire burden of characterizing someone who never appears on
stage; it is the letter from the object of his affections that "Mr. P. S." reads
in *Eros*:

> Dear John: How sweet of you to send me that sweet poem. I read it
> twice and thought it was simply sweet. No one ever wrote a poem to me
> before and I don't know what to think. I certainly never thought I was
> the kind of girl to inspire a poem, but you can never tell, as they say. Of
> course you may see me again, you silly boy. Why not? After the ball
> and the poem, I mean. Could you come around on Friday night, and
> we might go to the Dog Show. I love Airedales. Love. Thora (27-28).

From this it is clear that Thora is an open, unaffected, warm girl who lacks the wiles of sophistication, the subtlety of cleverness, and the elegance of cultivation. Repetitions of "sweet" and "love" contribute most to the humour, which comes from the simultaneous recognition that this girl is quite unremarkable and that she can nonetheless excite in "Mr. P. S." quite remarkable inner tumult. One other example of a short speech that works effectively in difficult circumstances is the "funeral speech" which Bad Bill Balmer pronounces over the corpse of Angus in *Righteous*: "Angus, you were a mean old bobcat while you were alive, but you were always loyal to the gang. As your heirs, in a manner of speaking — for we're dividing your share three ways — we say Thanks and Good Luck" (126-27). It characterizes Angus, who has not spoken but only grunted before his death, it is in character for Balmer, who displays both the pragmatism and the sentiment of a politician, and it is part of Davies's solution to the problem of carrying the play through an onstage death without loss of comic tone.

These short plays already show much of the skill and variety in style, dialogue, and character that are to be found in Davies's later work. His characteristic themes are here too, at least in embryo, and the variety of his approaches to expressing these themes is evident. A predilection for exploring the same theme in pairs of plays, one historical and one contemporary, is manifested first in *Hope Deferred* and *Overlaid*. The historical setting offers a new perspective on a problem which the audience will recognize as a contemporary one; it underlines the importance of the contemporary problem by showing that it has persisted through time and that changed circumstances do not seem to alter the essential effects of the dramatized attitudes towards art. The contemporary play depends for its effect more completely on the creation of characters who are recognizable and understandable and who feel their problems deeply enough for the audience to experience emotionally, not just intellectually, the force of the conflict between the opposing forces. This pairing of historical and contemporary plays on similar themes occurs again in *Fortune, My Foe* and *At My Heart's Core*, in *Hunting Stuart* and *General Confession*, and in *Question Time* and *Pontiac and the Green Man*.

The two themes most readily apparent in Davies's work are prominent already in these plays of the forties. Canada's need for culture, food for the spirit beyond what is provided by material well-being and moral satisfaction, is the subject of *Hope Deferred*. *Overlaid* is on the same theme, but it focuses on individuals who are deprived of food for the spirit instead of on historical leaders of a nation who are concerned with the needs of a nation, so *Overlaid* is about people anywhere, not just Canadians. If cultural deprivation is the most evident theme of Davies's early work, the dominant theme of his later work is Jungian: the need for acceptance by the individual of the totality of his personality. *Eros at Breakfast* certainly manifests this interest, and the resolute subjection of the intellect to other elements of the personality in that play suggests the source of Davies's fascination with the Jungian theme: his own sense of the importance of emotion and intuition in a rational age which tends to stake everything on intellect. "I really am not a very good thinker," he claims. "In Jungian terms I am a feeling person with strong intuition."[40] In the play's central conflict between emotion and intelligence, he stacks the deck in favour of emotion. The scene is set in the Department of the Solar Plexus, and that department is the only one represented by two characters. Though the spokesman for Intellect has a great deal to say, he is ultimately overpowered by the others, for in this situation physical and sentimental inclinations support the instinctual. *The Voice of the People* might be related to this theme in that it demonstrates the inadequacy of a personality which shows no evidence of intellect whatever, but the superficiality of the play suggests that this is too obvious to Davies to produce much thematic interest.

The two themes, the cultural and the Jungian, are in fact aspects of the same concern: a need for balance and wholeness on both the national and the individual levels. A third theme, rebellion, links the first two in Davies's work, and it is introduced first in *At the Gates of the Righteous*. The connection is not particularly clear until it is explored in *At My Heart's Core*. In *Righteous*, the point is made that the lower ranks are not well equipped to incite social rebellion. The implication might be that the upper ranks are, but Fingal's penultimate line, 'Is there no real revolt but in the mind?'' (129), hints at the idea that Davies was to develop fully later: the only really effective revolution occurs within the individual, at the "heart's core." Perhaps he meant that the inner revolution was more likely to occur among the privileged, who are most likely to be exposed to the best of human culture. *Righteous* touches briefly as well on the theme of Canada's cultural poverty with Balmer's conviction that he and Effie can go straight and contribute to society with "Science and Art: just what the country needs" (108). The irony is that their conception of science and art is represented by Bill's fascination with phrenology and Effie's laboured rendition of "The Maiden's Prayer" on the parlour organ. Ronnie, whose ambition to become a curate ended when he was caught with his hand in a mission fund, will contribute religion to fulfil the needs of Canadians as "a high-grade evangelist." The subjects of what is needed to enrich Canadian society and of rebellion against the narrowness of the Puritanical social code are both treated in *Righteous*, but only negatively; the comedy exposes the inadequacy of the characters' conceptions of enrichment and rebellion.

Davies's one-act plays are significant indicators of both the strictures on and the possibilities for Canadian drama in the mid-forties. They also reveal the fundamental interests and dramatic capabilities of a man who was to become one of twentieth-century Canada's most important writers. The plays were written for Canadian little theatres, so they are designed for productions limited by low budgets and lack of professional expertise. They also reveal Davies's assumption that a play written for Canadians needs "Canadian content," though the amount varies considerably.

All five of the plays were performed by little theatre groups, and some of them were done by many different groups. *Eros* won all the acclaim it was possible for a Canadian one-act play to win at the time, and *Overlaid* has achieved lasting recognition as a minor masterpiece in literary and theatrical circles, so although the conditions for Canadian drama in the forties may not have been especially hospitable, a determined and talented playwright did not find them inimical to creativity. Within the boundaries of what was likely to find a place on the Canadian stage, Davies was able to introduce subjects that he found compelling and would continue to explore in both novels and plays. Characteristic style is already in evidence; his satiric vein is apparent in all the plays, and his romantic side, prominent in *Hope Deferred*, is detectable in all except *The Voice of the People*. Davies may have felt the pinch of restrictive conditions on his creativity, but his interests and abilities found expression, and, especially in *Overlaid*, what it seemed advisable to write and what it seemed desirable to write merged very successfully.

3

Theatre of Wholeness and Canadian Little Theatre: *King Phoenix*

AS A WRITER of one-act plays for the Canadian stage, Davies was unquestionably a success. Little theatre groups who met at regional and national drama festivals saw the Ottawa Drama League productions of *Overlaid* and *Eros at Breakfast* and were eager to mount their own productions, particularly of *Overlaid*, which is relatively simple to stage. But Davies could not reach his full potential as a playwright with one-act plays. They afforded an opportunity for the satirist to express himself, but the romantic side of Davies needed more room. A one-act play is necessarily limited in scope: characters must be few and plot simple, for there is no opportunity to develop them extensively. Themes must lend themselves to expression without much elaboration, and technical requirements cannot be complicated, for often people who choose to perform a one-act play rather than a full-length one do so because their time and facilities are limited. In a full-length play, however, Davies could give full rein to his taste for myth and romance, for grand themes and bold theatrical effects. The one-act play is not really his medium, because it is not large enough to accommodate his conception of ideal theatre. "I try to create a theatre of wholeness," he says.[1] The statement is simple, but its implications are extensive. He speaks of the theatre as a temple, illuminating his perception of its function:

The theatre began, after all, as a temple; it was a place where people expected to experience the full range of human emotion; sometimes the outcome was joyous, and sometimes it was the revelation of what was godlike in man, who provoked feelings of the highest solemnity. Unfortunately, for several hundred years we have associated temples only with what is *good*, and we have narrowed our ideas of what is good to a meagre range of emotions. But the true theatre, the great theatre, is a temple not of goodness, but of *wholeness*, of the complete scope of human action and aspiration.[2]

Davies's perception of true theatre affects his choice of subject and the style of production he envisions for his plays, as well as connecting his love of theatre with the emphasis on the human need for wholeness that pervades all his work. Evoking the total range of human emotion means pulling out all the stops: Davies does not subscribe to the realistic understatement that has dominated twentieth-century drama, and he thinks in terms of a complete range of theatrical techniques, not simply the spoken word, for conveying emotion. His theatre is the equivalent of a full orchestra, not a string quartet. In "The Double Life of Robertson Davies" he acknowledges a fondness for period plays and elaborate settings.[3] He is impatient with those who profess an appreciation for "drama" but dislike "theatre," distinguishing between the terms by explaining that "very roughly, the drama may be called that part of theatrical art which lends itself most readily to intellectual discussion; what is left is theatre....Drama is immensely durable...theatre is magical and evanescent."[4] His emphasis on emotional appeal, rather than purely intellectual appeal, is consistent with his desire to be a playwright of the theatre, not solely a writer of books in dramatic form. He has gone so far as to say that his plays are "primarily for the exhibition of the art of acting"[5] in his desire to escape the label "playwright of ideas"; at any rate, he writes with an awareness of the actor's capability for conveying easily with a look or a gesture what might be cumbersome to put into speech.[6] In fact, according to his definition, "first-rate theatre" is not even dependent on an excellent play — for a playwright, he is remarkably modest about the part a script plays in the creation of theatrical art, but then, he is also a director. In his 1951 study for the Massey Commission on the state of theatre in Canada, he included in his description of first-rate theatre

a classic thoroughly understood and finely presented, a display of virtuoso acting in a play of modest merit, a fine piece of ensemble work in a play of Chekhov or Ibsen, a farce played with skill and gusto — any of these may, in its degree, provide that special pleasure, that sense of exhilaration and fulfillment which first-rate theatre can give....The theatre is a vigorous, living, and in a certain sense, a coarse art.... There are many kinds of excellence in the theatre, but all are recognizable by the completeness of the special effect which they produce upon the audience, and by the unmistakable deep satisfaction which they give.[7]

Davies likes to bring all the resources of the theatre into play to achieve that completeness and produce that satisfaction.

The implications of his desire to produce the appropriate effect on audiences pervade Davies's writing about theatre. A speech to architects asks — humorously — for better theatre design:

Give us colour, give us Muses, give us Joy! Oh, I know how much trouble you take to get the right seats, but you are caressing us at the wrong end. The *spirit* also demands its satisfactions, and man cannot live by foam rubber alone. Give us a whisper of grandeur, of excitement. Without it the theatre perishes.[8]

The playwright has little or no control over many of the ingredients of the total effect experienced by the audience at one of his plays. The design of the theatre is obviously one of these ingredients. The style of production is another, but it can at least be suggested by the playwright. Writing in 1953 of the triumphant beginnings of the Stratford Shakespeare Festival, Davies admired the ritualistic character of Tyrone Guthrie's productions, defining ritual as "conventions of gesture, movement and dance performed within a prescribed area in order to evoke the essence of something much greater than themselves." He expands on the advantage of this style of performance: "Ritual is man's way of evoking what is too great for realistic portrayal; ritual in these productions brings us to a high sense of the wonder, the beauty, the horror, the tenderness, the merriment and the overwhelming complexity and glory of life — in fact, it brings us to what is truly romance."[9] Guthrie's Shakespeare is one example of theatre that Davies admires; another is nineteenth-century melodrama. The powerful impression made on the young Davies by John Martin-Harvey's performances of nineteenth-century melodramas has been frequently acknowledged by Davies, who adamantly defends the worth of this theatre of archetypal emotion against the prevailing tendency to disparage it.[10]

Though he acknowledges other kinds of great theatre, recognizing that plays of Ibsen, Chekhov, Pirandello, and Shaw require another style of performance, Davies's own taste is for ritual and romance; he has never envisioned a realistic style of production for his plays. "None of my plays are realistic," he insists. "They're abstractions from life; they're not intended to be literal representations of daily life."[11] He is often dissatisfied with amateur performances, because amateurs "make a fetish of restraint when what they need is to cut loose." "The best actors of today have adopted a more robust style, and have left understatement to the movies, the radio and the amateurs," he observed in his 1951 report to the Massey Commission.[12] His preface to the 1950 edition of *At My Heart's Core* tactfully pleads for the style of performance he prefers. "The play ... is intended to be acted with some measure of the flourish and clarity of style which we are told distinguished the acting of 120 years ago, at its best. The play is not 'naturalistic' in the sense that it is a photographic reproduction of contemporary life, and a judicious dash of exaggeration is required for its successful performance."[13] Heightened effects, style, "flourish" in scene design, in actors' speech and movement are what he asks others to contribute to productions of his plays; heightened effects, style, "flourish" are what he attempts to contribute himself in the dialogue and action of his plays. He prefers "Total Theatre," which he thinks of simply as "Real Theatre":[14] singing and dancing as well as speech, freedom to stage whatever seems desirable, unbound by the shackles of realism.

In both function and style, Davies relates theatre more closely to dreams than to waking reality; not verisimilitude but psychological truth is the proper goal of theatre. In *A Voice from the Attic* he explains: "Theater is not realistic in a vulgar, wide-awake fashion: it is realistic as dreams are realistic; it deals in hidden dreads, and it satisfies hidden, primal wishes."[15] It reflects "not external realities, but rather those inner desires which... realism snubs and thwarts."[16] The appeal of the theatre is primal, he believes; "the more it partakes of primal quality in feeling, the more effective it is as theatrical art....The theatre is a house of dreams, in which audiences gather to share a dream that is presented to them by a group of artists who are particularly skilled in bodying forth dreams."[17] The effect of the dream is heightened because it is a shared experience. Hilarity is greater, tenderness more poignant, awe more profound when they are reinforced by the same feelings in others. Davies's assertion, when asked whether one of his characters speaks for him, that all the characters are part of the writer is related to the idea that the people of a dream are all projections of parts of the dreamer's personality. "Everything that is said in the play is being said by the playwright, being said from a different part of his nature....If he isn't particularly sympathetic to some characters, it doesn't mean he has condemned a particular kind of mankind, but only that there are elements in himself which he doesn't particularly sympathize with or trust. Like in a dream...."[18]

If the function of theatre as Davies perceives it is to permit people to experience fully their own humanity, and if the style in which he prefers to do this is that of the dream, more vivid than everyday reality, it is easy to understand his choice of material for his early full-length plays.[19] "What we expect to find in a dream, of course, are dream-figures and archetypal involvements";[20] the plays are in the nature of myth or fairy-tale, which Davies recognizes as "the distilled truth about what we call 'real life.'"[21] *The King Who Could Not Dream* (1944) and *King Phoenix* (1946-47) are set long ago, far away; they present kings and queens and magic. *Benoni* (1944-45) substitutes a gypsy and a conjurer for the kings and queens and uses the modern but romantic setting of the north Wales countryside. The romance, the primal mystery, the myth and ritual that Davies loves in theatre are much in evidence in these plays. *The King Who Could Not Dream* Davies describes as a play about two kings — Ethelred the Unready and Haroun al Raschid. "Ethelred's Queen sets off with her son (Edward the Confessor to be) on a pilgrimage to Jerusalem, to be present at the Second Coming, scheduled for the year 1000; she falls into the hands of pirates (as so many of those hopeful pilgrims did) and ends up in the court of the caliph; he is the precise opposite of her husband — decisive and masterful; she falls in love with him, but returns to England, and finds that Ethelred is what his circumstances have made him."[22] The play has never been performed or published; Davies seems to want it forgotten, having decided that "the play isn't good enough."[23] But though there seemed little likelihood of production for *The King Who Could Not Dream* or *Benoni*, and one-act plays about Canada were obviously more practical for a beginning playwright, Davies soon turned again to a full-length play of myth and romance: *King Phoenix*.

In his note to the published play, Davies says that *King Phoenix* was inspired by reading the twelfth-century account of King Cole by Geoffrey of Monmouth in *The History of the Kings of Britain*, which made him wonder why Cole "had come down through the ages as 'a merry old soul'."[24] He might well wonder; Geoffrey's account tells only that Cole took the crown after starting a rebellion against the reigning king and killing him in battle, then submitted peacefully to pay tribute to Rome because he feared to meet the Roman, Constantius, in battle. A month later, Cole died, leaving a beautiful daughter, Helen, whom he had trained to rule after him.[25] Geoffrey's account is recognizable in Davies's play only with respect to Cole's daughter; he even keeps her name, altered slightly to attain the graceful three syllables he favoured in naming his own daughters.

Cole is the play's hero, a figure both mythical and convincingly real. He is vitality personified. He is old enough that no one remembers life before he was king of Albion; he has outlived his grandchildren, yet he has the appetites and energy of a man in the prime of life. He is sexually vital; his lovely daughter, Helena, is only seventeen, and he mentions with pride that recently a charming visiting princess "made an extremely flattering suggestion" (124) to him. His supernatural vitality is emphasized by the fact that he seems to thrive on the slow, "sure" poison which the Archdruid Cadno has been subtly administering to him over the past two years. Cole should have died in four months, but the only perceptible effect has been that his white hair and beard have taken on a greenish tint, which associates him with the life of the plant kingdom: "Is not that a sign that I flourish?" he asks. "Do green things die? Only when they parch. Draw me another cup" (124). He drinks with gusto; his most prominent and devoted servant is his brewer, Boon Brigit. The gaiety of his spirit is his dominant characteristic, the essence of old King Cole. His mirth is "the laughter of the heart...a glory in the breast, a divine drunkenness, an o'ertopping of the gravity of tight-lipped men" (168).

In opposition to Cole stands the Archdruid Cadno; his name, Davies points out, is the Welsh word for fox, and he is the schemer who personifies intellect without feeling; in his youth he was "robbed ... of faith in anything except his own cleverness" (152). He lives a life of austerity, and he belittles passion. He is learned, a master of magic (the science of his day), and he is motivated by his hope to use his knowledge to make Albion a greater kingdom. Davies keeps the nature of the hoped-for progress vague: Cadno speaks only of standing on the brink of astounding advances. He dreams of taming nature, of seeing man's work dominate nature.

Cole, wishing only to perpetuate the golden era of his reign and feeling as if he might live forever, stands in the way of Cadno's dream of taking great strides into the future. He contrasts the "busyness" of such "little men" as Cadno, hurrying "hither and yon, multiplying and complicating their affairs," with his own serenity; he is not "chained to the chariot wheels of the Sun" (186). His strength is being, not doing. Cole never acknowledges openly Cadno's enmity, and Cadno's poison does not have its intended effect. The conflict between Cole and Cadno develops over Prince Leolin, who is betrothed to Cole's daughter, Helena, and thus is designated as Cole's successor. Leolin is a disciple of Cadno's who shares his vision of Albion's future, so Cadno intends to rule through him. However, Leolin is all honour and purity, and when Cadno commands him to kill Cole, Leolin respectfully but very firmly refuses. Having exposed himself and learned that Leolin is not so completely under his control as he had hoped, Cadno announces at the first opportunity that the gods have chosen Leolin as the sacrifical victim necessary to observe the rites of the spring equinox, when the new temple will be consecrated. Because of his devotion to the Druidic faith, Leolin makes no objection.

Leolin and Helena have to this point felt for each other admiration and respect, but no passion. With death staring him in the face, Leolin makes a tiresome little speech to Helena about honour and duty and the love that might have grown gradually ("like moss over a stone" [175], Helena mocks) had he lived. She has her father's spirit, and provoked by the recognition that he will die without ever having really lived, she goads Leolin, taunts him, bites him in the midst of his chaste kiss, and succeeds in arousing him to the passion he has never before experienced. She too is overwhelmed by passion, as she knew she would be if she could ever find anything in Leolin beyond the admirable but priggish sentiments he embodied. Now Leolin's impending death matters in a way it did not before. Cole, who has been besieged with self-doubt and intimations of mortality following a supernatural encounter with the ghost of a once formidable, now all but forgotten giant, appears to be too uproariously drunk to take seriously the plight of the young lovers as the moment for the sacrifice approaches. But he evades Cadno, and dressed in his ceremonial, godlike garb, wearing the wreath intended for the sacrificial victim, he mounts the altar, dances a magnificent ceremonial dance, and at the designated moment for the sacrifice, when the spring sunlight first touches the altar, he plunges to the ground. He survives just long enough to enjoy the prospect of living on in Helena's descendants and in the memory of his people and dies laughing at his perception of his death as his best joke. Helena dons the ceremonial makeup to appear "as if Cole had truly risen from the dead" (193).

Theatrical effects, the vividness of the dream, the awesome quality of myth and ritual are all present in *King Phoenix*. Four sets are needed, and Davies's emphasis on the creation in the theatre of a world of wonder rather than realism, historical or contemporary, is evident in his suggestion to set and costume designers to refer to Geoffrey of Monmouth's "dubious but fascinating book ... rather than to serious works on pre-Roman Britain" for their inspiration (106). The Archdruid's magic is on display from the opening scene, in which a very large barrel, rolling down a ramp and threatening to crush Cadno, halts at a gesture from him. Most effective is the scene in a moonlit sacred grove of oak trees where the voice of the oaks (audible but indecipherable) speaks and the ghost of the giant Gogmagog ("*huge, but shambling and faceless*" [147]) converses at length with Cole. This scene is markedly dreamlike. Set at night, it features the dimly perceived voice of the oaks speaking "for each man's ear" (145); three characters hear what each most fears to hear but what a part of himself knows full well. Then all depart but Cole, to whom the ghost of the evil giant, sadly but comically reduced to a whining slave of Cadno, tells his story, insisting that his reluctant listener face the truth: change is inevitable and mortality is a fact of life.

The theatricality of *King Phoenix* goes beyond striking sets and costumes, magic tricks, and giant puppets. Already a master of his craft, Davies constructed key scenes for maximum emotional impact. In the first act, Cadno's attempts to destroy Cole are established, he tries fruitlessly to get Leolin to murder Cole, and then after an argument with the merchant Idomeneus over the advisability of administering a large dose of what was meant to be a slow and undetectable poison, Cadno underpays him and uses magic to seize a pouch of powder from his robe. The indignant Idomeneus informs Cole that Cadno is likely to add a large dose of poison to his drink. The act closes with a ceremonial dinner during which emotions begin to build when Cadno announces that Leolin is to be the sacrificial victim for the next morning's consecration of the new temple. We share Idomeneus's outrage at Cadno's scheming and Helena's bewilderment at Leolin's dutiful acceptance of this development. Now, when Cole calls for drink and his cup is brought, Cadno stirs it ceremonially, "to exorcise any evil thing which may lurk in the cup," he says (140), and then offers it to the king.

A brief skirmish between Cole and Cadno over the possibility of having a taster drink first from the cup focuses our attention still more strongly on the likelihood that Cadno has poisoned it. Cole then compels Cadno to drink, which he does reluctantly. Noting contemptuously that Cadno has only half emptied the cup, Cole has it filled to the brim. *"All watch in amazement and IDOMENEUS with horror, as the old King slowly drains the cup to the bottom. His eyes never leave those of CADNO, who watches fascinated. At last COLE turns the cup upside down, and the King and priest stare at each other as the curtain falls"* (141). The act ends in admiration and amazement, fear and suspense, and we are far into the second act before the effect is dissipated with the revelation that Cadno seized the wrong powder, so although he and the king both believed the drink was poisoned, it was not.

Ritual plays a major role in *King Phoenix*. In part this is achieved by setting the play during the Druids' celebration of the spring equinox: the dinner at the end of the first act with its trumpet calls, rich robes, and ceremonial fare is part of the ritual, as is the procession in the last act. The setting of the last act is a tent filled with the properties and masks of the Druidic ceremonies; through an opening *"a monolith or two of the huge stone circle"* which is to be consecrated is visible (170). The specific Druidic ritual is generalized to encompass a number of regeneration myths: Davies closes the second act, as Cole attempts to reconcile himself to mortality, with a song of John Barleycorn; the phoenix image of the title is reinforced by Cole's death speech, which begins, "I shall live: and I shall die" (189); and Helena's startling appearance in the ceremonial regalia that makes her look like Cole is an image of regeneration. Cole takes over the Druidic ceremony and makes it his own, dismaying Cadno by deviating from the prescribed ritual, but turning it into a spectacle of his own which the people find more awesome and magnificent than the planned ceremony would have been.

As King Cole makes the Druidic ritual his own, Davies puts his personal stamp on the regeneration myth. The play's themes are characteristically Davies's themes, even though the regeneration theme of the phoenix and John Barleycorn is recognizable as the general theme of comedy, in which the old make way for the young, and joy and fertility prevail. Certainly, comedy is Davies's métier, and the play celebrates mirth in style, form, and theme. Though myth and ritual are popularly regarded as solemn things, Davies's humour goes hand in hand with the most serious elements of the play. Idomeneus's recognition that he has been shallow, his soul "light and false," combined with his discovery of the good and great in Cole, is expressed in an impassioned plea that Cole accept his allegiance. His self-discovery is an important moment, but even at the height of his impassioned speech, the soul of the merchant is comically revealed in his notion of the worst that could befall him: "Do not drive me away from you! Even if it should mean death, or monetary loss, let me stay near you!" (162). The ghost of the evil giant Gogmagog is wonderfully funny; Davies's "spook," which takes itself quite seriously and feels very sorry for itself, is a source of fun even though it is also the key to Cole's crucial acceptance of his own limitations.

Cole himself, of course, is the essence of mirth, and his laughter is heard at the two most solemn moments in the play: when the birth of Helena and Leolin's passion for each other is clouded by his imminent death and when Cole's own death comes. At the end of Act II, after struggling to reconcile himself to his own death and after Helena, Brigit, and Idomeneus have testified to the power of his joyful heart, Cole foretells the day "when the memory of my laughter will be all that will remain of me" (168). Davies and King Cole share one spirit in embracing humour as an essential good. Like Shaw in *Major Barbara* and *Androcles and the Lion*, Davies attacks "the old, fallacious idea that joy and merriment are not religious feelings."[26] In fact, religion without them is not worth having; the religion of Cadno and of Leolin before Helena takes him in hand is a limited and unattractive religion. Cole, the centre of his people's lives and their sustenance, is much more attractive, and his significance as the basis of life is suggested in two images: Cole as the well at which his people drink and Cole as the sun. Idomeneus observes that "a man of great spirit, complete in himself ... is a well at which lesser people fill their buckets" (166) and asks to fill his bucket at Cole's well. For the sacrificial ritual in Act III, Boon Brigit paints Cole's face like the sun, and after his death, Helena, who is not mourning because she shares Cole's spirit, is painted likewise. Mirth warms the hearts of the people; "laughter — laughter like his [Cole's] — is holy and great" (192).

As the comic style and form of the play are complemented by the theme of the enduring value of mirth, Davies's vision of theatre as a place of passion is complemented by a conflict between passion and intellect in which — as in *Eros at Breakfast* — intellect is clearly regarded as the inferior attribute. Cadno's dominant characteristic is intellect; that this is his misfortune is stated in so many words by Gogmagog: "I robbed Cadno of faith in anything except his own cleverness, and that's a terrible thing to happen to any man" (152). It is apparent too in the contrast between Cadno's cheerless life and the happy lives of Cole and Helena. Passion is quite beyond Cadno's comprehension; when he finds Leolin embracing Helena just before the sacrificial ceremony is to begin, he asks, "What is he doing with the Princess?" and Idomeneus' verbalization of the obvious, "He appears to be holding her in his arms," does nothing to illuminate Cadno, who wonders, "But why?" (179). He attempts — in vain — to set Leolin straight, pointing out that as his own pupil, Leolin must know that what he feels "is no more than desire." When Leolin, for the first time really in touch with his own heart, replies, "If this sweetness which I feel is desire, then desire is a holy thing," Cadno is contemptuous of him as "one of those fools who submits everything to the touchstone of his senses" (181-82).

Idomeneus, not an evil but a shallow man, is not contemptuous of Leolin, but rather "realistic" about love, observing that "love conquers all only in the tales of the minstrels," and replying to Boon Brigit's observation that for Helena now love is "all that life holds," "Ask your Princess in forty years if love is all life holds for her?" He admits, though, that his "bitter wisdom" is merely "a way of not feeling" (179), a way of shutting out reality instead of embracing the whole of life. Leolin, of course, is transformed by Helena — on the advice of Cole, who suggests that she bite him — from a man who knows only faith and reason, and who is in consequence admirable but limited, to a complete man who knows passion as well. For the first time, knowing the value of feeling, Leolin really comes to life; he is fit now to ascend with Helena to Cole's place.

Cadno had, in his own youth, undergone an equally important but opposite transformation: beginning, like Leolin, with faith and reason, his encounter with Gogmagog robbed him of faith, leaving him with reason alone, and he has become an evil man, spiritually mutilated, terribly incomplete. Interestingly, the only fruit of Cadno's intellect which he names specifically in outlining his hopes for the future of the kingdom is "a way of putting to work some of the power which is lavished on us by our

father the Sun" (117). Since Cole is identified with the sun, the implication
is that by means of his intellect Cadno can only labouriously generate an
approximation of Cole's personal power, for Cole is complete in himself,
that rare person who lacks nothing in himself and so has much to give to
others. The necessity of mirth, the necessity of passion: these are aspects
of Davies's larger theme of wholeness, the advisability of embracing and
encompassing all of oneself and all of life instead of rejecting the part that
seems undesirable.

What makes Cadno the villain is that he sets out to *destroy* what fails to
fit into his scheme of things instead of altering the scheme to accommodate
the embarrassing truths. The play's opening scene between Cadno and
Idomeneus introduces the central conflict between openness to all of life
and the destructive, narrow view of life. Idomeneus is all admiration at a
king so old having a child of seventeen, but Cadno frowns upon it as
"unnatural":

> CADNO: We Druids are deep students of the nature of things. We are
> not pleased by what is unnatural.
> IDOMENEUS: Understandably so: it makes you reconsider your
> opinions.
> CADNO: There you speak as an uninstructed layman, and as an
> infidel, of course. When matters do not agree with our body of learned
> opinion they are unnatural, and what is unnatural must be destroyed
> (113).

Cadno's approach would result in the destruction of the better than "natural" along with the worse: Cole's vitality, Leolin's honour, Helena's love
— all stand in the way of Cadno's notion of what is right and proper, so he
would destroy them all.

What is perhaps more difficult to see is that destruction of "the worse" is
not advisable either. In fact, at the end of the play, what Cadno represents is
not obliterated. The happy ending requires that Cadno be defeated, and he
is defeated in his immediate object of destroying Leolin as well as in his
hope to control the occupant of Albion's throne. We are even assured that
Cadno himself will not last long; Lug, the voice of peasant wisdom who acts
as a kind of chorus[27] and whose pronouncement is not likely to be
questioned, says with authority, "Cadno is his own poison: the belly is a
great revenger. The sight of the Prince on the throne will kill him before
summer" (192). But Cadno's vision of the Kingdom's future, his commitment to Druidic science, is shared by Prince Leolin. Leolin is Cadno's
student and inheritor of his ideas; Helena is Cole's daughter and inheritor
of his spirit. Together, they move into the future; they are last seen together

holding the King's oak crown *"above their heads as servants draw them out into the sunlight; cheers for them are heard"*(193).

Indeed, it is not Cadno's ideas only that will live on, but also the evil he personifies, though it is not in the spirit of comedy to belabour the fact. Certainly Cole's spirit triumphs, living on in Helena, while Cadno quails before her in Cole's image. But the phoenix image of the title is first associated with *Cadno*, who claims that Leolin, facing death, "will not go anywhere that I have not gone before him. We Druids ... must die and rise again before the last secrets of our priesthood are revealed to us. I have been to the land of the dead ..."(139). The spirit of evil cannot be disposed of once and for all. Like the spirit of good, it can be only temporarily defeated. This is why Cole insists that "there is no reform save that which each man makes in his own heart" (186), a theme which will recur in later plays. Other kinds of reform are only superficial.

Although King Cole is portrayed as the complete man, not the limited beings that Leolin, before his transformation, and Idomeneus and Cadno are in their various ways, he does undergo a painful self-examination from which he emerges wiser, with a greater understanding of his place in the nature of things. Cole is depicted as one who has enjoyed reigning in a golden age. The most striking feature of his fairy-tale story is that for him time seems to have stood still. Cadno describes him as "in love with the past" (115), Idomeneus, as "a man of repose" (166) — one whose very greatness makes change seem undesirable. However, mutability is a law of life. Life is not static, or it is not life. No matter how golden, Cole's era must pass; no matter how vital, Cole himself must die. Cadno is a shadow hanging over Cole's life, and he is part of the truth of life. That shadow must be acknowledged, accepted, and put into perspective. Cole must accept change; in particular, he must accept his own mortality. The second act of the play depicts Cole's struggle to come to terms with the truth. The voice of the oaks in the sacred grove whispers to him, "Cole, Cole, you are old, and your life is a dream; rouse yourself, King of Albion; awake, awake!" (146). The dream is time standing still; to awake means acceptance of death. Gogmagog furthers the process of Cole's coming to terms with reality. He was once thought invincible but now is virtually forgotten. Cole will suffer the same fate, though he struggles against it: "I am not old! I am not old! All who love me and all who hate me say it, but it is not true! ... I will not have it!" (153-54). In the second scene of Act II we see him much changed; *"his step is heavy and it is plain that all is not well with him"* (159). But there is still change to come; the Cole of the third act is not that of the second. Acceptance of mortality is not defeat, but necessity. Death is part of life, as evil is. Cole's death is also the means of life: Leolin's, Helena's with Leolin, Cole's own in Helena and her children and in the memory of his

people as the "merry old soul" of song. He will be remembered as one
"whose death was his best joke" (190), a means of defeating his enemy, of
perpetuating other lives, and of demonstrating the blessing of a great
spirit.[28] Cole's attainment of the appropriate perspective on death is a
triumph of the spirit. His loyal servant Boon Brigit's speech after his death
is *"ritual grief, half-chanted,"* and it is followed by Helena's refusal to
mourn, because she feels only "love, and the holiness of a great life nobly
ended" (190); instead, she carries on with life, perpetuating her father's
image and his spirit. Davies has taken a legendary figure who is remembered solely for his merriment and made him display all that is best in the
human spirit. His story is myth, romance, dream, and theatre as Davies
thought ideally it should be.

What sort of theatrical environment was there in 1947 in which to mount
a production of the best play an aspiring young Canadian playwright, with
all Davies's varied experience of the theatre, could write? Davies was
certainly not going to be satisfied just to publish his plays (even if publishers
of plays were easy to find); he wanted them performed. Theatrical production is a complicated affair: a play without actors, a director, and an
audience is no play at all, and for many plays — certainly for the sort Davies
preferred — costumes, makeup, special lighting and sound equipment,
sets, and properties are needed as well. Even if all these might be had, the
quality of every element is a factor in the success of a production. As a
playwright (and director and sometime actor) who arrived on the Canadian
scene in the 1940s, Davies has had a good deal to say about theatre in
Canada. When he first began writing plays he found not one professional
theatre that was interested in producing Canadian plays. The prevailing
attitude towards Canadian plays seemed patronizing, and Davies felt that
his greatest handicap as a beginning playwright was the lack of a theatre to
work with or a director who was interested.[29] Playwriting *"is* a craft and ...
it must be learned," he knew. "The best way to learn is to write a play and
see it through rehearsals and in performance."[30] Literary skill is certainly
an asset to the playwright, but so is a grasp of how what is written on the
page may be brought to life on the stage. Many of the twentieth century's
greatest playwrights were productively allied with specific theatre companies: Chekhov had the Moscow Art Theatre, Synge and O'Casey had the
Abbey Theatre, O'Neill had the Provincetown Players. Until recently,
Canadian playwrights have been less fortunate. Recognizing the limitations
of Canadian theatre, Davies thought first in terms of writing for London
theatre; he wanted to be a playwright, not specifically a Canadian playwright, and London was the capital of the theatrical world he knew. Unable
to get a showing there or in the few Canadian professional theatres, where
proven London and Broadway plays were the standard fare,[31] the little

theatre world offered Davies's only chance to have his plays performed.

He has described the little theatre of the forties, particularly the Dominion Drama Festival, as "one of Canada's cultural glories."[32] Much of Canada's talent — having no other outlet — was absorbed by it, and some of the amateur theatre societies prospered remarkably. Among them Davies cited in 1950 one which "owns a handsome, full-sized theatre, supports a studio for experimental work, gives assistance to promising young people, and employs several persons to attend to its business all the year round."[33] Certainly it was to his benefit to see his early plays performed, and some of the productions were good enough to win awards at the Dominion Drama Festival for both the productions and the playwright.

Although there were definite rewards in having his plays performed by amateur groups, there were drawbacks as well. One of the problems was that amateurs generally lacked the self-confidence and experience needed for new plays; it was easier to work from models. In a 1948 letter to Earle Birney about the problems of literature and the arts in Canada, Davies focused on theatre as his own "particular enthusiasm," and admitted that he was "somewhat depressed to find what a very small portion of the population is interested in the Little Theatre movement, and how small a portion of the interested group cares for anything more than amateur imitations of New York and London successes."[34] The Montreal Repertory Theatre's production in March 1948 of three of Davies's one-acts, *Hope Deferred*, *Overlaid*, and *Eros at Breakfast*, was indicative of the second-class standing of new Canadian plays among even the best of the amateur theatre groups. Like the Ottawa Drama League, the Montreal Repertory Theatre was making a deliberate attempt to foster Canadian drama. Canadian plays, however, were not featured among their main attractions; Davies's plays were performed in the Studio Theatre's series of more risky offerings. Sydney Johnson opened a review in *The Montreal Daily Star*[35] with a blast at the MRT: "What is the matter with the Montreal Repertory Theatre that it allows three brilliant Canadian one-act plays to be produced by The Studio instead of being given a major production? A repertory theatre devoted to the cause of drama has other duties than giving us the opportunity to see popular Broadway and London commercial successes." "Some of the speculation on the future of art in Canada expounded in *Hope Deferred*," Johnson noted, "is almost a sad reflection on the modified rapture accorded Mr. Davies' plays by the MRT here — though he, no doubt, will be as grateful to the MRT for producing them at all as we are for the opportunity of seeing them under any circumstances." The production was doubtless an exciting event for a man who was just beginning to be recognized among the knowledgeable few as a remarkable playwright; he and his wife made the trip to Montreal to attend both the Friday and

Saturday night performances. But though the MRT included many accomplished amateurs, including Leo Cicerci, who played Frontenac in *Hope Deferred*, Davies was quite conscious of the difference between amateur and professional theatre.

Davies's first novel, *Tempest-Tost*, is a humorous view of little theatre. By the time he began writing it in 1949 he had had considerable experience with little theatre, directing in Peterborough and seeing his plays performed by various groups, and the novel reflects both the joys and the frustrations of little theatre. A more straightforward account of Davies's reservations about amateur theatre is his report, published in 1951, for the Massey Commission on the state of theatre in Canada. Written in the form of a dialogue between "Lovewit," director and actor, and "Trueman," playwright, Davies's insightful, humorous, and urbane presentation must have cheered the members of the Commission in their labours, which led eventually to the establishment of the Canada Council for the encouragement of the arts, letters, humanities, and social sciences, the council which became the foundation of Canada's artistic life in the second half of the twentieth century. Davies found virtually everything wrong with the state of theatre in Canada, beginning with the fact that Canadian education failed to prepare people to appreciate classics of the theatre, so that when there were no such performances, they were not even aware that they were missing anything. He acknowledged that Canada's best actors were very good, but since there was stage work enough to support only a very few, most had to work in radio, which is poor training for actors, or stick to amateur theatre, where it is not possible to develop talent fully.

He waxed wryly eloquent on the subject of bad amateurs, apparently having suffered recently at the hands of some.[36] If he had judged all by the standards professionals should be judged by, asserts Trueman, he would have "slain the bad amateurs and chopped them into messes before the astonished eyes of their friends and relatives. When one has said that they, too, are God's creatures one has said absolutely all that can be said in their defence....A bad professional will bedaub your play with his own egotistical nonsense, but he will leave something of its original substance. But your bad amateur will ravish it and dance upon its corpse without any comprehension that he is doing it a disservice."[37] Davies's annoyance about the abuse his plays sometimes received at the hands of those who put together productions of them is most freely expressed through a persona. While Trueman voices his wrath directly, Marchbanks is ironic about little theatre productions of Davies's plays. In "The Double Life of Robertson Davies," Marchbanks remarks that little theatre people "show a tendency to cut and rewrite Davies' plays which he does not appreciate as he should. After all, it is a well-known fact that our Canadian Little Theatres are full of people who would write excellent plays if they could just find the time to do it; he ought to be grateful when they correct his many faults."[38]

Perhaps the greatest weakness of the amateur groups, which Davies noted in the Massey report, displayed in *Tempest-Tost*, and elaborated in an article published in 1951 on Canada's need for first-rate directors, was inherent in the non-professional, social nature of the groups. Fairness, team play, the democratic conviction that popular consent is the way to make decisions — these do not foster great art, he insisted, however fine they may be in other respects. A professional director with the moral authority earned by natural gifts and outstanding work is needed to lead a group to the greatest artistic success in theatre.[39] Valerie Rich, the professional director in *Tempest-Tost*, pronounces succinctly on the differences between amateur and professional theatre: "One of the nicest things about the professional theatre is that it is utterly undemocratic. If you aren't any good, you go."[40]

The dialogue form of "The State of Theatre in Canada" served Davies particularly well when he was of two minds about something, though in most matters Lovewit and Trueman necessarily agree. Davies's uncertainty about whether it was possible to be both a Canadian and a successful playwright is extended to uncertainty about the place of Canadian theatre in the larger world of theatre. Trueman argues that "a robust Canadian theatre would bring forth a large body of Canadian plays, some of them good enough for export." He notes that the civilized world takes an interest in plays by and about those of many distinct nationalities and insists that it is ridiculous to suppose that Canadians "are so cut off from the charity of God and the indulgence of mankind that they alone are of no interest to their fellow beings....If the plays are good enough, the world will like them." Lovewit is sceptical, persuaded that the universal prejudice against Canadian plays will leave them in the position of the "gifted young woman who asked a celebrated orchestral conductor if her sex would prevent her from getting a place in a first rate orchestra. No, said he; you will manage it if you are able to play twice as well as any of the men." Trueman concedes that we must simply hope to nurture playwrights of sufficient strength to overcome the prejudice. Finally, the hope Davies expresses in the report is not just to win a hearing for Canadian plays abroad, but to win for Canada "a proud place among the nations."

> I fear that her integrity, her good sense, her honest dealing and her indisputable political genius will not suffice to gain it for her. Think: do you know of any nation that the world has considered truly great which has not had one or many manifestations of great art? Canada will not become great by a continued display of her virtues for virtues are — let

us face it — dull. It must have art if it is to be great, and it has more real vitality, in my opinion, in the art of the theatre than in any other save music.[41]

The birth of the Stratford Shakespeare Festival, though it did nothing directly to foster Canadian plays, was a triumph for Canadian theatre. Davies acclaimed the opening season in an article in *Saturday Night*, for which he had begun writing a weekly "Books" page in January 1953. The article expresses his exultation about a theatre which is what he thought it should be: "a temple, devoted to gods [of] Pity, Terror, Tenderness and Mirth," featuring the work of a great director, Tyrone Guthrie. Davies concludes the article with a glance at the benefit to Canada's entire theatrical community, observing that the actors who took part in Stratford's first season have "tasted the wine of true theatre" and will never again be satisfied with "the sour slops of under-rehearsed, under-dressed, under-mounted, under-paid, and frequently ill-considered and ill-financed theatrical projects."[42]

In 1947, when he needed a production of *King Phoenix*, the bulk of Davies's struggle to make Canada a place where his plays and others would be competently performed was still ahead of him. He sent it to John Gielgud, whose refusal of the play was accompanied by the observation that people would probably think it was an allegory about Winston Churchill and Clement Attlee. A more important observation, with which Davies has since come to agree, was that a mythical era is difficult to realize in the concrete form of theatre.[43] *King Phoenix* was not performed until 1950, when Herbert Whittaker directed it for a little theatre group, the North Toronto Theatre Guild. Whittaker, another newspaperman who loved the theatre, and Davies had met in Montreal in 1948 when the Montreal Repertory Theatre produced three of Davies's one-act plays.

Whittaker too was fond of the theatre of myth and magic, so he was happy to direct Davies's play after he moved to Toronto. The usual limitations on amateur productions obtained: the play was rehearsed in a school and the actors' talents covered a considerable range. Whittaker thought that Ron Hartman was outstanding as the archdruid and the magic bits and the strong dramatic parts worked well, but the romantic parts were less successful, perhaps because the actors were weak.[44] Maxwell Wray, the regional adjudicator of the 1950 Dominion Drama Festival, praised Whittaker's production, but he was condescending about this "new play by Canadian Author" which he called "quite a good effort." He thought it was "very wordy," the content was "not very strong," and there were too many digressions from the story, and finally he damned the play for "a feeling of 'Artiness.' "[45] In *Love and Whisky*, Betty Lee's book about the

Dominion Drama Festival, Wray is singled out as an example of the least impressive adjudicators who reigned at the festivals; he seemed more absorbed in his own importance than in the responsible judgments and constructive criticism the adjudicator was meant to provide.[46] No writer is happy with a negative judgment of his work, but irresponsible criticism is especially infuriating, particularly when it is as influential as the adjudicators' judgments at the festivals were. Davies emphasizes the weight of the adjudicators' opinions in his introduction to *Love and Whisky* and in some of Marchbanks's sardonic remarks; apparently no one dared an independent judgment of a play's quality. Journal accounts were usually not reviewers' opinions but simply reports of adjudicators' comments. Wray's criticisms of weak content and frequent digressions from the story are obviously related, and they reveal that he simply failed to understand the central conflict in the play, from which there are no digressions. The "feeling of 'Artiness' " was more helpfully explained by Gielgud as the difficulty of bringing to life on the stage a concrete depiction of the mythical era in which the play is set.

Three years later Davies directed *King Phoenix* for the Peterborough Little Theatre. Brenda Davies played Boon Brigit and Davies himself appeared as one of her servants.[47] At the Eastern Ontario Drama Festival, the Kingston Cup for the best Canadian play went to *King Phoenix*, but adjudicator John Allen found "great weakness" as well as "great quality" in the "strange, sprawling, brilliant" play with its "passages of memorable brilliance made useless ... by passages of memorable banality."[48] Davies acknowledges that it is hard to cast, and not a perfect play, but still he believes that "there are some very good things in it, and the conflict between King Cole and the chief Druid is a very real one."[49] He speculates that the play's "sense of life as a mystery" may have made trouble for those who expect plays to explain life.[50] Another problem is the character of Lug. Davies, apparently not satisfied entirely with the "sense of life as a mystery," introduced Lug to explain a few things. Probably the effect Davies wanted is that this simple shepherd utters truths so basic that they are overlooked only by those who are too clever for their own good, like Cadno, or too sophisticated to retain common sense, like Idomeneus. But Lug's observations about the difference between "belly-joy" and "pain-joy" combined with the definition of love as "joy-pain in the belly" are more confusing than illuminating and might well account for Allen's comment about "passages of memorable banality." Lug's prediction that Cadno will die shortly because "the belly is a great avenger" is reassuring but still unsatisfactory, because it reminds us that Lug has little function in the play other than to utter such bits of earthy wisdom.

In most respects, *King Phoenix* is a success, and it shows Davies's command of his craft early in his career. Most characters are well drawn, memorable, and convincing. Such technical difficulties as exposition are handled with skill: character and humour are more in evidence than the mechanics of explanation. The scene of the runaway barrel, for instance, is a small gem; it provides an exciting break in the conversation, it reveals the Archdruid's power when his magic stops the barrel, and it also shows humorously how little regard Cole's camp has for the Archdruid when Boon Brigit's concern turns out to be not for the Archdruid, who might have been killed, but for the contents of the barrel, her best brew, which might have been spoiled by the rough ride. The emotional range of the play is considerable, and the very difficult conclusion to the play is a success, though it depends very much on the ability of the actor playing Cole. The death of the central character must be moving but not sobering, the appropriate outcome to permit the joyous spirit to reign. "Joke" seems not the right word for Cole to end on, since his mirth is grander than that of a mere joker and his death is trivialized by his own description of it as his "best joke," but the speeches and actions of the other characters between Cole's death and the final curtain put his death into the right perspective and give the play a much more satisfying conclusion than the "punch lines" to some of the one-acts provided.

King Phoenix was everything that Davies wanted a play to be in 1947, but it was not a popular success. He had difficulty getting it staged at all, and when it was performed, it was not altogether well received. The mythical era is part of the problem, and Davies has never since written a play without a sense of specific place and time, but another important source of difficulty may well have been lack of interest in a play by a new Canadian playwright which was not about Canada and was not simple to stage.

4

Cultural Poverty in Modern Canada:
Fortune, My Foe

Davies's next full-length plays were quite different from *King Phoenix*. *Fortune, My Foe* and *At My Heart's Core* are set in Canada, and both deal explicitly with the subject of Canada's cultural poverty. Both are ensemble plays, probably because Davies's experience with *The King Who Could Not Dream*, *Benoni*, and *King Phoenix* suggested that it was unwise to stake his chance for production on a star performer's interest. Beyond this, the two have little in common: *Fortune, My Foe* is as different from its predecessor in every respect as it could possibly be: contemporary and topical, explicitly Canadian, and easy to stage. In "The Double Life of Robertson Davies" Marchbanks reports that among Davies's first five full-length plays, *Fortune, My Foe* was the most popular, "for it has a comparatively easy stage setting, and the costumes are modern," and observes that Davies's "fondness for period plays, and for somewhat elaborate settings ... alarm[s] many Little Theatre groups."[1] With *At My Heart's Core*, written in 1950, Davies found an imaginative and effective compromise between the mythical grandeur of *King Phoenix* and the practical and topical *Fortune, My Foe*.

In the summer of 1948 the Arthur Sutherland International Players, a professional company, were performing in Kingston. Sutherland, an old friend of Davies's from Queen's, wanted to end the season with a Canadian play, and Davies had one underway. He finished it quickly, and rehearsed it for just five days before it opened the first week in September. "I drove the actors as hard as possible," Davies says, which was not as hard as I wished. They had the weekly Rep. habit of approximating the words they had to speak and though I did my best to persuade them that my dialogue was more carefully considered than their improvisations it was difficult to break long habit. The best actor of the group was William Needles, who played Szabo, and who was word perfect; I assumed that the considerable success he made in the part was owing to the fact that he said what had been written for him and not a recollection.[2]

The play proved to be extremely popular and its run was extended for a second week.

One factor in *Fortune's* success was doubtless its overt Canadianism, though Philip Hope-Wallace, the English adjudicator of the 1949 Dominion Drama Festival, observed that this "good Canadian play" is "so basically human that it could be enjoyed by anyone with any feeling in any part of the world."[3] Sutherland's desire for a Canadian play is evidence of a growing interest in fostering indigenous drama at the time, as is an article written the following year by the Toronto *Telegram*'s book editor, James Scott, in which he noted the scarcity of Canadian plays performed and published. Scott was concerned about the situation: "I don't believe any country can long continue to have a vigorous theatre when it has to derive most of its material from outside," he wrote.[4] The many fine features of *King Phoenix*, its well-drawn characters, witty dialogue, exciting action, and strong emotion, were not enough to guarantee success. Nor was the fact that the play was written by a Canadian enough to make it a "real" Canadian play. But *Fortune, My Foe* was self-consciously Canadian, about new immigrants, long-time residents, and native-born Canadians and their love-hate relationship with Canada, about the demands it makes on them, the rewards it fails to offer them, and the necessity to work for and have faith in a finer future Canada. Artistic deprivation in particular, the theme of *Hope Deferred*, and the more general cultural deprivation which is the subject of *Overlaid* are again the focus of *Fortune, My Foe*, but in *Fortune* Davies does not set his action far in the past as in *Hope Deferred* or in the country as in *Overlaid*, either of which might be considered somehow a special case not necessarily representative of the "real" Canada. *Fortune* takes place in the present in a university town, which ought to provide an opportunity for appreciation of the finer things of life if any place in Canada could but fails to do so. Another significant difference between *Fortune, My Foe* and the one-acts as a means for exploring this theme of cultural poverty is that the greater length and range of characters in the three-act play naturally allow for greater depth of treatment. *Fortune* gives us a number of variations on the hero who values culture, most notably Szabo, Nicholas, and Rowlands, who differ significantly in other important respects and so prevent over-simplification of the issues. The Philistine, too, is represented by a variety of characters, all of whom have pretensions to artistic or intellectual values of some sort but lack true understanding of what art is. This range of characters allows Davies to explore fully the nature and degree of Canada's cultural poverty and its effects on different individuals.

The play is set in Chilly Jim Steele's "equivocal establishment"[5] on the river, where he serves coffee or fruit drinks to all comers but encourages only the patronage of friends. One such friend is Idris Rowlands, a middle-aged professor from Wales whose love of literature and failure to establish a similar love in the hearts of most of his students has made him cynical about Canada, his adopted home. Another is Nicholas Hayward, a young and promising professor of literature, who is tempted to take a job in the United States, where he anticipates a better future for himself and Vanessa Medway, whom he hopes to marry, because his talents will be better appreciated — and rewarded — than they are in Canada. Rowlands accuses Nicholas of wanting to sell out his values simply for money and of sacrificing his loyalty to Canada for a girl who is not worthy of Nicholas's love. The central conflict is really internal; it is Nicholas's struggle, but Rowlands is a kind of alter ego, the advocate for another side of Nicholas which Nicholas will not recognize at the beginning of the play. Nicholas's argument with Rowlands and his romance with Vanessa provide the focus of the primary plot line of the play, but the secondary plot, with Franz Szabo as the focal point, provides the main interest for much of the play.

Szabo is a recent immigrant, a puppet master whose family has performed in Prague and who hopes to make a home for his beloved puppets in Canada. Chilly has taken the destitute Szabo in as a dishwasher, and he and his friends and patrons, particularly Ned Weir, a newspaperman who once saw the Szabo family's puppets in Prague and so recognizes Szabo as "a great man" (96), work to help him make a beginning as a puppeteer in Canada, bringing people who might be able to promote Szabo's career to see him.

While the two plot lines are separate, the problem of finding in Canada an environment which will nourish culture is common to both: neither Nicholas's sensitivity to literature nor Szabo's wonderful marionettes have a natural home here. The play ends with an apparent defeat but a triumph of the spirit in each plot; Szabo, at the centre of one story, is a significant influence on Nicholas, at the centre of the other. The fragment of a puppet show which Szabo and his friends present to win the support of locally influential Mattie Philpott and Orville Tapscott ends in disaster: the semi-educated pair, representative of Canada's cultural middle class, raise endless infuriatingly mundane objections to the show, the windmill scene

from *Don Quixote*. Finally, Rowlands, in drunken despair and outrage at
their insensitivity to the art before them, destroys the puppet show, "the
temple," because he cannot "bear to see it profaned" (153) and drives the
pair of Philistines out the door with his shouts of "anathema" and blows of
his stick. Rowlands has expressed Szabo's own feelings about the reception Philpott and Tapscott give the puppet show, but Szabo feels no despair.
When Rowlands warns him that Canada "will freeze your heart with folly
and ignorance," Szabo replies, "No, Professor, I do not think it will. I am
an artist, you know, and a real artist is very, very tough. This is my country
now, and I am not afraid of it. There may be some bad times; there may be
some misunderstandings. But I shall be all right....We [artists] must be
tough, and hopeful, too" (153). The primary plot is then brought to a
conclusion when Nicholas tells Vanessa that he has decided they should
not marry and he will abandon his pursuit of a job in the United States. His
admiration for the strength, determination, and hope which allow Szabo to
emerge unscathed from his encounter with Philpott and Tapscott inspires
Nicholas to a similar commitment, and he tells Szabo, "If you can stay in
Canada, I can, too. Everybody says Canada is a hard country to govern, but
nobody mentions that for some people it is also a hard country to live in.
Still, if we all run away it will never be any better" (156). Despite disappointments suffered by the characters upon whom both plots centre, the
play ends in their common affirmation of commitment to a future in Canada, a future in which Canada will be the better for the struggles of those who
decide to stay and do battle with the Philistines. This is, of course, the
choice Davies himself made.

The play's theme of Canada's inhospitality to her artists and scholars
and the necessity nevertheless for their commitment to her no doubt
contributed to its success, but ideas alone never made a successful play, as
Davies is well aware. He says of *Fortune*: "People who haven't got any
brains persist in describing it as a discussion of the low pay of Canadian
academics. This is utterly absurd. It's about a man who is torn with
emotion because he fears that if he's going to make the best for himself he
must leave Canada, but he doesn't want to. Another aspect of it ... is that
the girl he loves is very like Canada; she's as cold as an icicle, he's going to
get nowhere with her, but he's devoted to her and he can't leave her. That's
what the play is about: emotion, and when it's played that way it's very
effective."[6] While Davies is apt to de-emphasize the ideas in his plays when
he discusses them in his struggle to divest himself of the "Canadian
Bernard Shaw" label, the importance of emotion can hardly be over-
stressed. His characters are the key to his plays, for they are both the
source of emotion and the means of exploring ideas. Moreover, Davies's
characters are often the finest products of his creativity; their personalities

are frequently more memorable than what they say or what they do.

Nicholas Hayward and Idris Rowlands are best considered together, for Nicholas, younger and less experienced but sharing Rowlands's profession and his values, is a potential Rowlands. In Davies's words, "Nicholas and Rowlands are both romantics, caught in the characteristic bind of the romantic spirit. They want more from life than life is going to give them, so they're unhappy."[7] Each helps to illuminate the internal struggles, the suffering, and the hopes and dreams of the other. Despite their close friendship, each is excessively hard on the other; underlying the acrimony of their conflict are the self-doubts and fears both feel, for each recognizes within himself and feels threatened by the position of the other. After the first round of their argument over Nicholas's plans for his future, Nicholas, who has leaped to unwarranted criticism of Rowlands's banter with the old drunk who hangs about Chilly's place, apologizes, hypothesizing that the beginning of a new academic year has made him edgy. "No," Rowlands replies. "You find fault with me because you are discontented with yourself. And you are discontented with yourself because of what you are doing there [with the seventeenth-century joke book Nicholas intends to edit by way of opening the door to fame and fortune in the United States]. You are not the man, Nicholas, to leave Canada for money" (89).

Rowlands is no doubt correct about why Nicholas is so sensitive to criticism of his plans and consequently so edgy, yet there is much in Nicholas's argument which is never successfully rebutted directly by Rowlands or anyone else in the play. "Damn it all," he explodes at Rowlands, "why does everybody talk as though it were criminal for a scholar to want money? And what is sacred about the Canadian scale of payment for academic services? Is it disgraceful to want to make a name, to — to seek some recognition for whatever talents one may have?" Nicholas sees in the United States at least some promise of the realization of his ideal of civilization, "an ideal in which a high standard of living means something more than a high standard of eating," while in Canada, where "the questions that I ask meet only with blank incomprehension, and the yearnings that I feel find no understanding I know that I must go mad, or I must strangle my soul with my own hands." In Canada, Nicholas feels himself "despised because I do not teach anything useful. Despised because I want things from life which nobody else seems to miss. Despised because my abilities command so little money" (89-90).

In fact, Rowlands shares these feelings, which accounts for his cynicism about Canada. Much as he himself appreciates Szabo's puppets, he contends that they will hold no appeal for "the Canadian blockheads." He speaks despairingly of the twenty-five years he has spent trying to share with Canadian students "the treasures of a great literature," when only three among them all could recognize the wealth he offered, and those three have all left Canada for the United States. "God, how I tried to love this country!" he exclaims. "How I tried to forget the paradise of Wales and the quick wits of Oxford! I have given all I have to Canada — my love, then my hate, and now my bitter indifference. This raw, frost-bitten country has worn me out, and its raw, frost-bitten people have numbed my heart" (112). This is presumably what a future in Canada holds for Nicholas, yet Rowlands thinks he should stay.

Though Rowlands's criticism of Nicholas does not wholly invalidate the reasons Nicholas gives for leaving, the criticism is justified. Rowlands objects not just to Nicholas's intention to leave Canada, but to the calculation and compromise which Nicholas is permitting himself to fall into as a means of securing the recognition he yearns for. Nicholas has stumbled on a battered seventeenth-century joke book[8] which he intends to use as the key that will open the door to success. He will search out modern jokes which are equivalent to the old ones to show the similarity of humour in another age to humour in our own and will thus become known as an authority on humour. Rowlands mocks the "really up-to-date professor" who "sticks his nose into the silliest manifestations of everyday life and tells the public that they are more important than they really are." Nicholas, he claims, will sacrifice his potential to do good work to become "America's foremost academic buffoon" (79).

Though Nicholas protests that humour is worthy of serious study and Rowlands agrees with him, his point that Nicholas is not really approaching it seriously is well taken; Nicholas's own discussion of the work betrays his insincerity. He calls the old joke book rubbish which he hopes will prove a treasure to him. When he uses the analogy, "pitchblend is rubbish, but a precious substance may be refined from it," he means by "a precious substance" not the book he intends to write but the fortune he hopes to gain by it. When Chilly reports Rowlands's observation that "the better a book is, the less money it will make," Nicholas replies lightly, "Then I shall take care to write a very bad book" (77). Nicholas's calculation of the effects of his book has nothing to do with authentic contribution to mankind's understanding of humour:

I shall write a preface — scholarly but not over the heads of ordinary men, and witty, but not undignified — and my book will attract attention. I shall become known as a rising authority on humour. The *Reader's Digest* will ask me to run a monthly collection of old jokes, with explanations. I shall be a guest on the programmes of famous radio funny men. And I shall get a great deal of money (78-79).

Nicholas is proposing to base his academic career not on his real insights about literature — and Rowlands testifies that he is capable of truly fine work — but on what will "sell." Rowlands's criticism of Nicholas is justified, but the real villain is Canada, which forces its scholars to choose between resigning themselves to the indifference bordering on contempt with which they are regarded at home and selling out both loyalty to their country and what is best in themselves to seek recognition elsewhere.

What might have been a polite theoretical discussion of the plight of the scholar in Canada becomes a no-holds-barred battle because the emotions of both Nicholas and Rowlands are so deeply engaged in the dispute. Rowlands cannot leave Nicholas alone, though one might think that a grown man could be left to decide his future for himself. At every opportunity Rowlands, who is otherwise depicted as a reasonable and kindly soul, finds some means to throw up to Nicholas the error of his ways, either directly or by innuendo. Nicholas tolerates most of Rowlands's criticism rather well, but he is noticeably touchy on the subject of Vanessa Medway, who is the reason that more money seems indispensable to him and who is, Rowlands tries to make clear, the wrong woman for Nicholas. The quarrel between the two men moves through three phases in the first act, and it is only in the third phase, when Rowlands brings up Vanessa's shortcomings, that Nicholas shows any real anger. In the second act, Rowlands again ventures onto thin ice, observing that Nicholas should not leave Canada for love because "no girl who really loved you would insist on so much sacrifice to prove it. But Vanessa Medway likes to find out how much men will sacrifice for her; it enables her to compute her own value" (116). Now Nicholas is being made to face doubts about Vanessa which he has managed to keep suppressed, and his fury at being forced to contemplate the unbearable breaks over Rowlands:

> Do you think I don't know what's behind your scorn for England and the States? You never were asked to go to the one, or to return to the other. You're a sour, frustrated old man, jealous of any success that comes to others. You whine about your failure as a teacher in Canada, and hint that Canadian stupidity caused it. No, no, Idris; lay not that flattering unction to your soul; your failure came from within. And like every pulpy old mess who has botched his life, you are full of bitter wisdom which you are only too eager to offer to the young. I don't want any of it. In men like you the heart withers many decades before the faculties decay, and the process feels like the coming of wisdom. But real wisdom is sound and ripe, and yours is neither, for wholesome fruit doesn't grow on a cankered tree (116-17).

Humiliated, Rowlands makes his way out the door without a word and does not return until a week later, when he comes drunk.

How much truth and how much sheer vindictiveness is there in Nicholas's attack? There is some truth in it. Rowlands's sense of failure is clear enough; his proclivity to drink, suggested in Act I and demonstrated in Act III, presumably stems from it. But whether he failed to teach his students to respond fully to the treasures of literature or whether they failed to learn, his disappointment at being unable to achieve a goal the value of which he has never doubted is the same. Nicholas threatens to undermine the value of that goal; if Nicholas's proposed path is right, then Rowlands's struggles and disappointments have been pointless from the beginning. Rowlands is defending the proposition that honourable defeat in the pursuit of his goal is preferable to a success which can be achieved only by abandoning the one goal to pursue another. Canada needs her scholars and artists, though she may not appreciate them. If they give up the struggle to establish a foothold for themselves, to teach other Canadians the value of art and scholarship, there can be no hope for a better Canada. Rowlands's life has been sacrificed to the struggle, and he cannot bear to see a young man with Nicholas's promise abandon it. Where Nicholas is quite wrong in his attack on Rowlands is in his claim that the older man's heart has withered. Though Rowlands himself claims he now feels only "bitter indifference," that Canada's "raw, frost-bitten people have numbed my heart," Szabo at least can see through what is perhaps wishful thinking: "A numb heart would not feel so much because a young man of talent was going to leave his native land," he observes. "If you were truly indifferent to Canada, you would not care how its brilliance bled away" (112-13). For all his criticism of Canada's shortcomings, Rowlands gives the country his allegiance.

Davies says that all his characters are aspects of himself, but in *Fortune, My Foe* his ambivalent feelings about Canada can be seen most clearly in Rowlands. Superficially, the similarity between the character and his creator is suggested by Rowlands' nostalgia for the paradise of Wales, where Davies's father's family lived and where Davies chose to spend his honeymoon, and the quick wits of Oxford, where Davies studied for three years. In at least one production, the actor playing Rowlands was made up to look like Davies.[9] Rowlands anticipates the Davies who was himself to become a professor of literature in his emphasis on the importance of emotion: "Because I am a professor silly people suppose that my line is thinking. It isn't; it's feeling" (113). The strength of Rowlands's feelings initiates his conflict with Nicholas and also precipitates the climax of the play in which he brings down the puppet show and drives the Philistines out of the temple of art. His reconciliation with Nicholas is effected without words. Finally, they are united in their defence of art against the incomprehension of fools, which is what Rowlands wanted from the beginning.

What dictates the union of Nicholas and Rowlands and the separation of Nicholas and Vanessa at the end of the play is just the matter of emotion and sensitivity to art. Rowlands and Nicholas possess both; Vanessa Medway possesses neither. Her lack of sensitivity to art is suggested in her inability to understand why Szabo does not want her to handle his precious puppet, Punch, which she thinks of as only a doll, and her assumption (shared by Mattie Philpott and Orville Tapscott) that one could easily learn to make a puppet perform adequately in a matter of weeks. This in itself is inconclusive, since much puppetry is only craft at best, and no one really understands that Szabo is an artist until later. But Vanessa's attitude never changes. Her interest in Szabo's show is that of a society girl for a charity bazaar; she is never so caught up in Szabo's puppetry as Weir and Chilly and Rowlands and Nicholas are. She is not offensively insensitive like Philpott and Tapscott; she just seems incapable of more than a superficial response. This is true of all her emotions. Davies's stage directions specify the hauteur and contempt in her manner, attractive and beautifully dressed though she is. Rowlands understands her charm for Nicholas, but he is not in the least charmed himself:

> You think that [her cool and amused air] is superficial, and that Vanessa can be transformed into a very beautiful woman, and that you are the man to do it. You think that she will always be aloof and amused toward the world, but that toward you she will be the fulfillment of your heart's desire. Ice to the world and fire to you (99).

Rowlands's implication that there is no more to her than that superficial air, that she is all ice and no fire, is not contradicted by any word or action of Vanessa's in the play. Rowlands has more specific indictments: that Vanessa will not have Nicholas unless he has money, and that she is one of those women "who attract love only that they may reject it, and whose greatest pleasure is to wipe their feet on what better women would give their hearts for!" (101).

While Rowlands is essentially right about Vanessa, she is not a Medusa, though Rowlands makes the comparison. He offers a better comparison later when he suggests that it would be appropriate for Nicholas to dramatize "The Golden Asse" for Szabo to stage, explaining that "it is about a man who is turned into a jackass by a woman who does not understand the nature of her own enchantments" (105). A person who is incapable of strong emotion herself might well be unaware of the damage that can be done by arousing it in another. The critic who wonders whether Vanessa "can be made into a human person" in performance and places her among "the most objectionable female characters in Canadian imaginative writing"[10] may not have seen a good performance. If Vanessa is overwhelmingly glacial, Nicholas's attraction to her is incomprehensible. And the scene in which she explains her decision to part from Nicholas shows her to be neither wholly insensitive nor particularly unfair, though it reconfirms her essential superficiality. Nicholas is too serious for her; his constancy makes her feel, quite rightly, out of her depth. She is justified in pointing out that she cannot love him simply by making up her mind to do so and that it would be wrong of her to marry him without being sure she loved him, even though he might wish her to. She is perceptive enough to see that Nicholas would always feel, in his "heart's core," that she had turned him from his duty by encouraging him to leave Canada. Vanessa is not inhuman or grossly objectionable; she is just shallow, which makes her, as Rowlands says, the wrong woman for Nicholas.

Davies's observation that Vanessa might be compared with Canada is interesting, but she is certainly not an allegorical figure. Neither Nicholas's woman nor his country encourages him to make the most of his potential, to live a full and rewarding life. Yet he surrenders the woman but stays to struggle with and for his country. This may seem contradictory, but in part it is because the rewards offered by another country are not entirely satisfactory either. Like Canada, Vanessa is cool and incapable of appreciating Nicholas, but she is like the United States in the superficiality of her attractions. Wealth and fame are attractive, but for Davies the ultimate goal is enrichment of the spirit, not enrichment of the bank account or the ego.

Nicholas's decision to stay in Canada is influenced most of all by Franz Szabo, the immigrant puppeteer who is the centre of interest for both the audience and the other characters during much of the play. Szabo is a foil to both Nicholas and Rowlands; his attitude towards Canada is in command at the end of the play, and his attitude towards art is Davies's most important means of educating his audience. Szabo personifies the values which Rowlands and Nicholas have served and reaffirms their commitment to the service. As a character, Szabo's one fault is that he is too good to be true, but certainly he is effective in countering any prejudice the audience might have against immigrants. He is tolerant, humble, grateful, thoughtful, patient, wise, hard-working, and, most of all, optimistic about his future in Canada. Though Rowlands attempts to disillusion him about Canada's potential as a home for his art, Szabo counters every pessimistic suggestion. When Rowlands doubts that Canada can offer the raw material for a company of puppeteers, Szabo points out that ever since ancient Egypt there have been people who worked marionettes, and there is no reason to believe that Canada has no such people. When Rowlands suggests that movies might have replaced puppet shows, Szabo observes that Coca Cola has not replaced good wine. After Philpott and Tapscott have given Szabo's puppet show the most infuriatingly misguided reception imaginable and Rowlands asserts, "That's Canada, Szabo. That's what it will do to your puppets and to you" (153), Szabo's refusal to accept his judgment sets the tone of the play's conclusion, as he speaks about the necessity for artists to be tough and hopeful and about his faith in Canada's educated and uneducated, despite the folly of the half-educated. As a recent immigrant, Szabo is both the most vulnerable to Canada's harshness and the most determined to make a success of his life there. Caught in the red tape of immigration policy, he does not have the option of going elsewhere, so he must make the best of the country he is in. But though his optimism may be naive, his faith and courage are infectious, and both Rowlands and Nicholas find their own faith and courage renewed in turn.

The primary function of the minor characters is to contribute a range of responses to Szabo's art; they also provide most of the humour. Chilly Steele can be classed as a minor character only in terms of function; he is on stage much of the time, and his lines are numerous, for he comments on everything and everyone. He is, in fact, a kind of chorus, the natural philosopher whose succinct observations sum up everyone who enters his establishment and occasionally expand to more general truths: "When you want to know what a man is, imagine the exact opposite of what he seems; that'll give you the key of his character" (138). In addition to entertaining us with his unconventionally direct statements which are often disconcerting to other characters, Chilly's business methods provide entertainment. He sells everyone fruit drinks, then gives away the alcoholic fillip (from a bottle which he keeps off the premises in the river) on a selective basis, thus keeping on the safe side of the law and at the same time encouraging only that clientele of his own choosing. The "in group" then provides humour at the expense of primly respectable outsiders whose expectations of finding a seedy dive are frustrated. While the outsiders are not permitted to see the true nature of Chilly's place, it is in fact considerably less disreputable than they imagine it.

After Rowlands, Chilly is Davies's most successful creation in this play, an accomplishment which is all the more striking when he is compared with Lug, the shepherd in *King Phoenix*, who is meant to perform essentially the same choral role as Chilly does, but who is neither convincingly characterized nor fully integrated into the play, as Chilly is. Chilly is a practical, no-nonsense, natural man. He is self-educated and has none of the social graces, yet he claims language as his hobby, and he has read all of Shakespeare's plays. He can be hard-boiled, as when he calmly douses Buckety Murphy, who is making himself objectionable, with a bucket of water, but hard-boiled though he may seem, he provides Buckety with shelter and regular handouts, and he takes Szabo in and gives him a job. Most important, once Chilly is established as a simple and direct sage, uncultivated but sensible and good, is his response to Szabo's puppet show. Chilly is transported when he sees Szabo's pictures of his marionette theatre in Prague. He has never seen anything that appealed to him so much and is immediately bent on helping Szabo to get a similar theatre going for people on this side of the Atlantic.

Later, when a little marionette stage has been built and a scene from *Don Quixote* for three puppets has been prepared, Chilly's enthusiasm becomes reverence:

> You know how religion is: you've always suspected that something existed and you've wished and prayed that it did exist, and in your dreams you've seen little bits of it, but to save your life you couldn't describe it or put a name to it. Then, all of a sudden, there it is, and you feel grateful and humble, and wonder how you ever doubted it. That little stage makes me feel like that — quiet and excited at the same time (137).

Nicholas agrees with Chilly: "It fills a need in the heart. Why not call the feeling it arouses religious? Look at it: brilliant color, warmth and gaiety — qualities men once sought in the churches, and seek in vain, now" (137). The two speeches clearly contrast the natural man with the cultivated one: Chilly's phrasing and vocabulary are simple; Nicholas's are sophisticated. Yet Szabo's art evokes the same feeling in both men; it appeals to the educated and the uneducated alike.

Ned Weir is another character whose enthusiasm for Szabo's puppets helps to convey the sense of true art Davies needs to establish in the play. This cannot be done directly; the puppet show we see is only a fragment, it is repeatedly interrupted by the inane comments and questions of Philpott and Tapscott, the puppets are made on short notice, one of them is operated by an inexperienced puppeteer, and Nicholas reads all the puppets' speeches because Szabo thinks his English is inadequate and Weir is too nervous to memorize his lines. But Weir has seen Szabo's show in Prague, and in consequence his statements about it have some authority. Though it has been at least ten years since he saw it, he remembers it vividly and recognizes at once the great man in Szabo who appears to the others only as a destitute immigrant with a novel hobby. He helps to explain the effect of Szabo's art; when Vanessa calls the puppet theatre "a whole world of make-believe," he corrects her: "When you see it in action the effect is one of intensified reality, rather than of make-believe. You know when you look at people through the wrong end of binoculars how clear and fresh and marvellously detailed everything seems to be? It's like that'' (102-3). His very sense of the importance of Szabo's show adds considerably to the comedy of the third act scene of the puppet performance. Weir is coerced into assisting Szabo because a second puppeteer is required and no one else is able to come up to even the woefully inadequate level of ability to operate a marionette that Weir demonstrates. His acute sense of his own inability to do justice to Szabo's puppet prompts an attack of stage fright and a string of apologies that interfere with the beginning of the show, and the clumsy motions of his puppet contrast comically with those of the puppets Szabo controls.

The one minor character who does not react strongly to Szabo's puppets does constitute at least an indirect comment on the subject of art, and he also contributes a good deal of humour to the play. If Chilly is a choral figure, then Buckety Murphy is a counter-chorus or antiphonal voice, a figure who is peripheral to the plot, action, and theme, as he is to society, but who is ever present on the fringes of the scene. Buckety is a drunk, a social outcast whom Chilly permits to hang around as long as he causes no trouble. His usual position on stage reflects his peripheral position in society: though he rarely leaves the stage, for the most part he sits at the back, outside the large doors that open onto the river, sometimes facing the action, sometimes dozing with his back to it. Periodically, he pops into the action like a jack-in-the-box triggered by the word "drink" or attracted by a new visitor who may be good for a handout. Often his requests for handouts are humorously imaginative. His first venture is a piercing howl at precisely 5:02, which he claims is a birth cry, his customary commemoration of his birthday — and does that not call for a celebration? When Chilly spoils his pitch by noting that he has already had a couple of birthdays this year, he shifts to the claim that it is the anniversary of his wife's death and he needs the drink for protection from her ghost; each year on this day it gums horribly at him in his sleep in retribution for stealing her gold false teeth at the funeral and hocking them.

Buckety adds much humour to the play, but that is not his sole function. His patronizing approach to Szabo reminds us that too many Canadians patronize immigrants. Even though Buckety is friendly, he assumes his own superiority. Szabo knows better; he is kind to Buckety, and he makes a most perceptive comment about him. When Rowlands wonders why Chilly lets Buckety hang around, Szabo asks,

Did you ever visit any of the monasteries in Europe? They always had one or two sad people about them. Cripples or half-wits or fellows like poor Buckety. I think it was to remind the brothers that life could be

cruel, and that some misfortune might bring them to a similar condition. Do you think Chilly lets Buckety stay here to show his other
customers what drink can do if it becomes the master of a man? (111).

This — and compassion — may well be Chilly's reason for keeping Buckety
around, and Davies's reason for having him in the play is probably somewhat similar, though he includes him as a comment not on drink but on art.
Buckety has always about him pictures he posed for "at the height of [his]
career," pictures of himself as Hercules dressed in, at most, a lion skin and
displaying his physique to good advantage. These "dirty pictures" Buckety perceives as "art," and he concludes the story of his career as an artist
with the explanation that when he started to make money, he wanted to
expand his audience and so got some girls to pose.

> "Venus and Mars." That was the finish. Distributed them very careful-
> ly, of course, through private agents, and only to trusted persons. But
> somehow the cops got hold of a set, and that was the end of a high class
> artistic venture. And all because I was a dreamer, and wanted to give
> the public what was too good for it (108-9).

Buckety is unique in this play, but similar characters figure in Davies's later
plays and novels. If all his characters are aspects of Davies, then Buckety
and characters like him represent the ironic voice in a predominantly
romantic personality. There are ironic parallels between Buckety's description of his artistic career and Nicholas's plans for his joke book and his
sense that his talents are unappreciated in Canada.[11] Nobody dispels
Buckety's notion of art or even attempts to. Though for most of the play
Davies seems to be perfectly clear about what is art and what is not, there is
still in him an element of the revolutionary who is quite willing to permit the
introduction of the question implied by Buckety: who precisely is to say
that Szabo's work is art and Buckety's is not, that Canadian society is at
fault for failing to support the one but to be applauded for suppressing the
other? Yet Buckety also stands as an analogy to the sad souls about the
monasteries, as a cautionary note about the desirability of cultivating
discriminating taste.

Three other minor characters distinctly lack the taste to appreciate
Szabo's art, and these three represent the greatest threat to art and culture
which Davies perceives in Canada. Ursula Simonds, Mattie Philpott, and
Orville Tapscott have very clear and specific ideas about the function of art,
ideas which Davies wants discredited. They and their strong opposition to
Szabo's puppetry are made quite ridiculous, and in the process Davies's
ideas about art and the typically Canadian perspective on it are clarified.

The real threat is in the Philpott and Tapscott duo, but Ursula Simonds is introduced first to lay the groundwork for our perception of them. Simonds wants to make use of Szabo's puppets for political propaganda. To her, "your message is what makes your play. Get your message first, then clothe it in some little fable — the simpler the better — and there is your play" (119-120). She is a communist sympathizer who sees Canada as "a politically backward country" and Szabo as a man who has, with his puppets, "a means of helping to bring Canadians up to date in their political thinking" (120). An unattractive figure, lacking even a grain of humour and very defensive, Simonds is likely to be rejected as rapidly by the audience as she is by Szabo, who hardly relishes the notion of subjugating his art to the communist message.

Davies's audience is now prepared for the encounter with Philpott and Tapscott, who speak in the revered name of education and recreation, but who want Szabo to do essentially the same thing that Simonds suggested: to use his art to "sell" a message. Only the nature of the message differs; their suggestion is that Szabo "whip up a dozen little plays" (129) about children who do not eat a proper breakfast or will not clean their teeth. This complete failure to perceive the nature of his art leaves Szabo only momentarily speechless. They think in terms of learning all there is to know about puppets in a six-week summer course, of making them in long skirts with no legs for the sake of simplicity. Szabo calls their plan "cheap and nasty" and defines his position in a speech about art and the artist:

The puppet is a man, and I am the god who gives him life and a soul — a part of my own soul. I make him so carefully, piece by piece, that I know him better than I know my own body .... And when I know him, and make him walk and move his arms and dance I concentrate so hard on him that he is more truly alive than I am myself. He is myself.

He concludes uncompromisingly, "You are wrong, Mr. Tapscott, and if your nonsense is what your country believes, it is time your country got some sense!"(131). Davies fears that Tapscott's nonsense *is* what his country believes, and *Fortune, My Foe* is a part of his effort to correct that misapprehension, to give Canada "some sense." What makes the play art rather than a dissertation on Canadian Philistinism is the life he breathes into his characters, the reality of the emotions they experience. When Mattie Philpott denounces Szabo's opinions as "pretty radical," Nicholas joins the fray to defend him. "What's radical about decency, and honesty, and self-respect, and a refusal to cheapen art and drag it in the mud?" (131). The last two speeches exchanged between Tapscott and Szabo in this scene summarize beautifully the basis of the conflict: Tapscott claims that "in this country art is proud and happy to consider itself the handmaid of education," and Szabo counters (with Davies), "I shall always believe that education is something which helps men to appreciate art" (132).

The inadequacy of Canadian education, in particular its failure to help people appreciate art, is the real subject of the second encounter between Szabo and the Philpott-Tapscott duo, which occurs in Act III. Weir has persuaded the pair to consider Szabo's puppets on his own terms, so they meet again a week later for a showing of the windmill scene from *Don Quixote*. That this second encounter is ill-fated is evident from Mattie Philpott's first approach to the little stage, admiring it in her capacity as a crafts expert as "a very nice little piece of project work." "Don't touch it," Chilly snaps, and we are reminded of his reverence for Szabo's art as he asks, "When you go to church you don't expect to play the organ, do you? Haven't you any sense of mystery, woman?" (144). She has not, of course; she has no feeling for art, only a sense of the accomplishment in "project-work" (144). The enormous gulf between Tapscott and Philpott's perception of the puppet show and that of Szabo and his enthusiastic supporters makes for wry comedy. Szabo's self-important audience of two is easy to laugh at, but their inability to appreciate what they are offered, laughable though it is,[12] also means at the very least a temporary setback for Szabo, and it constitutes a condemnation of Canada. Just because they are so sure of themselves, because they speak with authority for the community on the subjects of education, recreation, and art, we see their views as those of the community at large. They object to nearly every line of the scene from *Don Quixote*. Some of the words are too hard for children; Don Quixote's reference to Dulcinea as his "mistress" sounds suspiciously immoral; Sancho Panza's realistic descriptions of his wife and the horse are too unkind. Even the gist of the action escapes them, which leads Rowlands to enquire whether they are entirely unfamiliar with *Don Quixote*.

What follows is Davies's most direct attack on Canadian education. He has already made it clear that Tapscott and Philpott believe that everything children are taught must be made as simple as possible, because "the minute a problem is created, interest wanes" (128), so the ideal educational technique will "reduce pupil-resistance by cutting down pupil-effort to the barest minimum" (130). Now Tapscott explains his acquaintance with *Don Quixote*: "I did it at the university."

ROWLANDS: Read it, you mean?
TAPSCOTT: No. It was on a general literature course. You're a professor; you ought to know that if we read all the stuff on those courses we'd have no time for extra-mural activities....The important thing in university life is rubbing up against other people (149).

Davies offers one line of defence of these Philistines, reminiscent of his characterization of Ethel in *Overlaid*, though she was more kindly treated. Weir says, "They're not bad souls, really. They have a simple belief in their power to do good." But Chilly's condemnation of them is more to the point: "A simple belief in the multiplication tables don't make you a mathematician; a simple belief in God don't make you a saint; and a simple belief in your power to do good don't make you fit to boss everybody and give them lip" (154). Szabo's comment is sweetly in character, but damning: "As for the half-educated — well, we can only pray for them in Canada, as elsewhere" (153).

The Don Quixote metaphor also helps to put the Philistines in the proper perspective. Philpott and Tapscott are like Don Quixote's giants; they are, after all, only windmills, though they seem to be terrible foes. The windmills get the best of Szabo momentarily, but his spirit, like Don Quixote's, is undefeated. His indomitable spirit, which is as vital as the arts that have flourished for hundreds of years and will not easily be entirely suppressed even by the indifference of semi-educated Canadians, gives new resolution to the others. Nicholas decides to stay and fight for the future of culture in Canada. Rowlands, the cynic who damns Canada and does his best to stifle Szabo's hopes in order to spare him disappointment, modifies his tune in the end. He closes the play singing the title song, which Davies added after he heard the fine singing voice of Glenn Burns, who played Rowlands in the first production[13]. It expresses the feeling at the heart of the play, mixed emotions about Canada, and while it hardly suggests blind optimism, it is finally on the side of hope rather than despair.

> Fortune, my foe,
> Why dost thou frown on me?
> And will thy favours
> Never greater be?
> Frown though ye may,
> Yet shall you smile again:
> Nor shall my days
> Pass all in grieving pain (156).

Though *Fortune* is in large part discussion drama, in which the opposing views of different characters on the issue of art in Canada are discussed at length,[14] there are touches of purely visual expression which are very effective. Davies's careful specifications for the setting suggest that much of the positive side of the argument about Canada is contained in the stage picture. The background is Kingston's skyline, seen across the Cataraqui River in an autumn haze.

*Two cathedrals, a domed City Hall, the towers of limestone churches
and a mass of river-shippings in the harbour make this one of the most
picturesque prospects in Canada, and in this light, one of the loveliest
.... When the audience has had a chance to drink in the peace and
beauty of this scene, the actors may begin to speak* (75-76).

This peace and beauty vanish in the third act scene in which Rowlands
breaks up the puppet show to save it from the desecration of the Philistines.
Davies directs: *"He pulls down the puppet show with his stick: CHILLY
and NICHOLAS seize the lamps, and as they dodge to avoid his blows the
light sweeps confusedly about the stage"* (152). Since the other lights have
been turned out in preparation for the show, the darkness in the mind of the
ordinary Canadian which is his response to art, the frenzy which is likely to
overcome the isolated Canadian defender of art, and the confusion which
reigns in the struggle between them are all conveyed in the stage picture.

Davies believes that the battle against the windmills must be fought for
the honour of Canada and for the idea of art, principles which have nothing
to do with New World Progress but are nonetheless important. This is
evident in the dialogue on the state of theatre in Canada Davies wrote for
the Massey Commission, in which he expresses the fear that Canadian
theatre may become

> a new playground for the professional do-gooders. Never forget those
> well-meaning enemies of art. They are the people who will not allow
> the theatre to be its own justification. The theatre is educational and
> recreative. But it is not so primarily. It is first of all an art, and it is as a
> form of art that it stands or falls. Let people get their hands on it who
> regard it as a means of spreading some sort of education dear to
> themselves, or who think that it is a social medicine, and you will kill it
> as dead as a doornail. But let the theatre develop freely and gloriously
> as an art, let it present classics and good modern plays, let it ravish the
> souls of its audiences with tragedy and comedy and melodrama, and it
> will educate and recreate them more truly and lastingly than the zealots
> think possible. The car of Thespis must not be turned into a travelling
> canteen, dispensing thin gruel to the intellectually under-privileged.[15]

Fortune certainly contains a message; Davies is educating his audiences
on a subject dear to him. It is also recreative; the antics of Buckety Murphy
and the pompous inanities of Philpott and Tapscott are fun. But however
important Davies thinks the message is, and however ready he may be to
work in a laugh line for the fun of it,[16] he could hardly be accused of
"dispensing thin gruel to the intellectually underprivileged." The artful

dialogue, the tight structure, the well-drawn characters with their hopes and fears and disappointments and faith and determination, together with the humour and the thoughtful exploration of an important subject, add up to a very fine play, and it was just the play that Canada's mid-century play-goers were ready for.

Accounts of the first production focus on public enthusiasm for the new Canadian play. In an article written for a little theatre magazine that fall, Charles Rittenhouse reflects:

> The most thought-provoking aspect of this production...was that it should have so far outshone all other offerings of the International Players. Here was a group of actors, mostly from Toronto's radio studios, anxious to make a summer's penny in provincial stock. Their stated policy was to present popular summer fare, such plays as *Claudia* and *Yes My Darling Daughter*. They produced these in the cheapest possible stock way, paying little attention to either direction or design. ... Then as a final gesture they turn about, select an untried play (and by a Canadian!), give it a first-rate production with designs by Grant Macdonald, and what happens? They register their first smash hit![17]

Another commentator tells essentially the same story: The International Players "played nine weeks of the usual Broadway hits. The tenth week they opened with 'Fortune My Foe' and suddenly found long queues at their ticket wicket where no queues had been before: they held the play over for a second profitable week."[18]

This, the first professional production of a Davies play, was soon followed by some impressive amateur productions. The Ottawa Drama League, which had scored a triumph in the Dominion Drama Festival with *Eros at Breakfast* in 1948, entered *Fortune, My Foe* in the Festival in 1949. At the regional festival, it won the best full-length play award[19]. At the national festival, for the second year in a row a Davies play carried off the top awards for Canadian drama. In addition, W. A. Atkinson's "beautiful interpretation of idealistic Prof. Idris Rowlands"[20] won him the award for best male actor in the Festival. (And to complete the Davies sweep of the top 1949 festival awards, Davies took the director's prize for the Peterborough Little Theatre's production of *The Taming of the Shrew*, which the regional adjudicator, Robert Speaight, described as "one of the most brilliant essays in Elizabethan stage-craft I have ever seen,"[21] and Brenda Davies won the best actress award for her performance in it.) A few months later, Robert Gill directed *Fortune* at the Hart House Theatre with an all-university cast that included Donald Davis as Rowlands and Kenneth

Jarvis as Szabo in "very outstanding performances."[22] By this time, sixteen months after Davies wrote it, the play's significance was so evident that B. K. Sandwell began his review of the Hart House production with the statement, " 'Fortune, My Foe' is so much the most important dramatic work yet written in Canada that is is difficult to think of any other as being in the same class."[23]

The next two decades saw over 100 productions of *Fortune, My Foe*, "a record no other play can boast,"[24] said Nathan Cohen in 1967. Part of *Fortune's* success is no doubt attributable to its topicality, and less than two decades after it was written, the play seemed dated; Cohen was calling it "a period piece," a reflection of a time when "cocktail lounges weren't allowed in most of Ontario" and "teachers really were underpaid, second-class citizens."[25] However, the passage of a few years more may complete the play's transformation from "smash hit" to "period piece" to "classic." Its interest reaches well beyond the specific time and place in which it is set. Even when the play was new, it was possible to see that "leaving Canada for money" was just "the local and temporal expression of the eternal clash between the unselfish pursuit of art or learning and the clamant demands of the ego for nourishment"[26] — an observation made by Sandwell in 1949. Any play that deals with social issues in a specific time and place "dates" in the way that *Fortune* has, but a play whose interest transcends time and place can reassert itself once the inevitable period in which it seems simply "old-fashioned" has passed.

5

Cultural Poverty in Colonial Canada:
At My Heart's Core

EVEN THOUGH *Fortune, My Foe* contains a theme that makes it more universal than the contemporary problem play it seems at first glance to be and it has vitality that triumphs over the pragmatism of the simple set and costumes, Davies may have felt that it was not entirely to his taste as a theatre piece because it is very literal; it has little of the archetypal dream, of the grandeur Davies admires in theatre. His next play, *At My Heart's Core*, written in 1950 for Peterborough's centennial celebration, retains most of the practical advantages of *Fortune*, with its Canadian setting and subject and its single set. However, the set with its indoor and outdoor acting areas has more visual interest, early nineteenth-century costumes are called for, and mythic overtones are manifest. The ambivalent feelings about Canada expressed in *Fortune, My Foe* are again central to *At My Heart's Core*, and a suggestion of the connection between the two plays is contained in a line from *Fortune*: "The only revolutions that make any difference to the world are revolutions in the hearts of individual men," Nicholas tells Ursula Simonds, and this can be seen as the basis for *At My Heart's Core*. Set in Upper Canada in December 1837, the rebellion led by William Lyon Mackenzie against the Family Compact is the background against which the main action of the play, dealing with the temptation of three individuals to revolt against the limitations of their lives as settlers' wives, takes place. The tension between duty and the desire of the heart, mind, and spirit for something which cannot be attained while duty is done is the core of this play, as it is in *Fortune*, and again, the subject of the intellectual and cultural deprivation Canada has imposed on its people is central. Thematically, the two plays have so much in common that they may be considered two ways of saying virtually the same thing, but the variations in setting, characters, structure, and tone make the two plays so different that they illustrate clearly the fact that Davies's "message" is not the whole play and lend support to his contention that his are not primarily plays of ideas at all.

Though the setting and the central characters of *At My Heart's Core* are historical, the historical event which occurs at the time of the play, the 1837 Rebellion, takes place offstage, and only one of the characters is directly involved in it. The events of the play are purely imaginary. What was of historical interest to Davies was the thoughts, the values, the attitudes of the settlers he portrays. Davies's three central characters, Susanna Moodie, her sister Catherine [sic] Parr Traill, and their neighbour Frances Stewart, are all women who left written records from which their attitudes may be deduced. Davies depicted them on the basis of these records[1] and contrived his plot to draw from each the secret longing at her heart's core and weigh it against the lot of the genteel settler's wife.

The action takes place on a day in December 1837 at the homestead of the Honourable Thomas Stewart and his wife, Frances, in Douro settlement. He, a Member of the Legislative Council, is for most of the play away in York to assist in quelling the rebellion, but he returns at the end of the second act. Mrs. Traill and Mrs. Moodie arrive at the home of Mrs. Stewart, where a young Irish settler has come the preceding night to give birth. Their discussion of the rebellion and their attention to the baby are interrupted by the arrival of the baby's father, Phelim Brady, who comes to claim his child and his woman. Mrs. Stewart objects on the grounds that a home where the frozen corpse of Phelim's wife is on the roof awaiting burial is not a proper place to take a newborn child, that Phelim and Honour are not yet married — the ceremony is to be performed by the priest who will bury the first Mrs. Brady — and that Phelim will, as he demonstrates at the first opportunity, beat Honour for producing a girl child. As the women, protected only by an Indian servant girl, who is quite effectively armed with a heavy skillet, wonder how to deal with Phelim, a neighbouring gentleman, Edmund Cantwell, appears. The ladies have no great faith in Cantwell, who is known to them only by reputation and who betrays a lack of proper values by his failure to work his large piece of land or to take part in putting down the Rebellion, but they accept his offer to help them deal with Phelim.

In Act II, the main line of the plot begins, as Cantwell in conversation with each of the ladies in turn brings to light their hidden dissatisfactions and by glorifying the secret image each has of herself strikes each with discontent. He speaks first with Mrs. Stewart, mentioning shared acquaintance in the better social circles of Ireland; in particular, he tells her of a hunting party with a Lord Rossmore who, Cantwell discovered when Rossmore was knocked unconscious in a fall, wears around his neck a miniature of Frances Stewart. Cantwell emphasizes the contrast between the woman she might have been "in the midst of that brilliant and fashionable society, with the light of a hundred candles falling upon her jewels" and the one she is, "sitting on a rush chair by the light of a backwoods fire" (43-44). She possesses all the graces to fit her for that other sort of life, he argues: "You are beautiful, highly born, witty, and possessed of that wonderful generosity of spirit — that quality of *giving* — which raises beauty and charm to the level of great and holy virtues. What need has the backwoods of these things? You should not be here. You chose wrongly" (44). This may sound like flattery, but everything we have seen of Frances Stewart confirms his description. Visibly distressed, she forbids him to say more and goes for a solitary walk, whereupon Cantwell turns his attention to Mrs. Traill.

Her work as a naturalist is the subject of their discussion; Cantwell reports to her the estimate of a Mr. Sheppard, who is writing a book on Canadian flora, that she has extraordinary scientific capacity. She has refused Sheppard's invitation to be one of a few expert collaborators in his work, because her duties as a settler's wife do not leave her time to do the scientific work. Cantwell urges the pity of "genius wasted": "You are able to do work which no one else can do. Why should you waste your time in tasks of which any woman is capable?" Her secret yearning emerges when Cantwell quotes Sheppard's assertion that "if Mrs. Traill could give all her time to her studies of natural life she could do for her part of Upper Canada what Gilbert White did for Selborne" (46). But she refuses to hear Cantwell insist that her husband's work as a settler should not take precedence over her scientific work, and she, like Mrs. Stewart, leaves him.

Now it is Mrs. Moodie's turn to be tempted to discontent, and Cantwell takes much the same line of argument with her as he did with her sister. He claims Byron's endorsement of his literary perceptions, admires her writing ability, and suggests that if she could devote herself to her writing, instead of working hastily when she is tired in what little time she can spare from the duties of a settler's wife, she might be the equal of Maria Edgeworth, whose writing she admires greatly. He attaches great importance to her work as a writer, elevating it above her concerns as mother, wife, and British loyalist, and calling it "art," and "sacred obligation," in contrast to the "chilly business" of her sister's science (54). Mrs. Moodie, who is of the three women the most susceptible to his arguments, does not walk out on him as the others did; rather, their conversation is interrupted by the others. He insists that he has only given words to what they have all naturally felt, and at this point Thomas Stewart enters, returned from York. He finds the three women overwrought, Phelim insisting on peculiar goings-on between the women and Cantwell, and Cantwell triumphantly proclaiming his success at tempting all three ladies.

The third act portrays Stewart most effectively as a wise, warm, fun-loving, sensible, and understanding man. He conducts a mock trial of Cantwell, trying to understand what he has done to distress the ladies so. Since the offence turns out to be a moral rather than a legal one, Cantwell is permitted to depart, and Stewart sets everything to rights by arranging the burial of Phelim's wife and his marriage to Honour, and telling Mrs. Moodie and Mrs. Traill that their husbands will be on full pay in the military for some time yet, which will considerably relieve them from the hardships of the poor gentleman farmer's life, and that Lt. Moodie is to have a government post. In a touching concluding scene between the Stewarts, their gratitude for each other and the love they share convinces Frances that her dream of Rossmore is only a romantic illusion and she does not really regret her choice of husband. And so they live happily ever after.

Indeed, the tone and structure of the play contain suggestions of the fairytale. The three parallel scenes between Cantwell and each of the ladies and the many hints that Cantwell is to be associated with the devil particularly contribute to this effect, as does the late entrance of Stewart to play the role of the charming prince who brings about the happy ending.

Cantwell is associated with the devil most obviously by Phelim, who introduces the idea explicitly: "him the wickedest fella in Douro and some says he's the Devil himself" (32). The ladies dismiss Phelim's assertion as drunken raving; only Cantwell seems to take him seriously in a sardonic fashion. "PHELIM: Beware, women, beware! He'll tempt ye! He'll have the smocks off ye! Didn't Barney Flynn see a goat fly out of his chimney last Hallowe'en? CANTWELL: Phelim is doing his best to warn you" (33). When Phelim is not reminding us to associate Cantwell with the devil, Cantwell keeps the idea alive himself: "I have been told that I have the cheek of the Devil" (49).

The more interesting evidence for seeing in Cantwell the devil himself is less explicit and less easily dismissed. Cantwell's entrance is accounted for realistically by his desire to hire a yoke of oxen and a driver from the Stewarts to aid in his departure from Upper Canada. But his first line upon entering is significant. He enters as Phelim and Susanna Moodie are discussing their roles as artists in time to hear Phelim's explanation of the difference between them: "My poems and tales are rooted deep in a mighty past, and yours are the thin and bitter squeezings from the weary fancy of a heartsore woman." "Who speaks of a heartsore woman?" asks Cantwell

(24), producing the distinct impression that he has been conjured up by the presence of someone in this state of mind — one who promises to be an easy mark for temptation. A discussion of temptation follows Phelim's allegations, at Cantwell's instigation: "If any of you have the slightest objection to eating with the Devil, I shall be happy to take my plate out on the step. I should not wish to put any of you needlessly in the way of temptation." Mrs. Moodie's brusque assurance that "if any of us are to be tempted, it will not be by you" is received with smiling irony: "I have received your assurance, madam, and I shall treat it with all the respect it deserves" (33). Mrs. Stewart and Mrs. Traill both feel that an advantage of their lives in the backwoods in the absence of temptation, but Cantwell, in the course of the play, shows them that they are quite wrong, that there is a kind of temptation for which the backwoods of Canada are the ideal setting.

There is a brief reference to a Mr. Cantwell in Frances Stewart's letters. In a catalogue of her neighbours, she mentions a man "who is a curiosity, and about whom there is an endless mystery — Mr. Cantwell. No one can find out exactly what countryman he is, but he has lived a great deal in Ireland, passed a part of his life in France, is well acquainted with literature and has a fund of anecdote and conversation. He married a nun, she left a convent in Cork to marry him. He is intimately acquainted with Lord Rossmore."[2] From this reference Davies retained every detail, but the sense of mystery is most important for its suggestion of a kind of archetypal Tempter. Cantwell is just the man to appeal to these ladies with the sort of temptation to which they are vulnerable. He is cultivated and he is from Home. Once the ladies have relaxed their suspicion of him sufficiently to let him in the door, they find themselves enjoying his conversation greatly. It raises their spirits "to hear English spoken in a fashion that recalls the society to which we were accustomed in our better days" (36-37), and they are excited by his acquaintance with Lord Rossmore and Lord Byron and Maria Edgeworth.

Not only does he remind them of Home, but this tempter has determined to turn his back on the scene of their trials, the backwoods of Canada; life here is too demanding for his taste. He tempts each of them in a general way at first and more specifically later to think of herself as Pegasus at the plough, to feel that her special talents are wasted in the struggle that this new country demands of its settlers. A traditional characteristic of the devil that Cantwell possesses is the ability to assume different guises as the occasion demands. As Cantwell begins his temptation of Susanna Moodie, Davies directs, "*his approach to her is that of the intellectual bully, in contrast to his air of calm reason when talking to MRS. TRAILL and the romantic air which he gave to his scene with MRS. STEWART*" (48). And once he has succeeded in tempting them all, Cantwell's "*manner is*

sharply changed to an air of contempt and amusement" (62). He knows
what approach will be most effective for each of the people he deals with.
He allows each of the ladies to see in him what she wants to see; only after
the damage is done does he allow the malice that motivates him to show.

On the realistic level, Davies gives Cantwell a motive for tormenting the
women: he resents the closed circle of the "in" group in Upper Canada
which has made no social overtures to him and his wife during the two years
they have been in the neighbourhood. "Perhaps you do not realize what a
tight, snug, unapproachable little society you have here in Upper Canada. I
am not surprised that you have brought a rebellion upon yourselves" (79).
Stewart, who seems otherwise quite perfect, is clearly uncomfortable
about the accusation; there is something in it. But Cantwell is out for
revenge, destroying the ladies' peace of mind out of malice. Their assurance that *he* couldn't tempt them betrays their conviction of their own
superiority, which gives credence to his motivation. Yet even in the midst of
the third-act revelation of Cantwell's realistic motive, the other, more
important level of meaning is apparent. Phelim is still shouting that
Cantwell is the Devil, and Stewart makes light of it: "We don't have the
Devil in the nineteenth century, and we certainly don't have him in this
country" (79). But the Devil is not so easily dismissed, and the air of
mystery about Cantwell remains. "Who are you," Mrs. Moodie demands,
"to cast our sins of omission in our teeth, and to stand in judgement upon
us?" "CANTWELL: That, Mrs. Moodie, is a matter which I prefer to
leave in doubt. MRS. MOODIE: And all that you said — you whose
opinion Byron valued — was flattery? No grain of truth in it. CANTWELL:
That also I prefer to leave in doubt." He exits still wrapped in mystery and
malice, triumphant in Mrs. Moodie's admission that "that doubt will gnaw
at me all my life" (80) and, as a parting shot, telling Mrs. Stewart that he will
not forget her message (her good wishes to Rossmore) in such a way as to be
sure that Mr. Stewart will overhear.

The mystery and malice are both appropriate for the Tempter, but the
play finally emphasizes the vulnerability within rather than the evil without. Whether Cantwell is just a man or the Devil himself, his significance is
that he objectifies the temptation that gnaws at the hearts of the three
women. This is made clear at the end of the second act, just before Stewart
comes to the rescue. Cantwell is discussing with the ladies as a group his
earlier conversations with each of them separately. "My transgression,"
he states, "was that I said what lay in *your* hearts, and you cannot forgive
me." When Mrs. Stewart refuses to heed his words, he replies, "But you
will always hear what your heart tells you. I have spoken your unacknowledged feelings; they will never be without a voice again" (59). When he is
accused of causing them pain, he replies, "I have done nothing but give

words to the pain which you have long felt," and when Mrs. Stewart again insists on the impossibility of any of them admitting the truth of his words, he answers, "I wish for your sakes that that were so, but you have admitted it already — at your heart's core" (60). That this is so and not just a wily defence of Cantwell's is shown by the three ladies' acute distress over the things he says to them. If they had not nurtured feelings of discontent in their hearts, they could enjoy the praise he heaps on them and shrug off his insistence that their lives are misspent and their talents wasted, secure in the conviction that they are doing what is best for them and their families in the world they live in. But they cannot easily dismiss the temptation to discontent. In the end Mrs. Stewart manages, with her husband's help, to resist the temptation. Mrs. Moodie cannot and admits that it will always torment her. Mrs. Traill occupies a middle ground of rational resignation, recognizing her dreams as "desires which can never be fulfilled and which are cherished all the more closely for that reason" (75).

The three women and the three parallel scenes of temptation allow Davies to avoid too limited a definition of the sort of deprivation which Canada's settlers suffered. Davies says the play "came directly from my sense of the intellectual loneliness of the pioneers who had left the world of the mind behind them, and tried to keep up their contact with it from the depths of the wilderness" (113). Frances Stewart's letters comment more than once on this, though her thoughts are more on her children than herself:

I have able and ready helpers in my dear girls; they are very expert needle-women, and can cut and make up better than I can myself. The disadvantage is that all these necessary occupations come in the way of mental and intellectual improvement, causing a want of ideas and conversation exceedingly perceptible among all the young people in this country. There is a dearth of intellectual pursuits and too much confinement to the business of the day.[3]

Davies's feeling that Canada is the worse for this deprivation is clear from such other plays as *Hope Deferred* and *Fortune, My Foe*. In *At My Heart's Core*, he is less concerned with those who have never known the joys of the mind and so do not miss them, like the Stewarts' children and the Philistines in *Fortune, My Foe*, than he is with those who have been accustomed to such privileges and are starved for them in their lives as new settlers. The lack is felt by all three ladies, in different ways.

Mrs. Stewart's sense of loss centres not in things intellectual but rather in the "brilliant and fashionable society" which is nowhere to be found in the life she now lives. Beauty and charm are her attributes, and these are

probably less valued in the backwoods than more practical talents, and
doubtless less valued than they would be in a society that had the leisure for
refining and admiring such graces. However, since everybody in the play,
from her husband to the reprobate Phelim, does respond positively to her
gracious manner, it would be difficult to argue convincingly that the
warmth she radiates to her companions is worthless, though she might have
shone more brightly as Lady Rossmore. We do see illustrated best in her,
partly because the play is set in her home, the particular hardship in coming
from a high social class into the backwoods, though the speech dealing
most directly with this subject is Mrs. Moodie's. She explains why the
humbler settlers seem often to have more success with life in Canada: partly
because they are accustomed to physical labour, but also "because we are
gentry we cannot live without a few of the comforts of life which the
humbler settlers have not known and do not therefore miss. These comforts make the difference between an endurable life and what we should
consider degradation....Good birth and gentle breeding carry with them
tastes and obligations which are costly to maintain" (50-51). She comments
on how the humbler settlers sponge on the gentry, who feel obliged to help
even when they have nothing to spare; Davies probably remembered
Moodie's amusingly rueful treatment of her illumination on this fact of life
in *Roughing It in the Bush*.[4] We see in the play Honour's easy assumption
that the Stewarts' is the place to go when she needs help, and she is not
mistaken; obviously the Stewarts are used to helping out.

Frances Stewart's loss of luxuries and elegance does not seem particularly serious compared to the Strickland sisters' lack of time for intellectual
pursuits. Davies orders the three temptation scenes from the loss that he
apparently feels is least significant, to the one about which he seems to feel
most strongly, and the ladies' ability to resist temptation varies accordingly. After Frances Stewart's temptation, he moves to Catherine Parr
Traill's and finally to Susanne Moodie's. There is not a great deal of
difference in the nature of the temptation experienced by the two sisters,
but Cantwell elevates the significance of art and the artist above that of
science and the scientist, because "art is what gives form and meaning to
life" (54). Cantwell's encounter with Mrs. Moodie is the longest scene of
the three, and the arguments he uses on her seem most persuasive. Indeed
one may well wonder whose side Davies is on, listening to his "tempter"
persuading the biologist and the writer to exercise their talents fully instead
of drudging away to help their husbands wrest a living out of their Canadian
backwoods farms. Does Davies not favour a writer using her talents as fully
as possible? Would Moodie's desire to do so not be good rather than evil?
At least one reader is so convinced that Cantwell's must be the Voice of
Truth that she complains that the women's efforts to resist the temptation,

their arguments in defence of the lives they are living, are "too effective."[5] But such an interpretation takes into account neither Cantwell's identification with the devil nor the obvious fact that Frances Stewart's refusal to succumb to temptation constitutes a happy ending. The complexity and ambiguity are not a mistake on Davies's part; they reflect his feelings about the part played by art in life and about the advantages and disadvantages of the early settlers' lives in Canada.

In choosing Susanna Moodie to be the artistic target for the devil, Davies selected a writer he does not admire. He has called her "a snob, a liar .... a self-righteous, egotistical woman" who "writes self-indulgently to make herself look great."[6] He describes her as one "who has tried to compromise with the demands of art and has ... seriously diminished her stature as an artist by doing so. Mrs. Moodie writes bad verses to support the Family Compact and would rather be thought a lady than a writer"(114). Susanna Moodie draws Davies's fire not because she does not devote all her time to her writing, but because he sees her as a hypocrite and a propagandist, one who uses writing to serve other ends. In *Roughing It in the Bush*, when she writes of pride in her first small successes as a writer, it is the money she seems to value most: "I actually shed tears of joy over the first twenty-dollar-bill I received from Montreal."[7] *Roughing It in the Bush* suggests that she wrote primarily to improve the lot of her family, and during the Mackenzie Rebellion, as Davies shows in *At My Heart's Core*, to serve a cause. Moodie's introduction in *Roughing It in the Bush* to the verses recited in *At My Heart's Core* as a sample of her writing would reflect clearly to Davies the utilitarian nature of her work: "As I could not aid in subduing the enemies of my beloved country England with my arm, I did what little I could to serve the good cause with my pen."[8] Davies's real objection to her as a writer, I think, is not that she fails to devote all her time and energy to her work, but that she fails to devote all her heart and soul to it. If she writes calculatingly to serve certain ends, whether they be to make money, to foster Loyalist fervour, or to project a cherished self-image, she is not an honest artist. This is a view Davies presents clearly in *Fortune, My Foe*; in *At My Heart's Core*, it is less of an issue but important to an understanding of Davies's portrayal of Moodie, the least attractive of his three women. Cantwell tempts her to devote all her time and energy to her writing, even if her husband and children must be sacrificed to it. But, given the real basis of Davies's objection to her, her writing would not be essentially transformed by such an opportunity. (In fact, it was not, since most of the writing by which Davies judges her was done after her departure from the backwoods, forecast at the end of the play.)

That there is much truth in the words of Cantwell should not blind us, as it does Susanna Moodie, to the fact that Cantwell's *is* the Voice of the

Devil.[9] After all, only a victim of enormous pride or naiveté assumes the
devil to be so stupid that he can be seen through easily. Davies's devil
begins with a valid argument about the importance of art and the desirability of doing the best of which one is capable. The temptation to evil lies in
the inclination to subdue the whole to a part, to violate the essential balance
of one's personality by over-emphasizing one part of it.[10] Elspeth Buitenhuis [Cameron] discusses Davies's advocacy of wholeness, of Apollonian
balance and restraint, convincingly in the concluding chapter of her monograph, *Robertson Davies*. She equates Cantwell's temptation with the
"Dyonysian forces of artistic genius and comedy," which are, in Davies's
work, generally restrained by the larger Apollonian order, in this play
represented by Judge Stewart.[11] It is in the excesses of Cantwell's pitch that
the evil lies. Perhaps Cantwell's villainy can be seen most clearly in the
light of Davies's exploration of evil in literature in "Masks of Satan." In his
discussion of the villain of melodrama, he portrays him as "the Hero with
the lid off....what the Hero would be if the Hero were not one of Nature's
Noblemen."[12] That Cantwell is urging Susanna Moodie to take "the lid off"
is most obvious in the penultimate speech of his temptation: "I tell you that
you may strangle all your children in their beds, murder Moodie with the
cleaver, trample the British flag under your feet and Almighty God will find
some mercy for you; but if you refuse, for an idiotic scruple, to write your
best, He will put you into hellfire and I, as a critic, will applaud His
judgement"(54).

Davies no doubt enjoyed casting his devil as a literary critic, and naturally, literary critics have some difficulty in recognizing the evil he embodies.
But Cantwell's phrasing sets forth vividly the logical extreme of his argument that Mrs. Moodie's husband and children ought to be sacrificed to her
ambition to become an acclaimed artist. Susanna Moodie might be a better
artist for subduing all her other values to the daemonic drive to create, but
she would not be a better person.[13] It seems to be Davies's contention that
what made her such a bitter, unlovable person may have been her inability
either to resist the temptation to which Cantwell gives words or to yield to it
entirely. For her, a happy ending can be brought about only by changing her
circumstances, by removing herself from the drudgery of the backwoods
settler's life so that she does not have to choose between her writing and her
family's welfare. This history contrived to do; Davies had only to include it
in his play.

The temptation of each of the three ladies is marked by "the note of a
horn...clear and mysterious in the still December air" (44), sounding
nearer each time. This is both theatrically and symbolically effective.[14] The
device is reminiscent of the sound of a snapped string used by Chekhov in
The Cherry Orchard to suggest the end of an era; in *At My Heart's Core*

the bugle call at the moment when temptation smites the heart of each woman suggests the call to revolt, to rebel against the bonds of domestic duty. Davies would have found the suggestion for the bugle in *Our Forest Home*, the edition of Frances Stewart's letters compiled by her daughter Ellen, where Mrs. Stewart comments that her husband "took his bugle with him to sound when he first came in sight to give notice of his arrival," and Ellen, recalling the Mackenzie Rebellion, remembers her father's "very active part in all preparations" and observes that "he always took his bugle with him on these occasions for he could sound the military calls as well as the most expert bugler in the army."[15] Using the sound of the horn to mark each temptation was an inspiration on Davies's part; the sound, which is louder each time it is heard (appropriately, because each successive temptation is stronger, more difficult to resist), is afterward explained as Mr. Stewart's announcement of his return home. Mrs. Stewart's failure to hear his signal, which her husband comments on in surprise, effectively emphasizes her absorption in Cantwell's temptation and the inner turmoil associated with it.

The sound of the horn is associated first with the call to rebellion and then, as it turns out to belong to Judge Stewart, with the saviour who comes to repel the force of evil. Stewart sits in judgment on Cantwell. The case does not fit within the legal framework of justice, however, as the offence is a moral one; the quandary posed by the attempt to pass legal judgment on such a matter, developed more fully later in *Leaven of Malice*, is touched on here.[16] But while Stewart is unable to act in a legal capacity, he is nonetheless the character whose wisdom and humour and understanding and authority enable him to resolve the problems of the play — insofar as they can be resolved at all. It is a human resolution, not a legal one. The concluding scene between the Stewarts in which Mrs. Stewart recognizes that her life with her husband is more rewarding than the illusory promise of a past romance convinces us because we have seen in Judge Stewart a man who is well worth the sacrifices his wife has made. As the embodiment of ideal attitudes and demeanour in the play, Stewart is reminiscent of Szabo, though their circumstances are quite different. Stewart's perfection, however, seems more appropriate than Szabo's, because *At My Heart's Core* is less realistic than *Fortune, My Foe*. The fairy-tale tone provides an appropriate atmosphere for such a character, who balances the diabolical Cantwell. Though he dominates the last act, he is saved from seeming boringly Virtuous and Wise by the relative brevity of his part and especially by his high-spirited humour.

Davies made a few changes in the play for the 1966 paperback edition. Almost all are insubstantial cuts, but two omissions are significant for characterization: one of the speeches made Cantwell seem too noble and one cast too much doubt on the integrity of Judge Stewart. The humorist in Davies tends to expose the other side of everything, but he made an effort to keep that inclination in check here. Cantwell originally had a speech in the third act which suggests that the judge should be judged: "In every court the wisdom and honour of the judge are upon trial and if the accused receives less than justice the judge is guilty."[17] No doubt the speech is an accurate statement of Davies's opinion, but it was not to his purpose to lead his audience to question Stewart's judgment.

Apart from his obvious affection for and appreciation of his wife, Stewart possesses two particularly noteworthy qualities. The first is a very special consideration of others' points of view, a fairmindedness which eminently qualifies him for his role as judge, both officially and unofficially. This quality comes out most strikingly in his attitude toward the rebellion. The ladies all have a conventional loyalist attitude toward the rebels, with the possible exception of Mrs. Stewart, who is concerned primarily that the disturbance end quickly and her husband return safe. Mrs. Moodie is particularly unsympathetic to the rebels and vociferous in her conviction that the world cannot be improved by rebellion against authority. Judge Stewart, who is the representative of government in their area and who has gone to help put down the rebels, might be expected to be at least as opinionated as Mrs. Moodie on the subject, but he proves to be anything but a typical loyalist. Lacking a uniform and leaving his gun behind, he has mingled with the rebels as well as with the loyalists and is quite jocular about the similarities: "I had never realized before what necessities uniforms are in a battle. Without them, how can a man decide whom he should kill? The loyalists looked such ruffians, and the rebels looked so mild that you couldn't tell which from t'other" (65-66). He is bitterly ironic about the loyalists' enthusiastic reprisals against the rebels. He is capable of a sober and sensible evaluation of the government he is part of, admitting that while he has no sympathy with armed outbreak against law and order, "a grave suspicion assails me that what we have at York is order without law. And that is tyranny." He surprises even his wife with the admission, "I don't really think that rebellion is such a very bad thing" (67). The statement is doubly qualified, but it reveals in him a greater objectivity and broader perspective than any of the others has. His sympathy for the rebels, despite his opposition to armed rebellion, anticipates his sincere concern for the rebellious feelings which have troubled his wife and her friends. Similarly, his honest judgment of the state of affairs in the outside world prepares us to accept his judgment of the little affair here at home: he judges Cantwell a scoundrel for maliciously arousing the women's feelings of discontent and so identifies Cantwell as the silver-tongued devil he is instead of leaving us to believe he might be Truth unqualified. Yet Stewart's recognition that rebellion can be valuable in keeping those in authority aware of the feelings of those they govern can also be applied to the situation of the three ladies. Just as Upper Canada's government will be the better for the rebellion, so Mrs. Stewart will be the better for having been forced to confront her rebellious feelings directly; thus, she comes to recognize exactly what part they play in her whole being. The rebellious element must be taken into account, not ignored, but it must also be put into proper perspective, not allowed to rule the country or the individual. Susanna Moodie, who cannot accept this view of the rebellion of Mackenzie's forces against the government, is also unable to accept her own rebellious feelings, and she will always be the worse for it.

The other quality which distinguishes Thomas Stewart is his spirit. Even though he is tired from his journey and his game leg hurts, his high spirits dominate the play from the moment he enters; this moment of his entrance marks the turning-point, when the comic spirit asserts itself and moves the play from the low point of the ladies' deepest discontent to the happy ending. The comic climax of the play is Stewart's spirited rendition of Joey Grimaldi's song, "Hot Codlings." *"He borrows his wife's cap, puts it on, and makes a Grimaldi grin – eyes flashing, and tongue lolling out like a dog's. As he sings the song he drums with knife and fork upon his plate, tankard and the table itself. MRS. STEWART smiles as though accustomed to such behaviour but the STRICKLAND sisters do not know what to make of it"* (69). Stewart reports the news of Joey Grimaldi's death more seriously than he did the news of the rebellion; the "prince of clowns" epitomizes Stewart's own sense of valued things from the old life which are not to be had in the new one. "Here in the backwoods we yearn for many of the things of home, and will you believe that I have yearned for a sight of Joe Grimaldi as often as anything?" (68). Cantwell seizes on this as he did on the women's sense of loss and shares in Stewart's regret at Grimaldi's death and in his enthusiastic imitation of the clown's song, but Stewart's judgment is not impaired by the shared sentiment or by Cantwell's flattery. He does not give himself up to regret for what is lost with the old world; though he feels the loss, he thoroughly enjoys that approximation of the things he valued which he can bring with him to the new world, specifically, his own imitation of Grimaldi.

Davies's choice of Joey Grimaldi as the focal point for Stewart's scene with Cantwell is interesting. With the three women Davies focuses on social graces, science, and art as important elements of the old world which the new world has no time for. Why does he add to this selection what Mrs. Moodie calls "this wretched clown"? (69). One might ask as well why, in *Fortune, My Foe*, Davies made his artist a puppeteer whose most dearly beloved puppet is Punch instead of a musician with an enthusiasm for

Mozart. The answer is that Davies wants to broaden what we normally think of as "culture," usually something that appeals primarily to the affluent or intellectual, to include everything that appeals to the *spirit* of all. "There was a great spirit in Joey," Stewart says, and spirit is one of the qualities which distinguishes Stewart himself. He contrasts markedly with Cantwell in that he has humour and high spirits and a rather homespun quality, despite his intellect, while Cantwell is cultivated, glib, and sophisticated. One of Davies's greatest concerns about Canada — our Canada, as well as the new land of the settlers — is that it appreciates only things of practical value, while things which feed the spirit are underrated. What feeds the spirit may be a great clown as well as great literature, it may be a Punch and Judy show as well as Cervantes. Davies is not a cultural snob. What is important is that the spirit — or the soul — requires sustenance as the body does, and Davies's fear is that in its efforts to provide material sustenance in ever-greater quantity and quality, Canada neglects spiritual sustenance. That this happened in the days of the early settlers Davies regards as pitiable, and his sympathy encompasses people he feels no particular fondness for, like Susanna Moodie, as well as those he admires, like the Stewarts.

The subplot of *At My Heart's Core*, featuring Phelim and Honour Brady, has generally been admired for its comic vigour but criticized for its failure to join smoothly with the main plot to produce a unified whole. Honour and Phelim, together with Sally, the Indian servant, provide farcical comedy which contrasts in tone with the romantic comedy of the main plot. Sally has two functions: one is to combat the stereotypical view of the Indian by giggling at everything instead of being wooden-faced and by providing domestic service to the settlers instead of violent assaults. The other, an amusing twist on her domesticity, is to defend the Stewart household by laying Phelim flat with a vigorous swing of her iron skillet when he becomes troublesome. Sally, armed with the skillet, is a convincing yet comic means of keeping Phelim in order, and later, of keeping Cantwell under house arrest. Phelim and Honour contribute to the farcical action as well, but more important is the comedy in the contrast between their values and social standards and those of the ladies. Honour feels no embarrassment about her relationship with Phelim, who is her foster father, the father of her child, and her husband-to-be (at the suggestion of his dying first wife, Honour's foster mother.) The comedy is in this very lack of self-consciousness, which results in a series of partial revelations that are first puzzling, then quite funny, as the light dawns on the ladies — and the audience. Given her casual attitude towards Phelim, Honour's sense of propriety about other matters is amusing too. She has, she explains, "a proper regard for the feelings of the dead," and so rather than give birth to her child in a house "with herself that was like a mother to me above on the roof friz as stiff as a cedar log" (16), she swallowed a pint of gin to soothe both herself and her child and took herself off to the Stewarts. And though Phelim gets the bulk of the commentary on the manners and attitudes of the ladies, Honour is the source of an amusing observation on Mrs. Moodie's reason for not wanting to be alone with Cantwell: "Gentry ladies can't trust themselves alone with a man. They're that frisky they'd be at him at once. It's all the rich food they eat" (49).

Phelim is the most important character in the subplot, not only because he provides the excuse for Cantwell to stay on the scene and identifies him explicitly with the devil, but because his contributions to the themes of revolution and art have significance for the development of the main plot. Phelim's refusal to budge from the Stewarts' door until Mrs. Stewart yields up his "wife" and child, his rejection of her insistence that he first bury his wife, marry Honour, and go to work, constitutes a rebellion in miniature which is paralleled with the Mackenzie Rebellion taking place offstage. Phelim, we are frequently reminded in one way or another, is representative of "the people," and the Stewarts, of the privileged few who control the government. For instance, when Phelim observes that the gentry folks all side with the government and describes the delight Moodie and Traill must take in larking off in their old uniforms, leaving their farms and their wives and their debts behind them, Mrs. Moodie observes that "he is railing so bitterly because he is on the losing side in the little battle that is being fought right here" (40). And when the ladies and Cantwell go into the Stewarts' home for dinner, leaving Phelim to his determined seige on their doorstep, Act I closes with Phelim peering through the window, exclaiming, "B'God, it's the Family Compact sittin' down to their food! And where's the common people? Out in the cold, every time; out in the cold! Hurray for Mackenzie and responsible government!" (34-35).

The interaction between Phelim and Mrs. Stewart in particular shows us directly the state of affairs which constitutes the background to the action. Phelim is powerless but bent on his right to have his own family in his own home. He is not a bad sort in his way, but he knows what he wants and he is not about to knuckle under to authority and do without it. Mrs. Stewart has a different idea from his about what is right and proper; she has — or her husband has — legal authority over Phelim: the fact that he is a squatter and could be removed from "his" land is held over his head, and she has the power (in Sally and her skillet) to enforce her will, so she refuses to give him Honour and the child until he conforms to her standard of behaviour. Her motive, to do her credit, is at least in part to protect Honour. The implication is that the Family Compact rules with the intention of doing their best by the people under their government but under the assumption that they know what is best better than the people do. Mrs. Stewart admits, "Probably what I am doing is quite illegal, but I know it is right. MRS. TRAILL: If it is right it cannot be illegal. One can only deal with people like that by telling them what is good for them, and seeing that they behave themselves accordingly. CANTWELL: That is the simple principle of government, madam, which has given rise to the regrettable revolution" (30). Davies draws a sympathetic picture of characters on both sides of the miniature rebellion. Phelim is a rascally old reprobate, but nonetheless likeable. He is the natural man, true to his own conception of rightness, intelligent though uncouth, not awed by authority but responsive to kindness. He taunts Mrs. Moodie, who inclines to steamroller tactics, but he is respectful of Mrs. Stewart, who treats him politely. Mrs. Stewart embodies the best of authoritarian government. She worries about how cold Phelim must be, stubbornly maintaining his stand outside her door, and decides to take him a cup of tea. Mrs. Moodie protests: "But Frances, you are punishing Phelim for his wickedness and trying to bring him to a better frame of mind. How can you do that and give him cups of tea at the same time. MRS. STEWART: Set it down to Irish irrationality, Susanna. CANTWELL: It is the sort of irrationality which makes our system of government endurable. If we will not permit people to run their own affairs, we are obliged to be very kind to them to make up for it" (38).

Judge Stewart settles this miniature rebellion very easily when he returns, simply by making arrangements for Phelim's late wife to be buried and for Phelim and Honour to be married. The other grounds of disagreement, Phelim's inclination to beat Honour and his refusal to go to work, are ignored, or perhaps cursorily dealt with in Stewart's instructions to Honour to "keep this man in order, and if he lets a rebellious thought out of him ... tell me at once" (81-82). The Mackenzie Rebellion was dealt with almost as summarily. The subplot is clearly related to the 1837 Rebellion, then, as is the main plot. Critical complaints about lack of unity in the play are acounted for by the fact that the two plots are related to each other only indirectly, through the third story of rebellion which forms the historical background of the play.

The two plots indirectly related by the subject of rebellion are more directly related by the subject of art, for Phelim and Susanna Moodie are explicitly compared and contrasted as artists. Phelim makes the comparison; Mrs. Moodie could not have conceived of classifying herself and Phelim together in any way. "I'm one of your own kind," he tells her. "I'm a story-teller." He cannot read or write, but he sees himself as "the latter-day heir o' the great bards and story-tellers of the old land" who can tell "a story will pass away a whole night from dusk to dawn" and "make up a new song for a wake or a wedding as quick as the fiddler can play."

"You and me is two branches o' the same old tree," he assures her, and they suffer the same fate in the new land: "You and me is both in one losin' battle. We're the songbirds that aren't wanted in this bitter land, where the industrious robins and the political crows get fat" (41). Though he begins by classifying himself with her, her snobbery evokes a spirited declaration of his own superiority. "MRS. MOODIE: I am not a vain author, but I think that there is a difference between the productions of an educated and disciplined taste and a rigamarole of memorized fairy tales! PHELIM: How wise ye are! There's a big difference, and it's this: my poems and tales are rooted deep in a mighty past, and yours are the thin and bitter squeezings from the weary fancy of a heartsore woman" (24). To the genteel characters of the play, Phelim is beneath even the common settlers, who are more industrious and more presentable than he, but Phelim considers himself their superior: "Isn't a poet and a story-teller miles beyond and above them common fellows is diggin' the ground and pullin' out stumps?" (27). Phelim's role in this play is similar to Buckety Murphy's in *Fortune, My Foe*, but Buckety is a passive social outcast, while Phelim is in active rebellion against social constraints, defying both religious and civil authority as well as disdaining conventional mores.

Davies defends Phelim's claim to artistic superiority, calling him "a real artist and a real Bohemian" who "will do no work but that for which he believes himself divinely fitted." In this Davies draws "a sharp contrast to Mrs. Moodie, who has tried to compromise with the demands of art. ... There is no doubt in my mind," Davies concludes, "as to which is the greater artist" (114). Yet in this statement Davies provides a one-sided view of an issue which is presented with greater complexity in the play; it is worth noting the context of Davies's statement, which is a defence against the accusation that he is unfair to the lower-class settlers in the play. All we know for certain about Phelim is that he does no work at all, explaining that no one in this new land wants his art. All we see him do is drink and talk and attempt to beat Honour. He is characterized chiefly by irresponsibility. He wants Honour back to "tend him," but he, who has left the corpse of his wife frozen on his roof for six weeks, appears to feel no duty to anyone. Phelim is in a sense an image of the temptation Susanna Moodie struggles against: to free herself of the claims duty makes upon her and refuse any work except her art. With Phelim as the model of one who has made this choice, it is easier to see why Davies suggests that Moodie's temptation is a temptation to evil, despite a fairly general assumption that devotion to Pure Art must be a fine thing. Though the suggestion has been made that the temptations are not evil at all but only seem so to the bourgeois mind, Phelim weighs against this interpretation, for it is he who first identifies Cantwell with the devil, and his is hardly a bourgeois mind. Cantwell and

Phelim are the two who speak for Pure Art in this play, and there is a hint of the old saw, "It takes one to know one," in Phelim's insistence that Cantwell is the devil. Certainly Cantwell makes no effort to tempt Phelim, who is rather a lost soul already. Though they could not be more different superficially, they have in common, in addition to their advocacy of dedication to art, their failure to thrive in the new world or even to make an effort to thrive.

Fortune, My Foe and *At My Heart's Core* are strikingly similar in their treatment of the theme of Canada's cultural poverty. In both, central characters are tempted to repudiate Canada's demands on them, to turn their backs on the hardships imposed on them, not so much physical or economical hardships (though the latter enter into *Fortune, My Foe* and both into *At My Heart's Core*) as intellectual and spiritual ones. In both plays, the temptation is objectified in a character who personifies both the allure of the heart's desire and the drawbacks to it: Vanessa is superficial and Cantwell is irresponsible. Both plays depict Canada as a scene of sacrifice but also of hope. However, the differences are significant, and they add up to a better play in *At My Heart's Core*.

Although both plays show Davies's ambivalent feelings about Canada, *At My Heart's Core* goes beyond *Fortune, My Foe* in exploring ambivalent feelings about art as well. Consciousness of the difficulty of defining art is apparent in both plays: Buckety and Phelim present their claims to artistry along with Szabo and Susanna Moodie. But the question of the role art should play in the life of an individual and a society is given much more complex treatment in the later play. One cannot utterly condemn nineteenth-century Canada for its neglect of art in favour of more practical concerns in the light of a passage like Phelim's "In the old land...the people were that wretched they'd be glad of a tale or a song to beguile them from hunger and the thoughts of death and injustice. But here the poorest ruffian of them all has his bit o' land, and his pig, maybe, and the ones with good arms and good heads on them is thrivin' so fast they never feel the need of a story at all....They're a strange lot entirely, with the blush o' health on their cheeks and the maggot o' respectability in their brains. They're wantin' schools for their young ones, and for me it's 'Get away wid ye, Phelim; don't be wastin' our time wid yer talk'" (27). *Is* a song or a tale to be preferred to a school for children? *Should* one sacrifice the welfare of one's family to nurture one's art? *Is* a person who refuses to feel any obligation except to art a better person than one who tries to strike a balance among different obligations?

Davies is a humorist, an ironist who cannot long rest with a simple view of anything. Always, the opposite intrudes. In *Hope Deferred*, his earliest play on the place of art in Canada, Davies kept things simple with his example of art — a classical play, — and with his heroine's easy choice of her art over her country. *Fortune, My Foe* is more complex in its definition of art and in its treatment of the hero's choice. *At My Heart's Core* is the most complex of all in its exploration of the definition and function of art and of its value relative to other values on both a national and an individual scale. It seems very likely that Davies was wondering at this time what place art should take in his own life. He had a wife and three small daughters; he had a demanding job as editor, vice-president, and publisher of the *Peterborough Examiner*; he was writing and directing plays and working on his first novel. He may well have felt something of Susanna Moodie's yearning to give all of himself to his art as well as her sense of duty to her family. His later work shows more clearly the values that bore on resolution of this problem, but the problem itself is quite clear in *Hope Deferred*, *Fortune, My Foe*, and *At My Heart's Core*. The resolution is in striking a balance among conflicting demands, in creating harmony out of conflict by recognizing wholeness as the ideal, and this is suggested first in *At My Heart's Core*. Looking back, Davies says, "I never had to choose between art and duty, and I protest against the poseurs who talk about having given *all* to art; my family life sustained me when I was writing, and my work sustained them, because my wife and children knew I was working away at something we all thought important. Artists have to be kept human: they achieve this in various ways. My way was by daily contact with life through my job, and daily contact with real emotion through my family."[18]

Among the marked differences between *Fortune, My Foe* and *At My Heart's Core* is the relationship between the main plot and the subplot. In *Fortune* the tone does not change from one to the other, and the outcome of the main plot is dependent on the subplot. If unity of action or tone is assumed to be the measure of a good play, *Fortune* will be judged superior in this respect. But a farcical subplot that contrasts with a romantic main plot is a feature of plays which have remained popular and critically acclaimed for hundreds of years. Such plays are *Twelfth Night*, which Davies directed for the Peterborough Little Theatre the year after he wrote *At My Heart's Core*,[19] and *A Midsummer Night's Dream*, which he identifies in "Jung and the Theatre" as "one of the very greatest dreams" of humanity.[20] The result of the combination of contrasting elements is, at its best, a play which delights because of its variety as well as its depth; this *At My Heart's Core* does.

Another striking difference between the two plays is that one is contemporary and one is historical. This need not in itself define a better or worse play, but in several respects the historical play worked better for Davies. One is that he could write the sort of language he likes and is particularly good at for his nineteenth-century upper-class characters; the wit and polish of their speech seems more appropriate for them than for his twentieth-century characters. Vincent Tovell's review notes: "The charm of this most entertaining play lies mainly in its dialogue, which is literate and very polished. The scenes between Cantwell and the ladies are witty and graceful, suggesting the period perfectly, and the outlandish extravagances of Felim [sic] contrast beautifully with them."[21] Another advantage of the historical setting, observed by Michael Tait (who also remarks on the linguistic advantage), is that it puts a distance between Davies and his subject which allows him to develop his theme of the cultural povery of Canada with some detachment.[22] In this respect, At My Heart's Core is a better play; by contrast Fortune, My Foe seems rather sour and sullen, though the ebullience of Chilly Jim and Buckety Murphy's antics and the warmth of Franz Szabo lighten the tone of the play. Also a contemporary play is likely to be more quickly dated; the complaints about greater rewards for scholarship elsewhere no longer seem justified. At My Heart's Core allows one to share Davies's mixed feelings of sympathy for and criticism of early Canadians and to contemplate our own situation in comparison with that of the settlers, feeling both that naturally some change for the better has occurred and also that there is no longer any excuse for Canada to neglect nourishment of the mind and spirit; to do so suggests that Canada is characterized by second-rate mentality, by mediocrity, rather than by hardship and the necessity to make sacrifices.

A third way in which At My Heart's Core seems a more successful realization of Davies's playwriting ideals is not solely a function of its historical setting, but the historical distance between the audience's present reality and the lives of the characters seems to make a mythical flavour easier to realize. King Phoenix embraces the mythical but suffers somewhat from insufficient sense of even historical reality. Fortune, My Foe is real and immediate, but it has little of the sense of a shared dream of humanity that Davies saw as theatre at its greatest. At My Heart's Core succeeds in capturing both a sense of historical reality and a feeling of mythical grandeur.

Davies directed the first production of At My Heart's Core at the end of Peterborough Summer Theatre's 1950 season, using the facilities and actors of the young summer stock company that he had been encouraging with praise modified by kindly-phrased criticisms in his reviews for the Peterborough Examiner. Brenda Davies and the role of Mrs. Frances Stewart were apparently made for each other; the charm of her performance won praise both in Peterborough and in Ottawa, where she recreated the role with the professional Canadian Repertory Theatre the following January. John Primm as Cantwell and Donald Glen as Thomas Stewart also gave fine performances in both productions, the latter scoring a particular hit with his rendition of Joey Grimaldi's "Hot Codlings." Edmonton, Alberta, and London, Ontario, productions followed quickly. Davies was disappointed in the London Little Theatre production, which was "literal and dowdy." In the final scene, which he "meant to be touching," "Mrs. Stewart rubbed her husband's leg till it hurt — comedy as Little Theatres understood it."[23] Still, reviewers of productions everywhere as well as reviewers of the published play were enthusiastic about Davies's success in bringing Canada's pioneers to life in this warm and witty play, which many hailed as his finest to date.[24]

6

A Masque for U.C.C. and A Jig for the Crest

WITH the production of *Fortune, My Foe* in 1948 and *At My Heart's Core* in 1950, Davies was beginning to make a place for himself in professional theatre, though the plays were produced by ephemeral summer stock companies. He was also beginning his career as a novelist with the publication in 1951 of his first novel, *Tempest-Tost*. But he was not too busy making a place for himself among Canada's most important writers to comply with a request from the Headmaster of his old preparatory school, Upper Canada College, to write a play for the boys to perform in the spring of 1952 as part of the celebrations for their Jubilee Year.[1] Davies, whose first book was about boy actors in Shakespeare's day, knew that boys could play very effectively parts that were written with their abilities and limitations clearly in mind. His second book, *Shakespeare for Young Players*, was an expression of his interest in drama as a means for enriching youth. His foreword to the teacher in *Shakespeare for Young Players* stresses the value of the poise and self-assurance to be gained from acting experience, and his foreword to the pupil centres on the process of becoming a more interesting person as a result of acquiring ideas and the ability to express them well through close study of fine dramatic literature.

   A Masque of Aesop, which Davies offered as a tribute (complete with all royalties from book sales and performances)[2] to "a school which I deeply admire" (vi), reflects his ideas about drama for young people. It is a delightful romp, witty and exuberant. It is also enriching; he does not condescend to the boys by giving them something simple and childish —

one reviewer notes that it might as well be played by adult actors.[3] Classical allusions and sophisticated vocabulary offer the boys the chance for an intellectual stretch, and the themes, familiar from his earlier plays, show Davies making the most of his chance to impart to Canadian youth the values he cherishes. At the same time, the play is full of fun, ranging from Apollo's embarrassment by his disreputable aunts, the Parcae, to the Cock's reference to the *Breeder's Digest, the Creeder's Digest*, and the *Bleeder's Digest* in answer to all his chicks' questions about life. Davies's notes to the educational edition of the play published in 1955 maintain the balance of instruction and fun. The first footnote, for instance, explains that "Grege" means "The Crowd," an important character because it expresses Public Opinion; the note goes on to explain the footnoting process, calling the indices "clawmarks of the Owl of Minerva, who was the Goddess of Wisdom," which "guide you to the bits of priceless wisdom at the bottom of the page" (5). His second footnote, however, is without information, an indirect ironic comment put in solely "to warn you against a slavish dependence on . . . scholarly apparatus" (5). Some notes reinforce themes of the play: "Blasphemy means speaking against God, and it is also used to mean contrary to the majority opinion. It is extremely important to distinguish between these two usages which are frequently confused" (11).

The play is set at the Temple of Apollo at Delphi, and the action is precipitated by the rage of Delphi's citizens against Aesop, whom they are determined to put to death for the impropriety of his teachings. Apollo insists on a fair trial for Aesop at which he will be judge. The trial encompasses dramatizations of three of Aesop's fables: "The Belly and the Members," "The Town Mouse and the Country Mouse," and "The Cock and the Pearl." These are witnessed by Apollo, the three Parcae, who control men's fates, the citizens, who protest against everything (like Philpott and Tapscott watching "Don Quixote" in *Fortune, My Foe*), and Aesop, who explains his intentions. In the end, Apollo, God of Light and Truth, who is particularly interested in the arts and the affairs of boys, finds in Aesop's favour. He rebukes the citizens because "concerns of self and petty advantage have so blinded your eyes and stopped your ears that when a great teacher arises among you, he seems to you to be deformed, and his words seem blasphemy. Yet they are not blasphemy against the Truth, but only against your false beliefs" (49). He reveals Aesop, who has appeared as a "small, lame, hump-backed, wretched little man" (14), transformed into an upright and noble teacher, but he rebukes Aesop for the arrogance of his wisdom and his scorn for his fellow man, expressed by making the objects and animals of his fables wiser than mankind. Apollo then pronounces his sentence: "For centuries to come your writings shall be the delight of children, but only the wisest among them will remember your fables and interpret them wisely when childhood is past. For the greatest teacher is he who has passed through scorn of mankind to love of mankind" (49).

Davies calls his play a masque, "a form of entertainment which we have allowed to disappear, but which permits a freedom difficult to achieve in a play of conventional form" (v). The masque, which Davies would know from his familiarity with Renaissance drama in general and the work of Ben Jonson in particular, was a freely structured entertainment in which music and dancing and spectacular scenic effects were at least as important as drama, usually written for a special occasion to honour royalty and performed in part by nobility. Davies had to minimize special effects because Upper Canada College was not equipped for them, though the play calls for imaginative costuming and Apollo uses thunder to control the irate mob. The set is very basic — a platform, steps, and a backdrop — except for an empyraeum high above the platform. Davies suggests draping it with star-spangled blue cloth in which are openings for the Parcae's heads. Bearing the abilities of his performers in mind, he kept the dancing simple, but songs are featured prominently, for which original music was written by H. E. Atack and J. A. Dawson. Like the Renaissance masques, *A Masque of Aesop* was written for a special occasion, and though it was not designed to flatter royalty, Davies works in that feature of the masque by having Apollo jocularly identify various members of the audience as Juno, Mars, Bacchus, and others of distinction. Apollo's transformation of Aesop from a wretched cripple into a noble and upright figure is another feature of the play drawn from the Jonsonian masque. As in some of Jonson's masques, features of the antimasque and the masque are blended; in Davies's play the burlesque of the antimasque dominates, with the conclusion providing the dignity and grace of the masque proper. Davies capitalizes on the freedom from conventional form, using the fables to give featured roles to a large number of boys and to provide varied entertainment without elaborate plot or complex characterization.

A Masque of Aesop pits the opinions of the mob of citizens against the truth of Aesop, endorsed by Apollo. The mob ("Grege") and their spokesmen, three citizens and the leader of the crowd, are the objects of Davies's satire, aimed, as in *Fortune, My Foe, The Voice of the People*, and *Overlaid*, at those narrow minds which are confident of the correctness of their views simply because they are held by the majority. When Aesop replies to Apollo's enquiry about the nature of his terrible transgression, "I have told the truth," the four spokesmen protest, because Aesop "has the insufferable impudence to think thoughts other than those which we recognize as sane, safe and sanitary" (12). The first citizen feels that Truth is his personal property because he is the editor of a widely circulated journal

(Davies cheerfully includes one of his own profession among those he mocks); the second, because he is a priest who speaks in Apollo's name; the third, because he is a successful businessman who has mastered arithmetical facts. The leader of the crowd, as a representative of organized labour, is in principle opposed to everything the others say, but he is also opposed to Aesop as an unsettling influence in society, because "unless society is reasonably stable my followers cannot threaten it with the horrors of instability" (15). They interpret Apollo's brief account of the mountain who laboured mightily to bring forth a mouse as an attack on the Royal Commission. They are pleased with the moral of "The Belly and the Members" (though they object to the lack of refinement of the term "belly") only so long as they can interpret it solely as a plug for nationalism; they are outraged to find that Aesop means it also to endorse internationalism. They are distraught by the implication of "The Town Mouse and the Country Mouse" that luxury is not worth the sacrifice of peace of mind, because the idea threatens an economy based on the consumption of luxuries.

This first three-quarters of the play amounts to a very entertaining preparation for the key fable, "The Cock and the Pearl." The narrowmindedness of the citizens' views has been established, and Davies's thrusts at democratic foolishness culminate in an exchange between the Parcae and the Leader of the Crowd that introduces an idea treated more fully in *A Jig for the Gypsy*. As a mindless proponent of democratic equality in all things, the leader of the crowd objects menacingly to Aesop's suggestion that there is anything, like peace of mind, that everyone is not equally likely to have:

> LEADER: Something everybody can't have, eh? Who says so?
> THE PARCAE: We do!
> LEADER: And who are you?
> CLOTHO, *with sinister emphasis*: Just the Fates, dearie.
> LACHESIS: Just the Allotters and Disposers.
> ATROPOS: Nobody has any peace of mind until he had made a little shrine in his heart for us. Not an easy shrine to build, dearie (37).

Acceptance of the uncertainties and inequalities of fate is essential to peace of mind and irreconcilable with insistence on the equality of all people in all things. Some have longer lives, some, greater peace of mind, some, a better grasp of Truth.

The last fable, "The Cock and the Pearl," reinforces the theme of the whole play. The Cock, a self-important character whose idea of the begin-

ning and end of all wisdom is to "Keep an eye on the Main Chance," drills
his chicks in his philosophy:

> Let every action be
> Prudent and tactical;
> Tether your wits
> To what's sober and practical;
> Though you have wings, do not venture to fly!

The Cock gets all he wants of art and philosophy from *The Reader's
Digest*.

> I never take any chances
> In the portion of life where Romance is;
> I'd probably lose my shirt!
> I shun the mercurial
> And cheer for the stolid;
> Many heads put together
> Are sure to be solid:
> 'Go slow and in circles' is my battle cry (39-40).

His admiring hen and chicks are gratified to have "such a practical down-
to-earth, shoulder-to-the-wheel, nose-to-the-grindstone Father and Husband" and to live "in a world where everything is digested and only needs
to be swallowed" (41). The Cock attempts to devour a large piece of grit,
which turns out to be a Pearl. The Pearl's efforts to convince him of his good
fortune in happening upon a thing of perfect beauty are wasted; he can see
nothing in it but a useless, inedible piece of grit. The Cock with his
utilitarian fixation on physical well-being is as oblivious to the value of the
Pearl as the citizens with their limited perspective are oblivious to the
wisdom in Aesop's fables.[4]

Upper Canada College's production did justice to Davies's masque, and
the *Globe and Mail* reviewer found it "the ideal medium for a school
performance — literate without being pompous, witty without being frivolous and suffused with the sort of naive homespun wisdom that derives the
greatest conviction from the interpretation by a very young cast." "The
cast was splendidly costumed and meticulously disciplined," and under
direction which showed "great imagination and attention to detail," the
boys performed "with confidence and intelligence."[5] A revival in December 1954 drew equally high praise,[6] and the masque's great appeal has led to
many other performances by the College and schools, drama clubs, and
summer camps across the country.[7]

The published play, handsomely illustrated by Grant Macdonald, also delighted reviewers, though two dissenters considered it less witty than some of Davies's earlier work.[8] Others found it "entrancing," "a little masterpiece of light satire," and one thought it "perhaps his happiest invention to date," observing that "very few writers in Canada have as sure a sense of the comic as Mr. Davies or as much theatrical imagination" to which he adds "a felicity of speech that he puts to better use with each new play."[9] *Aesop* is a delight with its quirky lyrics and the attractive variety of its dramatized fables within the unifying framework of the quarrel between Aesop and the citizens over which Apollo presides. There is not much to the characterization of Aesop; his fables rather than his personality are the centre of interest. Apollo is the central character, and he is both human and divine, funny and impressive, as he tries to keep the squabbling, imperfect humans in order. In the lightness and brightness and sheer fun of *Aesop* Davies succeeds in satirizing without bitterness those facets of Canadian character which received harsher treatment in *Fortune, My Foe*. Though the setting is remote from modern Canada, Davies freely incorporates numerous references to features of modern Canadian society. The anachronisms are part of the humour, but they also remind us that the qualities of human nature which Davies satirizes in the citizens of Delphi are all too evident in our own society.[10]

Davies was generous with his talent in writing for the amateurs of Upper Canada College, and he was still directing a play every year for Peterborough Little Theatre, but the early fifties saw a spurt of growth in Canadian professional theatre, and Davies's dramatic work grew with it, both in quantity and in quality. The Stratford Shakespeare Festival was born in 1953 after a year's gestation. Partly because of his close friendship with its first director, Tyrone Guthrie, and partly because it promised to contribute significantly to his dream of strong Canadian theatre, Davies worked for its success in many ways. He was on the Festival's Board of Directors for its first nineteen years, many of them years in which he was the only member of the Board who was a director and had read all of Shakespeare's plays.[11] He wrote pieces for the Festival's souvenir programs, gave lectures on Shakespeare, and for each of the first three years of the Festival in collaboration with Tyrone Guthrie and Grant Macdonald, he produced a book to record permanently the achievement of the Festival.[12] Davies's chapters contain thoughtful analyses of the plays and of Stratford's productions.

He wrote reviews of the Festival plays for *Saturday Night* or the *Peterborough Examiner* nearly every year from 1953 through 1967, reviews which were designed to arouse and sustain enthusiasm for the Festival. Not that they were undiscriminating, for Davies was clearly more enthusiastic about some productions than others, and he commented forthrightly on weaknesses as well as strengths, but in his reviews he was out to accentuate the positive and minimize the negative, because he felt that on the whole the Festival did excellent work and deserved support.

In addition to his work for Stratford and his journalism, Davies was writing a second novel, *Leaven of Malice*, published in September, 1954. Though he was furthering the cause of Canadian theatre, his own creative work was not furthered by the Stratford Festival; his creative impulse was finding its outlet in fiction. But the Stratford Festival was not the only centre of growth in professional threatre in the fifties. A number of groups in Toronto were establishing permanent companies. It was the Crest Theatre, founded by Murray and Donald Davis, which provided Davies with an incentive for a new period of dramatic productivity. *Benoni*, written in 1944-45, had not been performed, except by BBC radio in 1952.[13] Its Welsh setting and the Welsh flavour of the dialogue diminished the play's appeal for Canadian producers. But the Davises, whose summer stock company, the Straw Hat Players, had produced *Overlaid, Fortune, My Foe*, and *At My Heart's Core*, were of Welsh ancestry, their mother was a gypsy, and the play appealed to them.[14] Davies revised it, and the Davises opened the Crest's second season in September 1954 with the play, now called *A Jig for the Gypsy*. Barbara Chilcott, the Davises's sister, took the lead role of Benoni, the gypsy fortune-teller. Donald Davis played the impish Jack the Skinner, and the director was Davies's friend Herbert Whittaker, who had directed the first production of *King Phoenix*.

Davies had been inspired by the part of Wales his father came from, "an especially beautiful part of the Border Country of North Wales." For Davies, its people had "a special degree of charm and even of romance."[15] The romance of *A Jig for the Gypsy* is largely in its central character, Benoni. The satire which dominates most of the shorter plays, including *A Masque of Aesop*, is in *Jig* as well, largely in the minor characters. Commentators on Davies's work have frequently remarked on the combination of satire and romance in his plays and novels. Patricia Morley describes Davies's style as "the result of the tension between his romantic and ironic points of view."[16] Mavor Moore sees in Davies's development "the traditional struggle between Romantic and Classical impulses (one all heart, the other all brain)."[17] Elspeth Buitenhuis [Cameron] classifies the novels as "satiric romance," in which the writer "must walk a tightrope between two forms which are at opposite ends of human experience": romance, which involves a quest "for some object or vision normally understood to stand for an ideal" and satire, which rejects the ideal "by pointing out what men are really like as opposed to their romantic ideals."[18] Satire springs from the critical intellect; romance, from the feeling heart. Oversimplification can make the combination seem an impossible contradiction, and Davies is as guilty of this as anyone in his insistence on himself as a man of feeling rather than a man of intellect, although the importance of his ideas is apparent in all his writing. Much of his best writing, that which contains the greatest depth and breadth of his comic vision, expresses both mind and heart and includes both satire and romance, though many of the shorter plays, including the masques, are more exclusively satiric. In plays of larger scope, as in the novels, he satirizes one ideal while promoting another, ridiculing the inadequate ideals of the narrow-minded and conventional majority and offering in place of them the ideals of wholeness and individuality and the personal freedom to develop as fully as possible. *A Masque of Aesop*, which concentrates on satire of the citizens' bigotry, concludes with the vindication of Aesop, the man whose perceptions go beyond the narrow views of his fellows, but even Aesop is reminded of his limitations, his failure to become a greater teacher by passing "through scorn of mankind, to love of mankind" (49). For Davies, who has a good deal of the teacher in him, the scorn of satire, which perhaps comes most readily, is usually not enough. His love for what is best in man is expressed in romance.

In *A Jig for the Gypsy* the two modes of satire and romance are both clearly present and the themes of love and politics are developed to expose the inadequacy of narrow ideals and to offer instead more satisfying ones. The play presents two worlds, that of the free-spirited gypsy fortune-teller, Benoni Richards, and the more familiar humdrum world of politics and conventional young love. Benoni is set apart physically by the isolation of her cottage on a hillside a mile and a half from town. The play is set outside her cottage, and the action is developed by a series of visitors who bring the outside world and its values into conflict with her way of life. Richard Roberts, a local grocer dedicated to Radical ideals, is inspired to have his candidate's fortune told by Benoni, knowing that if her reading of the tea leaves suggests victory for Sir John Jebson, the people will be eager to cast their ballots for him as the contender destined to be victorious. Roberts's daughter, Bronwen, persuades Benoni to tell Sir John's fortune, and the reading, as they had hoped, lends itself to the interpretation that Sir John will win the seat held for the past seventy years by the Tories. It suggests too that Sir John will receive a Cabinet post. Jack the Skinner, a poacher who makes himself at home at Benoni's place, is sent to spread the news in town; Roberts, Sir John, and his secretary, Edward Vaughan, depart in high spirits, and Bronwen stays to ask Benoni's advice about fulfilling her secret yearning for Vaughan. The first act ends with Jack's return to announce the success of his mission — Sir John is now the favourite — and Benoni is famous, a public figure whom the Tories would gladly stone if she set foot in town. Left alone, Benoni broods and shudders in the gathering darkness.

The second act expands on the effects of the fortune-telling through visits from the town photographer, a Radical who wants to display Benoni's photograph in his window, and the Church of England curate, sent by his Tory archdeacon to persuade her to sign a retraction. Vaughan, converted from cold scepticism to eager interest by Benoni's reading of Sir John's fortune, wants his own fortune read, for he has political ambitions and Sir John's victory will mean his own first step up the ladder of political success. Bronwen circumspectly follows Vaughan, and the ensuing encounter between Bronwen and Vaughan arouses his passion but throws her into confusion and uncertainty. The act culminates in the arrival of a Tory deputation consisting of Jesse Fewtrell, the Earl's valet; Davy John Thomas, the town's mayor; and Gwalchmai Price, the ironmonger. They tell Benoni that if she does not retract her words and Sir John wins the election, they will see to it that she loses her house and land, for she has no legal evidence that she bought it as a freehold. After they have threatened her and Fewtrell has insulted her outrageously, Fewtrell taunts her with the information that they are spreading word that Conjurer Jones had a vision in which he saw the Tory incumbent returned to Parliament, "so it's you against Conjurer Jones, and magic against magic" (69). At this, Benoni explodes with a gypsy curse that Fewtrell's "flunkey's back may never straighten," that he may "cringe in body as [he does] in soul" (69-70). He steps back, trips over Jack, who has knelt behind him, and the act ends with Fewtrell hobbling off painfully as Benoni screams her curse.

In Act III Bronwen asks Benoni to tell her the truth of the gossip about a thirty-year-old love affair between Benoni and Captain Rhodri Lloyd, an affair that ended when Lloyd went to the Crimea, where he was killed. Benoni's relation of her affair of the heart strengthens Bronwen's suspicion that Edward Vaughan is not the ideal match for her. Then Price and Thomas bring the news that Sir John has won the election, and Benoni is to be out of her cottage in the morning. They also want her to take her curse off Fewtrell, who has been crippled since he left her place. Roberts assures her that he will write to Sir John to intervene, but Vaughan brings word that Sir John presumed upon the fortune Benoni told for him so far as to ask Gladstone for the postmaster-generalship, and humiliated to find he is not to have it, he is angry with everyone involved in "the gypsy fiasco," even Vaughan, whose position as Sir John's secretary is now in doubt. Roberts, who has worked for more than thirty years for the Liberal victory without expectation of personal gain, is disillusioned by these developments. Bronwen admits to Vaughan that she has learned enough about herself to know she cannot marry him, and the three go, sadly leaving Benoni to her fate.

The final scene, played in a thunderstorm, has a supernatural air. Conjurer Jones appears in a clap of thunder and a flash of lightning to propose an alliance — marriage, in fact. Fewtrell, he explains, induced him to sign a description of a vision about the election by threatening to cut off his livelihood. Moreover, he tricked Jones with fine print that says if the Tory candidate does not win, Jones will lose his trade anyway. Jones's proposal is that he and Benoni join forces and take the curse off Fewtrell in exchange for a promise that Jones shall again be given the trade he lives from, and Benoni can live at Jones's place. Though Benoni is at first reluctant, because Jones is an old man who hardly promises to excite the kind of love she once felt for Lloyd, he eventually persuades her with the same view of love and marriage Benoni expressed to Bronwen — that marriage means more than sex, and that common interest is the best foundation for marriage. Their common interest is in magic: "Magic must close its ranks or vanish. Married, we'd have the best magic hereabout between us" (93), he argues. It is evident that Jones, though not a Prince Charming, is a remarkable man; Jack perceives him to be "a true mate" (93) for Benoni. They have a gypsy wedding "over the broom," and the play ends with Jack, Benoni, and Jones, *"not quite creatures of this earth, and certainly not of this sober age of 1885"* (98), celebrating the marriage and magic, drinking, laughing, singing and dancing, heedless of the rain.

Politics and magic may seem an unlikely pairing, but Davies sees nothing incongruous about combining them in the central device of the play.[19] The dialogue includes a number of allusions to politicians who armed themselves with magic. Alexander the Great consulting omens before battle, Arthur seeking Merlin's counsel, King Saul visiting the Witch of Endor. There is also mention of one who did not: Caesar, who disregarded the soothsayer's prediction and lost his life in consequence. The characters of *A Jig for the Gypsy* provide a spectrum of attitudes towards magic, politics, and love. Davies aims his satire at those who either dismiss life's magic altogether or presume upon it as if it were a guarantee. His sharpest satire, however, is reserved for those characters who use politics to serve their own ends — typically, self-aggrandizement. The two chief vehicles for Davies's satire, one from each political camp, are Sir John Jebson and Jesse Fewtrell. Both are characterized by their inflated opinions of their own importance and by their readiness to sacrifice others to their own interests.

Sir John Jebson is not Welsh but English; the country in which he is campaigning means nothing to him but a potential seat in Parliament. He is sceptical about the "flummery" of having his fortune told, doubting that anyone could "take such nonsense seriously" (11) and fearing that it will make him look ridiculous. Roberts persuades him that it will help to get him elected, so Sir John resigns himself to it with ill grace and utter disregard for Benoni's feelings, interested only in getting it over with quickly so he can get on with his campaign. But when Benoni has proceeded past what he considers irrelevant parts of the fortune to the Lion, which he immediately identifies with Gladstone, and tells him that a very powerful man will tell him something of great importance to him, which is taken to mean a Cabinet post, Sir John is captivated. Now he reproves the others for interruptions and listens to the rest of his fortune, however apparently irrelevant, with the greatest politeness to Benoni, assuring her that he is in no hurry at all. The fortune includes the prediction that "you will succeed in a task where many a one before you has failed" (17) — surely a reference to the contested seat, which the Tories have held for seventy years. Sir John admits to being quite convinced of the dependability of Benoni's reading, yet always cautious in matters of self-interest, he asks to be left "a back door" (19) when the news of his glorious fortune is spread.

In his rapture over Benoni's perception, Sir John waxes poetic on the "quicksilver in the veins" which is Welsh blood; "no wonder we are a people of strong intuitions and prophetic gifts." In response to the others' evident amazement at his sudden transformation into a Welshman, he explains that his grandmother was Welsh, "and when I first looked upon these hills, and streams, a month ago, something in my heart stirred, and a voice deep in my breast said, 'This is home' " (21). This pose is too much for even his staunchest supporter, who implies that while Welsh credulity may embrace a reading of tea leaves, it would be strained too far by Sir John's bogus sentimentality, and no report of it is to be circulated. Davies completes his characterization of a foolish and selfish politician by showing that even at the height of his transport, Sir John is above all concerned with self-preservation. He declines to pay Benoni her usual fee of one shilling on the ground that there must be no hint of bribery and suggests that there may be a gift after the election. Subsequent reports that he acts foolishly in presuming upon the fortune, that he is less pleased about winning the election than displeased about failing to gain a Cabinet post, and that he blames everyone else for his disappointment and so cannot be expected to do anything for Benoni, even when the fortune that helps him to a seat in Parliament proves her undoing, are quite consistent with what we see of him in his single scene in the first act.

Even more fiercely portrayed is Jesse Fewtrell, the Earl's valet, who prefers to describe himself as "his Lordship's personal attendant" (62), "a man of some influence. Very near his lordship himself" (67). He affects the Earl's mannerisms, cuts his beard in the Earl's fashion, dresses above his station, dusts Benoni's chair with his handkerchief before sitting on it. He treats Jack and Roberts with contempt, but his most despicable behaviour is towards Benoni. He pulls up her petticoats to show her bare feet, pulls down her hair to let fall the coins she keeps in it, and concludes his taunt about matching Conjurer Jones's magic against hers with "How do you like that, you decayed beauty, you cast-off gentleman's plaything, you withered old gypsy faggot?" (69). When Benoni curses him, our sympathies are entirely with her. Fewtrell's obsession with his own superiority and his insistence on preserving the decencies where he himself is concerned, combined with his utter disregard for human decency where Benoni is concerned make him ridiculous and contemptible; he richly deserves whatever misery he suffers.

Sir John and Fewtrell appear in only one scene apiece; both are caricatured in the manner of the best classical satirists. Writing of Ben Jonson, Davies defends him against complaints that he lacks compassion and his characters are all rogues or fools: "Jonson's idea of comedy was the classical one — that it exposed and scourged follies. ... He would have thought it bad art and probably immoral to present a fool as someone who might be admired or even indulged."[20] Davies's treatment of fools is reminiscent of Jonson's.

Orville Tapscott and Mattie Philpott, those representatives of middle-class taste in *Fortune, My Foe*, are fools of the same order as Sir John and Fewtrell; they too appear for a relatively short time and are broadly caricatured. Such characters, at their most successful, are funny and memorable, not realistic or appealing. There are a number of other such characters who appear in only one or two scenes of *A Jig for the Gypsy*; they broaden the scope of Davies's political satire by showing how politics is stirred into business and religion, and particularly how self-righteous and hypocritical those who cloak their politics with religion can be. Most successful among those characters is the photographer, Pugh, who fusses about interminably, trying to capture what he considers to be the appropriate image of Benoni for his shop window, certain that he will thereby earn himself the distinction of becoming an innocent victim of Tory vandalism. "He lights up like a lamp at the very thought of being hard done by," Benoni observes (39).

Pugh does receive the broken window he invites, but the real innocent victim is Benoni, and this is her primary function in Davies's development of his political theme. Benoni initially agrees to tell Sir John's fortune simply because she habitually tells fortunes for those who come to her for that purpose. Other than the shilling which is her usual fee, she has no personal interest in it, and she considers politics to be no affair of hers. She is concerned only that she might be expected to guarantee a fortune that predicts victory, but their intention is only to spread the word if the fortune seems promising and keep it secret otherwise. She is reticent when Sir John and his secretary, Vaughan, belittle her and her abilities, but she, like Sir John, is persuaded by Roberts, who compares the proceedings to great conquerors' consultation of the omens before going into battle. As soon as the reading is over and the politicians are gone, Benoni begins to suspect that she would have done better to refuse to tell Sir John's fortune. It occurs to her as gypsy intuition rather than reason; Bronwen thinks Benoni should feel proud to have helped Sir John, but Benoni has "a feeling" that Sir John is bad luck to her. Reasonable grounds for the feeling are provided by Jack when he brings her word that the effects of his report of the fortune are all that Roberts hoped for, and as a result "the Tory roughs are lungeous to stone you if you so much as set foot in town" (30). Benoni is deeply disturbed, though Jack, like Bronwen, assumes that she can only gain in the end from having helped the victorious candidate. This turns out not to be the case; Benoni's forebodings prove correct. Though Roberts does his best to help, she is ultimately the victim of both parties; Sir John's selfishness leaves her at the mercy of Tory rancour.

To the extent that these politicians promote their own self-interest by victimizing others, they are evil. But there is another dimension to their dealings with Benoni which is perhaps less readily perceived and more important: to the extent that they fail to understand the nature of her magic, they are deluded about the nature of the world they are trying to run. They try to harness the magic; they want it to provide guarantees. "I didn't say Sir John would be elected," Benoni points out.

> VAUGHAN: Yes; you did.
> BENONI: No. I never talk like that. I've been dukkering for thirty years, and I know better.
> VAUGHAN: You said that he would succeed where many had failed.
> BENONI: Does that have to mean in the election?
> VAUGHAN: Yes! It must or you are a cheat (44).

When Vaughan cites cases of surprisingly accurate fortunes Benoni has told and concludes that her gift is "proven," she is annoyed at his notion that proof can be applied to magic: "Don't use that word when you talk of dukkering! Oh, you want the best of old and new! You want an old gypsy fortune, and you want a guarantee and a songbook with it, like a box of Beecham's Pills!" (45). Vaughan has political ambition, and he wants his own fortune told so he can plan. Benoni refuses with scorn: "Ambition means risks, and you don't want any risks, is that it?. . . Certainty and guarantees. That's what every ambitious young adventurer wants nowadays....Oh man, man, you'd put Fortune in a yoke, wouldn't you?'' (45-46). Others tie the vague and general terms of Benoni's "dukkering" to specific facts and then hold her responsible for them, though true to the nature of fortune-telling she offers no guarantees.

What happens to Conjurer Jones is an extension of her case: he is badgered and tricked into signing what is in effect a guarantee, a contract under which his intuition that the Tories will win must prove true or he loses his trade. In consequence, Jones is particularly bitter about the insistence on certainty that banishes the romance of the unknown from the world: "These are bad old days for magic. Guarantees they want! And security they want, and the winds and stars hampered like a ram with his head in a bag'' (93). There is more to the world than what is provable and predictable; those who refuse to accept this truth are Davies's villains and fools. His choice of politicians to strike a contrast with the like of Benoni is clearly influenced by his observation that "a politician is always looking for some kind of advantage, some kind of angle. So their perception is likely to be shallow.''[21] If such people were able to diminish the world to fit their perception of what it is or ought to be, it would be the worse, as the individual who rejects part of himself is the worse for not admitting the whole of his being.

Sir John makes a fool of himself by acting as if the fortune Benoni tells were guaranteed. He assumes he will be elected and given the Cabinet post he covets. Others are equally gullible: the implication is that Jesse Fewtrell hurt his back in the fall he took, and what keeps him ailing is his belief that he is under a curse. The healing power of nature and the change of attitude that will occur when he hears that Benoni has taken the curse off can be expected to effect a cure. Belief in magic gives the magician much of his power. Gwalchmai Price dares not cross Benoni in Act III for fear that she might curse him, even though she gives no hint of intending to do so. Benoni can control Fewtrell partly because chance (assisted by Jack) happened to be on her side and partly because Fewtrell himself believes in her power. Sir John wins the election because the people believe he will, and so they vote for him to be on the winning side. It happens because of Roberts's insight into the nature of the people he is dealing with. He predicts that having Sir John's fortune told "may have quite a magical effect on the uncertain vote" (14). Does this make him a magician? It might seem so, to someone who does not understand the way it works. Magic is intuition or perception or control which is not understood. Once it is explained, it is no longer magical. To someone with lesser power, the possessor of greater powers seems to be a magician.

Benoni is perfectly honest about the limitations of her magic. "Dukkering'' is not done in terms of provable fact, though after a fortune seems to be realized, it may be remembered that way, as the outcome of the election no doubt will be. Many of the things Benoni finds in Sir John's tea leaves are irrelevant to the action of the play and are neither proved nor disproved. Of the two things she says that are interpreted as having immediate relevance, one is "proved" by the event, and the other is "disproved." The rest are forgotten. This is probably typical of good fortune-telling; believers can find something worthy of their belief. Benoni admits to having told some remarkable fortunes in her time but implies that there were many other fortunes that are now forgotten. Some of her fortunes are grounded in her astute perceptions about the people she is dealing with: she does not need tea leaves to tell her than Bronwen can have Vaughan if she really wants him or that Vaughan will limit his own future by trying to tie it down. In truth, Benoni is quite realistic about her powers; others romanticize them. She believes in her own strong intuitions, and often — not always — she is right. She may not know just how the intuition works, but she trusts it.

Such "magic" is widely practised — by Davies himself, for instance. In one interview, Davies discussed having mentioned in *Fifth Business* that the Bollandists wrote in purple ink. He knew little about the Bollandists, and a man he met later who knew the Bollandists well asked, "How on earth did you know that they wrote in purple ink?" Davies said, "Well, I divined it." He maintained this line with the interviewer: "I could have just said that they wrote in ink. But it seemed to me — welllllll, *purple* ink. And they do."[22] The interviewer commented that Davies had taken quite a chance, and Davies the magician was content to leave it at that. Yet in another interview he referred to the same incident, saying that he neglected to tell the man that about nine of every ten people in France and Belgium write in purple ink. "I let him think it was magic."[23] Nine out of ten is not really very "chancy," and so stated, the power of divination seems unremarkable. But the suggestion of magic is more interesting, and probably the man who knew the Bollandists was fascinated.

Benoni's intuitions, whatever their source, have the same fascination for her customers. She has earthy wisdom, understanding, and personal morality (not social conventionality) which make her remarkable; she is rightly respected, as Richard and Bronwen Roberts respect her, but to regard her as infallible is folly. Those who see her as only a cheap fake, on the other hand, reveal their own utter lack of discernment. The fool who sees her as a cheap fake and the fool who regards her as infallible can be the same person, converted from the one to the other when he feels personally affected by her magic, like Sir John Jebson and Jesse Fewtrell. Davies's attitude towards Benoni's powers is balanced, neither dismissive nor credulous. Writing of superstition in 1978, he linked it with "man's yearning to know his fate, and to have some hand in deciding it." When he was a university student, he recounts, "a gypsy woman with a child in her arms used to appear every year at examination time, and ask a shilling of anyone who touched the Lucky Baby; that swarthy infant cost me four shillings altogether, and I never failed an examination." Then, he thought he did it for a joke; in his maturity, however, he feels less inclined "to stand aloof from the rest of humanity" in the matter of faith in magic.[24] His fascination with gypsy magic is more evident than ever in his novel *The Rebel Angels* written thirty-six years after the first version of *A Jig for the Gypsy*.

Benoni is significant in Davies's development of the political theme as a victim of the politicians' machinations, but more importantly, her values provide marked contrast to theirs. Despite the necessary ambiguities of the fortunes she tells, her personal dealings are straightforward and honest. She says exactly what she feels and does not strike poses or act in a manner calculated for personal gain. Unlike Sir John and Fewtrell, she does not seek power over others. Her powers are used to fulfil the needs of those who seek her out and once, in the case of Fewtrell, in self-defence. What she wants most is to be left alone to live her life as she chooses. The setting and structure of the play emphasize the fact that others seek her out, either in hopes of benefitting from her powers or in an attempt to force her to do their will. As a victim of the politicians, she demonstrates the evils of the social meddling that interferes with the attempt of the individual to live life as she chooses in a way that harms no one.

Benoni personifies the blend of realism and romance that Davies advances as ideal. Hers is the untutored voice of common sense that is embodied in Lug of *King Phoenix* and, more successfully, in Chilly Jim of *Fortune, My Foe*. And just as the untutored Chilly Jim can open his heart to the beauty of a puppet show in which the "half-educated" middle class sees nothing, Benoni is open to the magic of the uncertain, unprovable dimension of life which the narrowly earnest and conventional middle class rejects in its pursuit of security and certainty. As Davies sees it, life is full of magic. "People won't see it, but it's there and I'm trying to persuade them to take another look to see what's right under their noses. . . . Everybody's life is a great big tissue of coincidence. . . . You wake up in the morning and think about somebody, then come down and find that they've written you a letter, and that sort of thing. A lot of people are scared of coincidence — they call it magic. It is not magic, it's the real texture of life and they're scared of it. They want life to be manageable and simple and very much under their control and it isn't and they can't stand it."[25] Benoni, the gypsy fortune-teller, is part of a tradition which lives amicably with the world's uncertainties, unlike those who seek to control all elements of their physical, social, and psychological lives.

The two people Benoni affects most significantly she affects in terms of changed values and attitudes. These two are Richard Roberts and his daughter Bronwen, who are involved in politics not for the purpose of adding to their own power but from an idealistic desire to improve the lot of the people. They are the only two who respect Benoni as an individual with rights and feelings and abilities of her own, the only two who feel strongly about her victimization. Roberts, whose idea it was to have Benoni tell Sir John's fortune, is practical about the results he expects; in contrast to Sir John and Vaughan he is neither scornful of Benoni's powers nor credulous. Like Benoni, he is square dealer, honest in personal relations and respectful of others' rights. The penultimate scene of the play features his shift from a perception of himself as a political, social being to focus on himself as an individual, a change brought about by his recognition that the political victory which he has worked for throughout his adult life has devastating consequences for someone to whom he feels responsible. His key speech develops the theme of the precedence individual concerns should take over social concerns, a theme which is developed most fully in *Question Time* (1975). Disillusioned with politics, Roberts says to Vaughan, who still aspires to a political career, "We're too much concerned nowadays with helping other people: we don't do enough to help ourselves. If a man wants to be of the greatest possible value to his fellow-creatures let him begin the long, solitary task of perfecting himself. Look within, Edward, look within" (85).

Davies is not particularly interested in politics, because he does not see political activity as the key to a good life. Though some of his ancestors were involved in the Radical movement in nineteenth-century Wales, *Jig* is not a play about a political movement. The only admirable character in the play who is involved in politics[26] in the end gives up his endeavours to improve the country and takes up the work of self-improvement. The play's central character is not a political creature at all; she is markedly an individual, noteworthy for the wisdom she has gained from personal experience and the integrity which comes from a clear sense of her personal values uncontaminated by any notion that her values should be imposed on others or that conformity with the social norm is laudable. People who use politics for self-aggrandizement are satirized; the ideal is to concentrate on the self, not on others or what one looks like to others.

A second theme of the play is love, and Davies treats the lovers as he treats the politicians, satirizing shallow and conventional notions of love and offering instead an ideal of love which is grounded in self-understanding, an ideal for which Benoni is the spokeswoman. Bronwen and Vaughan are the young people whose false love is satirized. Vaughan, as secretary to Sir John Jebson with hopes for a political career of his own, figures in the political theme too, as one who is so lacking in imagination that he first scorns Benoni's fortune-telling and then sees it as a means to gain certainty about the direction he should take to ensure success. In the end his position with Sir John is no longer secure, but unlike Roberts, he learns nothing from the experience and changes not at all. Lack of imagination cripples him, and so does lack of self-understanding. Bent on furthering his career, he is so unaware of his sexual self that his sudden recognition of Bronwen's interest in him knocks him off balance and leaves him quite overwhelmed by the rush of emotion she inspires. Having kissed her on impulse, he declares himself bound to do what is right — that is, to follow the dictates of conventional morality — and marry her, though he assumes that so swerving from the singleminded pursuit of his career will be his ruination. Reminded that Gladstone speaks glowingly of his wife, Vaughan is happily reconciled to his fate, but Bronwen is less than enraptured by his behaviour, and though she initiated the romance, she now needs to reassess her feelings, a process in which she seeks Benoni's advice.

The romance Davies satirizes is characterized by superficiality and posturing. Bronwen is transported by Vaughan's fine words — not even his, in fact, but Ruskin's — and high-minded ambition. Actually, his high-mindedness is more a case of head in the clouds; it explains his failure to take any notice of her at all. When he does notice her, she finds the resultant rush of passion unbecoming to such a noble being. Vaughan feels contempt for his own flash of passion, and it does not change him. He sets about "to discuss everything; to plan it as thoroughly as possible; to foresee everything" (55). Now his ardour is all honourable and restrained, and he proposes to help Bronwen discipline her own "irresponsible imagination" (86). But while this stance should appeal to the Bronwen we meet at the beginning of the play, she is undergoing a transformation, aided by Benoni. Her view of love changes, as does her father's view of politics.

Bronwen is intrigued by reports of an old love affair between Benoni and Captain Rhodri Lloyd. Benoni's description of that affair is pointedly in contrast with Bronwen's affair; hers was *real* romance, "true love...as sweet and fair as the daffodils in the spring. If it hadn't been so I wouldn't have lived with him" (76). True love is always immodest, Benoni tells Bronwen, who is so concerned with her own modesty that she cannot relinquish it to enrapture Vaughan as any gypsy girl might do. "This world is terrible hard on immodesty" (25), Benoni learned, but still she lived with Lloyd without marrying him. "I was a gypsy: he was a Lloyd of Lundy. Both good in their way, but very different. There was only love to keep us together, and that's not enough for marriage, whatever you may have heard. We had a few years of delight and we didn't follow it with forty years of the bitterness of a bad match" (76). Benoni cautions Bronwen against throwing herself away on Vaughan, for Bronwen, Benoni observes, though she is "a silly girl, full of soft notions," has "aristocracy of soul" (77). Bronwen begins as a romantic idealist, apparently without a scrap of common sense. She is unwilling to do anything that might be considered indecorous to attract Vaughan's attention, though she is obsessed with her fancy for him. When Bronwen protests that Benoni lacks refinement, that her (perfectly accurate) assessment of Bronwen's feelings for Vaughan is "common and vulgar," Benoni chides her for middle-class foolishness: "You belong to the class where everything in life that's important either seems coarse to you or is beyond your understanding" (26).

Under Benoni's influence Bronwen learns to know herself better, and she becomes more realistic, though paradoxically, she comes to hope for a more truly romantic attachment than Vaughan offers. Davies's satire promotes realism, but the realism leaves room for — in fact, demands acknowledgment of — true romance. In an article on theme and structure in Davies's drama M. W. Steinberg sums up Davies's position on reality and romance in this play: "To be truly joyful one must learn to live with reality, and one must avoid creating abstractions, ideals, supported by a host of taboos, which obscure or reject reality....Actually Davies is not so much anti-romantic as opposed to conventionalized romanticism, or sentimentalism, which is in fact the arch-enemy of true romanticism. This in part is the gist of Benoni's advice to Bronwen."[27]

The final scene of the play is essential to balance the negative view of satire with the positive view of romance, and in its own right it is entirely successful, but because it does not blend easily with the rest of the play, it causes critical headaches. The supernatural atmosphere contrasts startlingly with the greater realism of the rest of the play, and though it is necessary to establish the contrast, the change of tone seems too abrupt. Setting can help to prepare for the shift, however, and one reviewer of the Crest production noted the effectiveness of John Wilson's combination of "a fine fairy-tale quality with attractive realism" in the setting.[28] Conjurer Jones enters the play only in this scene, though he is mentioned in the first act and figures prominently, if indirectly, in the second. Jack Karr, in an otherwise enthusiastic review of the play, protests that the introduction of Jones "as a makeshift tidier-up of the ruins that lie round about....hardly seems a straight game of cricket."[29] Steinberg concurs, finding Jones's marriage to Benoni "dramatically....inappropriate because Conjurer Jones seemingly is introduced at the end only to help Davies dispose happily of Benoni."[30] No one seems to object to the introduction of Judge Stewart to tidy up the mess created by Cantwell and Phelim in *At My Heart's Core*, but he enters at the closing of the second act and dominates the whole of the third, so the conclusion seems less contrived. The real problem is that while one can agree with Benoni that love is not enough to sustain marriage and common interest is necessary, a marriage of convenience in which love figures not at all is less than perfect. However, since the end of Roberts's political efforts and the end of Bronwen's love affair are satisfying only intellectually, not emotionally, the happy ending is still to be brought about. Strictly on the basis of plot, Benoni could just as well contrive her own trade-off with Fewtrell: remove the curse in exchange for legal title to her home; Conjurer Jones's part in that arrangement makes it excessively complicated, and since Benoni had no yen for marriage, he is not apparently necessary.

Davies introduces Conjurer Jones for another reason, the same reason that he has Benoni's explosive curse at the end of Act II sparked by Fewtrell's taunt that they have set Conjurer Jones's prediction against hers, "magic against magic." The crisis is precipitated by the inroads made against the world of magic by the representatives of the constrictive society that Benoni struggles to keep apart from. The happy ending must be a closing of the ranks of magic against the outside threat, a victory for the forces that struggle to keep hearts and minds open to the wonder of the world and free from the petty constraints that dominate small minds. The magic of *A Jig for the Gypsy* differs from the magic of *King Phoenix* in that here it is not associated with the intellect. As the science of the time, magic in *King Phoenix* was an intellectual attainment, possessed by the villain of the play. Davies used it for its theatrical value; the effects were exciting, and it helped to create the atmosphere he wanted. In *Jig* there are no showy effects of magic, and its metaphorical value is primary. The magicians do not do tricks, and they are not intellectuals. They have strong intuitions and sensitivity to the world around them which are not blocked by conventional views. Inner truth is more important to them than received truths, so they prize their individuality.

The importance of nature and its relationship with magic are underscored by the setting of Benoni's home, by the thunderstorm of the last scene, and by Jack's presence at the finale, in which the climax is built around not just a pair of magicians, but a trio that includes the "natural" man. Benoni is close to nature, and her home on the hillside isolates her from society and its concerns, notably politics. There is comic value in the struggles of politicians from both camps to climb the hill to reach her, but their inability to deal comfortably with the natural world that is her element is thematically important as well. Though she makes some money from telling fortunes, her living is ensured by the sale of milk from her goats; her living is from the land, and she provides nourishment for others, which makes her more of an Earth Mother than a supernatural figure; her magic is

part of the natural order of things. Benoni revels in the falling rain: "When I
have the rain on my cheek on a night like this I feel a love for the whole
world that's blood relation to the love I had for the youth who opened my
heart years ago" (97). The importance of nature is emphasized by the
inclusion of Jack in the concluding scene; he too is to live at Conjurer
Jones's, and he makes no claim to be a magician, so the celebrating trio is
not representative solely of the intuitive, magical power, but also of natural
man, unbound by social law. Jack the Skinner is a poacher, looked down
upon by the proper middle class, but good-humoured, high-spirited, and
more youthful in appearance than usual for his years. Michael Peterman, in
"Bewitchments of Simplification," relates Jack to Davies's description of
the Mercurius archetype, "the rogue who is sometimes benevolent and
sometimes a trickster, an enemy to the law and the revenue officers, but a
great friend to people of noble spirit, and to lovers."[31] Peterman notes that
the expression of Jack's "inner happiness and cleverness" in a particularly
vital language "helps to suggest the specialness and inner richness of
Benoni's hill-top world."[32] Jack's role seems incidental, yet Donald Davis
found in it the material to make "a very big thing"[33] of it in performance.
The part bears a resemblance to Phelim's in *At My Heart's Core* and
Buckety Murphy's in *Fortune, My Foe*. Outside the social code, these
characters assume the licence of the privileged fool. Herbert Whittaker has
suggested that this is the role Davies himself likes,[34] which is perhaps why
such a character as Jack is more prominent than one might expect from a
plot summary.

Jack lives outside the law, and Benoni has no faith in law — she will not
attempt to regain her property through legal channels. Also, she will not
have her marriage solemnized in either a religious or a legal ceremony,
though she does not regard it as a "supple" arrangement. It is a bond
between two individuals, not a concern of society at large, and she and
Jones are married in their own private gypsy ritual. The last speeches
assess the problems of their world, giving a verbal summation of the
necessity for the union of Jack, Jones, and Benoni against the dominating
forces of society. "Too much old politics, isn't it?" Jack reflects. "Too
many pieces o' paper. Too many Nosey Parkers, isn't it?" (96). The
problems are elaborated in an extended metaphor introduced by Jones:
"The world shouldn't be a tight-laced corset on a man! It should hang loose
about him, like my magic cloak." The choice of how to live is up to the
individual; if he feels constrained, Benoni comments, he has only to reject
"the tight boots of vanity, and the strangling stiff-bosomed shirt of envy, and
the crotch-binding old trousers of other people's opinions" (97) and dress
comfortably to suit himself. To know oneself and be oneself is to be happy,
and the conclusion of the play is the traditional ending of comedy in that it

celebrates renewal, symbolized by marriage. In this case it is specifically a renewal of the possibility for freedom and individuality in the modern world. The last moments of the play are wholly joyous, as *"the curtain falls on the three of them, laughing and jigging, heedless of the storm"* (98).

The production of *A Jig for the Gypsy* by the Crest Theatre marked the beginning of a brief but exciting period of creative co-operation between Davies and the Crest management. The Crest was a landmark in the development of Canadian professional theatre, for during its thirteen seasons it established the possibility for long-term, regular operation of a theatre built on Canadian talent. Murray and Donald Davis were among the first students of Robert Gill when he became the first full-time director of Hart House Theatre in the University of Toronto. The brothers wanted the opportunity to act professionally, and they created this opportunity for themselves, founding a summer company called the Straw Hat Players in 1948, and when they wanted to assure themselves of a living by acting steadily the year round, founding the Crest.[35] The Crest was to be a theatre for Canadian talent; the Davises used Canadian actors, often importing directors, designers, and technicians from Britain and the United States on a resident basis to train and develop native talent.[36] Though the Davises were more concerned with employing Canadian actors than Canadian playwrights, and most of their plays were popular English and American fare, they did produce some new plays by Canadian writers, and the first of these was Davies's *A Jig for the Gypsy*. Davies, who tells many a wry tale about the abuse of his plays by amateurs, was pleased to work with professionals who treated him as a collaborator in the effort to mount the best possible production of his play.[37]

The result opened on 14 September 1954 to a full house which included Ontario's lieutenant-governor.[38] It was enthusiastically received, an auspicious beginning for the Crest's new season. Barbara Chilcott, fresh from an appearance as the Shrew at Stratford, made a sensation as the gypsy. She loved playing the role, which she recreated with enthusiasm nineteen years later in the Lennoxville Festival's revival. Davies "writes marvelous parts for women, which few men do," comments Chilcott, contrasting Davies's "positive, life-supporting women" with less fulfilling roles by other playwrights.[39] Chilcott's Benoni was a mistily magical, earthy, and tempestuous character who drew raves from the critics. Members of the supporting cast, notably Donald Davis as Jack and Max Helpmann as Richard Roberts, were also favourably mentioned. Apart from some reservations about the resolution of the play and the difficulty of handling the Welsh dialect, the critics as well as the entertainment-seekers proclaimed the play a success, noteworthy especially for its extraordinary characters and sparkling wit.[40] Before the Toronto run ended, *A Jig* opened in London in a production by the Questors, an amateur group which had in its twenty-five-year history established a reputation for professional quality. Among the more experimental groups in England, the Questors produced on the average two new plays among their seven major productions each year,[41] and they thought well enough of Davies's play to open their silver jubilee season with it. Certainly a London production was a triumph for Davies, and that together with the success of the Davises's production stimulated him to a fresh burst of dramatic creativity.

7

The Magic of Self-Discovery in
Hunting Stuart

INSPIRED by the success of *A Jig for the Gypsy* and by the evidence of the Stratford Festival and the Crest that Canadian professional theatre was finally coming of age, Davies wrote two more full-length plays in the next two years: *Hunting Stuart* in 1955 and *General Confession* in 1956. Thematically and structurally, these plays show an advance in Davies's development. The thematic change reflects Davies's fascination with Jungian thought. Discussing other writers, humorists in particular, Davies has commented on the evidence for Jung's perception that mid-life often brings about a change in people, either towards greater strength as new meaning is found in life, or towards diminished strength as the goals and values of youth are clung to when they are no longer appropriate. In *A Voice from the Attic* (1960) Davies writes of the "humorist's climacteric" at which the source of humour seems to change and the writing becomes fuller-flavoured — or the humorist loses power and faith in himself. In either case, he notes, the change "rarely leaves them humorists pure and simple." The change is not just increased experience of life, but "an alteration in the writer's attitude toward himself which shows in his means of expression and the themes he chooses."[1]

Davies's own climacteric coincided with his absorption of Jung's writings, beginning sometime in the early fifties.[2] The extent of Jung's appeal for Davies was not apparent to critics until 1972, when both *The Manticore* and *General Confession* were published. But Davies acknowledged in the mid-seventies having spent "much time, over the past twenty-five years, in the study of the work and thought of Dr. C. G. Jung."[3] One cannot find a sudden shift in Davies's thought as a result of discovering Jung; rather, Jung appealed to Davies greatly because he developed in provocative ways ideas that Davies had already begun to explore for himself.[4] Even in the one-acts of the forties there is the conflict between feeling and intellect of *Eros at Breakfast* and the need to attend to the neglected part of the self in *Overlaid*. The ideal of wholeness, the preference for encompassing what seems to be an undesirable element rather than attempting to obliterate it, is a feature of *King Phoenix* and *At My Heart's Core*. Davies's interest in such ideas predisposed him to fascination with Jung, as did his conviction that the mode of romance or fantasy had merits beyond those of realism. And the tone of all Davies's writing with its combination of humour and serious ideas shows that he shared Jung's view that "life is crazy and meaningful at once. And when we do not laugh over the one aspect and speculate about the other, life is exceedingly drab, and everything is reduced to the littlest scale. Then there is little sense and little nonsense either."[5]

A Jig for the Gypsy was written many years before its revision for production in 1954, and it has more in common with *King Phoenix* than it does with the plays of the fifties. Benoni and King Cole share the vitality that is a manifestation of closeness to nature and an instinctive, intuitive sort of wisdom by which they are distinguished from the limited, incomplete characters who surround them. Both plays were conceived theatrically as star vehicles and thematically as an exploration of the contrast between the complete, superior human being and more commonplace types. Neither is set in Canada; though Davies has said that he wrote *A Jig for the Gypsy* for the Davises, he actually wrote it first at a time when he still thought of his plays in terms of English theatre rather than Canadian. He resurrected and reworked the play for the Davises, and this revamping of the play in the fifties, though it involved no major alterations,[6] no doubt accounts for some of the ways in which it is more sucessful than *King Phoenix*. The minor characters are more sharply drawn, and the dialogue is less ponderous. The structural failings of *Jig* could not be easily remedied in rewriting, and it is structurally inferior to the plays written in the early and mid-fifties. Jungian thought touches the play most obviously in Roberts's climactic speech, in which he turns his thoughts at mid-life from social involvement to individual improvement; the speech as it now stands emerged from extensive cutting and focusing when Davies reworked the play.

The plays of the mid-fifties, *Hunting Stuart* and *General Confession*, show significant differences from earlier plays in theme and structure. *Jig* and *King Phoenix* contrast a complete human being with other, lesser people. *Fortune* and *Heart's Core*, dealing with cultural poverty in Canada, have characters more significantly fixed in their cultural environments than those of the other full-length plays. *Hunting Stuart* and *General Confession* present the Jungian theme that man is a vastly more complex creature than he may seem or than he himself imagined. Both plays focus on a process by which a man's knowledge of himself is greatly extended. The theme appears in Davies's plays well before it finds expression in his novels. Even the development of Monica Gall in *A Mixture of Frailties* (1958) is dealt with primarily in terms of wholeness and balance and the necessity to surmount the restrictions that characterize provincial Canada, themes of the early plays. Only in the novels of the seventies does Davies treat in depth the self-exploration of an individual's later years that is central to the plays of the mid-fifties.

In structure, the two plays of the mid-fifties are remarkable for tightness and unity. One set is used for each. Though each play has three acts, an act break is only a dropped curtain following a dramatic climax; no dramatic time elapses before the curtain rises on the next act. There are no subplots, no concerns of minor characters that assume enough dramatic importance to require resolution at the end of the play. In these plays the minor characters have a part in the revelatory process and are themselves obliged to reconsider their own values and assumptions.

Hunting Stuart is about the discovery of a Canadian civil servant and his family that he is directly descended through the male line from Bonnie Prince Charlie and is therefore heir to the Stuart line and pretender to the throne of England. In the first act, Henry Benedict (Ben) Stuart is overshadowed by the women in his family; the dramatic conflict develops as a showdown between Ben's wife, Lilian, and his Aunt Clemmie. Lilian is diligently striving to become Somebody in the sphere of women's affairs, and she had hopes that the paper she is scheduled to deliver to her club in the evening (entitled "Some Canadian Pioneer Families Connected with the Nobility and Gentry of Great Britain") might mean her election to the national executive. She feels hampered in her struggle for success by her husband's Aunt Clemmie, whose heartfelt urge to serve others tends to find expression in advertising testimonials for products that are unmentionable in Lilian's polite society. Today Clemmie is featured as the "Flush of Youth Lady" in a quarter-page newspaper ad for a laxative, and Lilian is so unnerved at the thought of how her fellow club members will take her paper on notable families (with its "one trifling reference" to her own family) in the light of the publicity Clemmie has garnered that she feels she must withdraw the paper and resign from her position on the club's executive. Despite her daughter Carol's efforts to bring Lilian to a reasonable perspective, the conflict between Lilian and Clemmie becomes a brawl by the time Stuart arrives. He is having some small success at soothing the women when Carol's suitor, Fred, comes, and the conflict veers to a skirmish between Lilian and Fred, who reveals much more intimate knowledge of the Stuart family than Lilian thinks proper. Lilian is further alienated from Fred because he disparages her cherished notions of the importance of family; his psychological studies have led him to value the environmental factor and dismiss the hereditary factor in an individual's composition. The first act closes with the arrival of a couple of distinguished strangers who question Stuart about his family background and then astonish everyone by addressing him as "Your Majesty."

The second act opens with the strangers' explanation that they are scientists who have traced the royal Stuart line, apparently lost after the death of Bonnie Prince Charlie in the eighteenth century, to Ben Stuart. Reactions are mixed. Clemmie is instantly convinced and delighted, and she is eager to act as guinea pig for the scientists' investigations into inherited traits, since she apparently has royal blood herself. Fred and Carol are sceptical, and even if Stuart is of the royal line, they do not see that it matters: he is just what he is. Lilian's reaction is most complex; divided between the difficulty of yielding up her old pride in herself as the better connected member of the family (descended as she is from two generations of postmasters while her husband was just of dubious immigrant stock) and a yen to be connected with royalty. The greater prestige of the latter position wins her over.

Fred's strident scepticism leads eventually to the scientists' offer to provide proof by administering a dose of powder which arouses a patient's memories of his ancestral past. The amount of powder determines how far into the past the mind will go, and the subject will think and act as his most direct male ancestor. Fred acts as Minor Guinea Pig in proving the powder, and he displays the personality of a nineteenth-century phrenologist, a "tentshow bump-feeler,"[7] in Lilian's phrase, intent on selling copies of "The Secrets of the Brain Revealed" for twenty-five cents apiece.[8] Fred appears to suffer no ill effects apart from a touch of grouchiness which later proves to result from the embarrassment of remembering the experience, so Ben, the Great Guinea Pig, takes the dose designed to evoke in him the personality of Bonnie Prince Charlie. That it proves the scientists' claim is eatablished beyond question. *"From his first words we are conscious of a great change in him; this is a confident, aristocratic, charming, wilful and utterly selfish man"* (57). Among other things, he is an expert cook and a card-player and is left-handed, none of which is true of Ben Stuart, all of which is known of Bonnie Prince Charlie. This Stuart casts Lilian in the role of his mistress Walkinshaw, and much of the ensuing action develops in her the conflict between her recognition that it is advisable to play along with his eighteenth-century whims (lest he, in his imperious character, beat her soundly) and her insistence on her rights as his twentieth-century wife. The others too are drawn into Bonnie Prince Charlie's sphere in various roles. Dr. Shrubsole's wife and fellow scientist, Dr. Sobieska, is introduced to Stuart as a cousin (which she is, for the Chevalier's mother was a Sobieska). The act ends with Stuart leading his attractive cousin into the bedroom with the obvious intention of satisfying his "imperious" sexual need, despite Carol's and especially Lilian's frantic protests.

In the third act, Lilian, who is unwilling to sacrifice marital tranquility to scientific investigation and unmollified by Dr. Shrubsole's claim that the man in the bedroom cannot really be considered her husband, frets until a crash and a shout from the bedroom testify to Dr. Sobieska's expertise in unarmed combat: there appear to be limits to both her scientific curiosity and her romantic enthusiasm for the royalty to which she is distantly related. Nonetheless, Lilian's panic mounts as it becomes clear that she has no power at all over this unfamiliar Stuart. Shrubsole and Sobieska want to take him off to their Foundation for five years of research into hereditary traits. Lilian, increasingly unwilling to accept the reality of Stuart's royalty, which at first seemed attractive because of the prestige it would bring her in the eyes of others but now proves to be most unattractive in terms of her relationship with Stuart, demands more substantial proof, which sets the stage for the climactic scene.

Dr. Shrubsole undertakes to test Stuart for the Royal Touch. Clemmie has a rheumatic hand which she has been unable to straighten for years, and though science prefers a less suggestible subject, none of the others has any physical complaint, so she is chosen. With the utmost ceremony that it is possible under the circumstances to provide, the Royal Touch is applied in a genuinely moving scene, and Clemmie's hand is cured. Then Stuart comes to himself, the scientists withdraw to await his decision about their invitation, and Fred and Clemmie go home. Carol puts in her plea for Stuart to leave things as they are — she wants to be ordinary — and Lilian, now interested neither in London (scene of her fantasy about sharing their secret with England's reigning family) nor in New York (locale of the scientists' Coffin Foundation), tries to draw Stuart back to pure domesticity by inviting his assistance as she tidies the bedroom. But as the play closes, he looks at the genealogical chart that establishes his identity and the royal snuff box that held the powder which allowed him to realize his vast, formerly untapped potential and then phones for a seat on the next flight to Scotland, explaining that he is going on "Government business" at "the highest level" (101).

Hunting Stuart has a contemporary Canadian setting, unlike any of the earlier full-length plays except *Fortune, My Foe*. Each of Davies's plays is strikingly different from the last in setting as well as in the central device of the plot, and often in tone and character relationships as well; Davies is not one to satisfy himself with variations on a formula, and each new play gives evidence of the range of his creative ability as well as of his ability to learn from mistakes and avoid repeating whatever aspects of his last play seemed least satisfactory. Sometimes these "mistakes" were less matters of dramatic construction than of offence against popular taste or practical problems that caused difficulties in production. The Welsh flavour of *A Jig for the Gypsy* had caused some trouble with dialogue. The late appearance of Conjurer Jones to act as saviour had aroused critical ire, and there had been some comment on the frequency with which characters dropped into and out of the play. *Hunting Stuart* is set in familiar, contemporary Ottawa, so its characters employ familiar, contemporary language. And each of its seven characters is introduced in the first act and is onstage for most of the next two acts.

In some respects, a Davies comedy is recognizably a Davies comedy, despite striking variations in other features. Again in *Hunting Stuart* among the chief objects of satire are the narrow-minded characters who are mulishly bourgeois and critical of anyone who does not subscribe to their middle-class ideals. Lilian is chief of these; her daughter Carol plays a supporting role. The other four characters surrounding the central figure of Ben Stuart are all comic figures. One, Clemmie, is a full-scale "character." Like Buckety Murphy of *Fortune* or Phelim of *Heart's Core*, she behaves outrageously, judged by commonplace standards, but she is a warm and appealing character. The other three, a psychology student and two scientists, introduce a new satirical target for Davies: scientists.[9]

Lilian is in many respects a familiar figure in Davies's work: the Puritanical woman of Scottish descent who is grimly set against sensual pleasure and devoted to Duty as she perceives it. *"There is not a free or unconstrained thing about her,"* the stage directions specify; *"her hair is tightly done, and her clothes are tight; her mouth and eyes are tight"* (4). When Davies is asked about the characters he dislikes in his plays, he denies that there are any such — but it is Lilian he comments on first: "Even such apparently unsympathetic [ones] as Lilian," are not bad people, he contends, excusing her on the ground that she has not had much opportunity to understand life.[10] In her case, this means that life in the circle of civil servants has not been conducive to developing much in the way of meaningful personal values. Her aspiration in life is to play a part "in the world of active, thinking, vital women who are spreading their influence everywhere, and making themselves felt in the councils of the nation" (14). She wants to be Somebody, but she has no idea whom or to what end. Lilian lacks taste, as the furnishings of the Stuart apartment show, but this play is not about Canadian middle-class failure to nurture the arts. What is significant about Lilian is that she is aggressively, vehemently bourgeois, limited in values, in aspirations, and even in her fantasies. She is uncomfortable with anything out of the ordinary, as she suggests when she tells Carol, ''Your father is very handsome, of course; sometimes I've thought him too handsome, for the civil service, anyway. ... 'Nothing in excess' is the creed of the gentleman, my father always said'' (10).

Lilian thinks of herself as ambitious and high-principled, but her vision is so limited that she has no conception of what these qualities might really mean. Clemmie mocks Lilian's air of superiority: ''my lady; *she's* born to the civil service; *her* father was postmaster in Arnprior'' (18). The civil service epitomizes the bourgeois because of its soullessness and its subservience to British royalty. The family motto in which Lilian takes great pride is ''Ower leal'' — more than loyal. She insists that she is loyal to her husband, but her very insistence is disloyal in its display of the great strain she is under in being loyal to a man of foreign descent whose family, in the person of Aunt Clemmie, is such a cross to bear. When her disloyalty to Stuart comes out in Fred's casual revelation of Carol's confidences about her family, including her mother's disappointment in her father's failure to advance, blamed on his coming from foreign stock, Lilian simply accuses Carol of being disloyal by betraying her confidence. Lilian considers herself loyal by definiton.

Where her loyalty really lies, where her soul is most convincingly anchored in civil service, is amusingly revealed in her instinctive solution to the problem of what to do about the discovery of her husband's claim to England's throne. Recognizing that a claim to the throne could at the very least assure Stuart of a fortune in guest appearances, Lilian's priorities suggest another line of action: they will lay all their evidence at the feet of the Queen and assure her that they would not think of embarrassing her by making it public (though doubtless it would leak out, at Lilian's club, for instance). The Queen's gratitude would lead to a private visit to the palace, an exchange of Christmas cards, and perhaps, quietly, such official honours as an O.B.E. and permission to use something like an upside-down crown on personal stationery. Lilian's greatest fantasy is not of being in the first rank herself but of gaining a nod of approval from her Queen. And in fact, the more real Stuart's royalty becomes, the less capacity Lilian has for dealing with it; her final wish is to dismiss it altogether and try to get back to her old life as the wife of a well-behaved minor civil servant.

Davies's defence of Lilian on the grounds that her life has not given her the opportunity to be anything better is at least partly belied by the contrast between Lilian and Stuart in the play. He has had no more opportunity than she to rise above the civil servant mentality, but unlike Lilian, he does not glorify the second-rate. Though he tries to put the best possible face on his promotion to "Number One C.I.P." (Correspondence in Pendency) in a speech which delightfully satirizes bureaucratic paper-shuffling, he does so because he knows it will mean a lot to Lilian, and he admits later that "it's nothing very great" (30). The one talent Ben Stuart claims is a talent for happiness. He sees his life and his family clearly, and he is content, unlike Lilian, who compares her lot unfavourably to her ideals and is perpetually frustrated. Stuart may be content to be second-rate, but when he is faced with the fact that he has the capacity to be very much more than that, he embraces it. This is a consequence of the other talent he has but does not mention: his talent for realism. He has no false ideals to prevent him from accepting the new reality of his greater self as happily as he accepted the old. Lilian, however, finds the greater Stuart quite incompatible with her ideals and is unable to accept the reality. The new Stuart is a blatantly sexual being, and sex is for Lilian something best kept under wraps. Confident of the divine right in all his feelings and actions, the new Stuart is ruthlessly self-assertive beyond anything Lilian, used to compliance, or at least gentle and polite treatment, can cope with. The reality of the complete man is simply too much for Lilian, who is comfortable only with the eviscerated man; she is unable to embrace the whole of human reality, because she has idealized a part of it. She would rather have her nicely domesticated minor civil servant than the unfettered totality of a personality whose royalty brooks no constraints. Ben Stuart at the end of the play is not Bonnie Prince Charlie, but he has found the qualities of Bonnie Prince Charlie within himself, and he is able to accept them as part of himself.

Lilian has a wonderful foil in Clemmie; they bring out the worst in each other, and each is more comic by virtue of the way her personality clashes with the other's. Neither is a caricature; both are convincingly human in their very different ways. The newspaper testimonial for Flush of Youth that Lilian finds so embarrassing is a source of pride for Clemmie. She feels "called" to serve humanity by alerting sufferers to the existence of products that might cure their ills. She is delighted to attract the attention that horrifies Lilian. Clemmie's unlimited adoration of Ben, her emphasis on life and positive thinking, and her call to help suffering humanity are more attractive than Lilian's negative emphasis on everyone's failure to live up to her ideals, but some of Clemmie's good traits are carried to excess. Her testimonials, however suffused with the glow of good intentions, are fraudulent: "After baby came I was in agonies with nerves, hallucinations and female disorders of every description" is a claim the childless Clemmie defends as a matter of creative imagination and psychic conviction that "if

I'd ever had a baby I'd have had all of that" (21). Clemmie's creativity is reminiscent of Buckety Murphy's artistry, and Lilian's view that she is an imposter who should be turned into the Medical Association has as much validity as Clemmie's notion that she is serving humanity. Clemmie's talk of universal love is all very well, but it is transparently meaningless when it comes to her feeling for Lilian: "I don't say I like her personally but I like everybody on principle because that's the right way and the healthy way to live, and so she can sniff and sneer at me and poison herself with hatred all she wants, but I'll go right on sending out rays of universal love" (13-14). Clemmie's "strong, strong love" for Lilian leaves her room to refer to Lilian in such loving terms as "negativizing snob" and "gas bag." It is no wonder that Clemmie's insistence on "positivizing" in Lilian's direction makes Lilian see red.

Ben's first act entrance is a perfectly crafted moment. Clemmie is determined to stay and wait for Ben, who always brings her a bottle of "medicine" for her crippled hand on payday. Lilian, in no mood for tolerance because of Clemmie's "Flush of Youth" ad, wants passionately to get rid of her. Clemmie combats Lilian's inhospitality characteristically: "I'm loving you right this minute. I'm beaming love toward you just as hard as I can. I'm positivizing, Lil, right straight at you." Lilian, "*goaded beyond endurance*," seizes Clemmie and tries to evict her forcibly, but Clemmie is too solid to be budged. At the height of their struggle, with Clemmie insisting, "I love you! *I love you!*" and Lilian shouting, "Shut up! Shut up! *Shut up!*" Stuart enters "*unnoticed*" (16-17). Davies has a flair for creating theatrically effective dramatic moments, and this is one such. The twenty-year-old conflict between Clemmie and Lilian is vividly demonstrated, and Stuart's entrance shows visually what the stage directions specify verbally, that he plays "*second fiddle to everyone*" (17).

With the satire of bourgeois mentality well launched by the middle of the first act, Davies diverts part of his satiric energy to his second target when Fred enters. Satire of scientists was something of a new line for Davies. His studies of Freud and Jung enabled him to recognize the ways in which the genuine scientific insights can be distorted by inept followers into absurdities and led him to turn his satire on those who reduce human beings to fit a scientific theory or turn them into scientific laboratories. Davies is a devout humanist, and though he respected Freud's work, he objected to Freud's reductionist view of man.[11] More to his taste was Jung's view that the collective unconscious means each individual has bottomless depths. Davies laughs at those who easily assume they have plumbed the depths. Fred is a nice enough young man, and he attempts to stay out of family quarrels by being perfectly objective. He can do this, however, only as long as his feelings are not engaged. He needs to be shown both that perfect objectivity is not possible and also that current scientific theory is not inviolable Truth. His assumption that heredity means nothing and environment determines personality is discredited in the play. In the episode in which Fred sees through his ancestor's eyes, Fred is subjected to the painful (and improving) experience of seeing his pet theory disproved and discovering that the psychological scientist of today may be the derided charlatan of tomorrow. He also sees his relationship with Caroline, which he has regarded as a process of accumulating knowledge of each other and adjusting accordingly, in the light of sexual appetite. The best of Fred is the honesty and flexibility which permit him to accept — with a struggle — the new truths instead of clinging stupidly to the old ones.

The Doctors Shrubsole and Sobieska create additional dimensions to Davies's satire of the scientific study of humanity. Shrubsole is satirized for the myopic vision with which he sees people as guinea pigs and seems unfailingly surprised to find that most of them think of themselves otherwise. Shrubsole and his wife are studying heredity, for which purpose the ideal subjects are those with the most fully documented family histories: royalty. To the scientists' chagrin, "there is not a crowned head in Europe who has not declined our proposal to live for five years, under hospital conditions, at the headquarters of the Coffin Foundation" (37). Shrubsole regards Stuart, "with the profoundest respect," as "the Great Guinea Pig" (36), and he hopes to persuade him to devote five years of his life to this role. The most amusing test of Shrubsole's scientific faith is his wife's disappearance into the bedroom with Stuart in the personality of Bonnie Prince Charlie. He attempts earnestly to regard the sexual act scientifically rather than emotionally. He has complete faith in his wife's ability to keep the encounter under scientific control because of her expertise in unarmed combat, but he has to consider the possibility that her scientific interest in this unique experience may prevent her from making use of her combat training. Happily for his scientific objectivity, she does not try it to the uttermost, for a number of his comments and queries after the event reveal that even this scientist is irreparably human at the core.

Dr. Sobieska shares Dr. Shrubsole's role as a scientist who seems to think that scientific research should be everyone's first priority; it is she who observes scornfully of all Europe's reigning monarchs that in declining the Coffin Foundation's invitation to spend five years as guinea pigs, "They were like mules" (37). But though Dr. Sobieska calls upon others, especially her husband, to be objective, she herself is a comic reminder that science and romance are not incompatible. The "scientific" powder which can place someone in the personality of an ancestor has a romantic container, a gold snuff box which Dr. Sobieska treasures because it symbolizes a connection between her family and Bonnie Prince Charlie. Sobieska herself is *"a woman of startling magnetism and perhaps also of beauty; she is superbly dressed, with costly furs"* (33). Shrubsole says she is "of a strongly romantic nature" (45). Her romantic reaction to Stuart at the end of the first act and the beginning of the second gives theatrical impact and comic value to the revelation of Stuart's royalty, which without Davies's flair for theatricality might have been dryly expository. Overwhelmed by the living, breathing embodiment of all her scientific theories and "a thousand years of divine election" (35) she curtsies deeply to Stuart, covers his hand with kisses, and hails him as "Your Majesty" when he has not the faintest notion what she is going on about. Dr. Shrubsole attempts to bring his wife to some state which will not embarrass Stuart and she, confessing to being "utterly unstrung," begs Stuart to "disregard" her, which is obviously impossible as she either fixes him *"with a burning regard"* or *"casts herself at Stuart's feet"* (34-35). Eventually, Shrubsole decides "we had better allow her to remain on the floor [where] she obviously feels happier" (35), and following several minutes of stage business and dialogue which are bewildering in the extreme to the Stuart family, Shrubsole finally gets around to a comprehensible explanation of Dr. Sobieska's behaviour. Her romanticism and her magnetism plus the licence with which she is endowed by her scientific credentials make her a formidable sexual threat to Lilian, and the reality of Stuart's sexuality is a key factor in Lilian's reluctance to accept this new, royal Stuart.

Davies has said that the initial idea for *Hunting Stuart* came in the vision of a woman like Lilian, who makes much of her own ancestors and is a little ashamed of her husband, and a man like Ben, who appears to be nothing much, finding out that after all he is the one with the splendid ancestry.[12] The conception is rooted in the comic delight of taking a snob down a peg. In the play, Clemmie makes the most of this opportunity. Contemplation of the comic situation he had imagined gave dimensions to it that were influenced by his reading of Jung and Davies's own reflections on what man is. Jung postulates nothing like the ancestral memory Davies uses in his play. That was in part a zany and fantastical solution to such problems as "How does [Stuart] find out that he has royal blood? How can it be demonstrated on the stage?"[13] Shrubsole begins his explanation of the proof he intends to use for demonstrating Stuart's royalty by asking, "You have heard of the theory of a collective racial memory?" (44). From that he goes one step further to claim that not only racial memory but also ancestral memory resides within each of us. Davies deliberately equates science with magic as Shrubsole gives a plausible explanation for his magic powder — and then Davies refuses to let us take the proceedings for anything but a joke when the carefully measured dose of powder is administered like snuff. The powder and its effects are wonderfully theatrical and purely fantastic, surely not meant as scientific theory of any kind. The truth that is revealed by the proceedings is metaphorical truth. As in *A Jig for the Gypsy*, magic is metaphor. Here, it purports to be a means to reveal ancestral memories. That, taken together with the assumption that our inheritance does affect what we are, suggests that the powder reveals unsuspected dimensions of the inner man, or opens up a restricted personality.

The play's theme is developed on two levels. The first argues simply that for all the emphasis on environment in our modern social-psychological assessment of people, heredity is an undeniable, though perhaps concealed, factor in making us what we are. The central metaphor of the play, specified in the playwright's ideas about the set design, is that, as Fred finally concedes, "Heredity is the old house we all have over our heads; environment is the junk we put in it" (99). This is developed first in Lilian and Carol's discussion of the importance of families to a courting couple, and it re-emerges in the discussions over whether Carol's shortcomings are to be attributed to Lilian's family or Ben's and again in Carol's reaction to the discovery that Fred's ancestor was a lascivious charlatan. Davies describes the effect he wants the setting to have:

> *Our first impression is one of clutter and fussiness of a rather pathetic sort; so much has been done, and done so badly, to make this room home-like and fashionable in the convention of the ladies' magazines. But the room itself resists both the striving toward fashion and the trend toward vulgarity.... Here is a challenge, then, for the scene designer. Let him give us a room in which the good old quality of the house is swearing at the cheap decorations of its present occupants. Let him give us a setting which is capable of being hideous, pathetic, and, when occasion demands, noble* (3-4).

Ben's environment consists primarily of his wife and the civil service, both ramparts of mediocrity, suggested in the furnishings of the house. His heredity is the noblest, suggested in the quality of the good, old house itself. Twice, once in the climactic scene and once at the very end of the play, Davies calls for the essential nobility of the house to be emphasized. The Stuart ancestry displayed in Bonnie Prince Charlie seems not altogether noble, at least in the chivalric sense. The man can be lusty, moody, drunken, and violent. But in the climactic scene, when the legend of the royal Touch is tested and proved, all of the spiritual qualities of the concept of the divine right in kingship are manifest. Stuart agrees to Touch, because even though he does not wear the crown, "kingship is not a matter of the crown, but of the spirit" (96). For the ceremony candles are brought and the electric lights are turned off. "*In the candlelight, the cheapness and trumpery disappears, and only the bones of the setting are visible; thus revealed, the old house has its own nobility"* (96). As the twenty-first Psalm is read, affirming the bond between God and King, Clemmie is brought before Stuart, and Stuart's gentleness and love for his "subject" appear: "But this is my nurse, my earliest friend, and the guardian of my childhood: why did no one tell me that you were ailing, my dear?" He touches her hand and, *"moved, leans forward and kisses her cheek"* (97). As Clemmie, awed, reveals that her twisted hand is now straight, Stuart faints, signalling the expiration of his time as Bonnie Prince Charlie. Shortly afterward, at the conclusion of the play when Ben Stuart is alone on stage, the house is again darkened. *"Once again the handsome structure of the old house is seen, and the hideous furnishing is bathed in kindly oblivion"* (101). By Stuart's attention to the genealogical chart and snuff box and his call for a passage on the next plane to Scotland, we know that he will not suppress his royal heritage as Lilian and Carol would have him do, nor will he turn it over to science as Shrubsole and Sobieska wish; he will use the knowledge of what he is as *he* chooses, not as someone else advises; this is his royalty asserting itself.

On another level, the theme of the play is open to a more general interpretation. What happens to Ben Stuart is that he finds in his inner being resources he did not know he possessed, and the experience of being directly in touch with his inner self frees him from limitations with which he has been living, however contentedly. Though the plot of the play puts a good deal of emphasis on Stuart's royalty, there are a couple of hints that a person need not be descended from kings to be enriched by contact with the hidden resources of his inner being. One, emphasized by Stuart's assenting echo to Dr. Sobieska's statement, is that kingship is a matter of the spirit. Another universalizing statement is Dr. Shrubsole's reply to Lilian's frantic insistence that the man with Bonnie Prince Charlie's personality is "not a king. He's *not*! He's my husband." "Every man is a king at some time," Shrubsole observes. "And if nobody will acknowledge it, he dies — whether he cuts his throat or by a long, slow withering through the years. It is extremely important to secure and cherish the moments of kingship. Be generous" (78). There is a suggestion too that the best of kingship is within the reach of many who wear no crowns in Carol and Ben's comments on the Royal Touch that cures Clemmie's hand. "CAROL: That business with Clemmie — it doesn't exactly make you a king, does it? I mean, she loves you so much that you could do anything with her. STUART: Perhaps that, multiplied by thousands, is what it means to be a king" (100). An ordinary man may win the devotion and confidence of only a few people, but it gives him as much power over them as a king might have, together with the responsibility to exercise that power in their best interests. And, of course, Fred too experiences the personality of an ancestor, hardly a royal one. Though he is embarrassed by the experience, Fred is improved by it: he gains a better perspective on himself and his profession.

Clemmie both summarizes and generalizes the revelation of the magic powder: "I never thought life was as simple as you did, Lil. I always knew there was a lot behind everybody, if we could just get at it. And here we are, see? All of a sudden life stops being gray and messy, and gets bright-coloured and exciting" (81). The essence of the magic powder's — and Davies's — revelation is not that Ben Stuart has royal blood but that the most apparently ordinary man has a bright-coloured and exciting life buried within him. This theme became the foundation of Davies's portrayal of Dunstan Ramsay in *Fifth Business* fifteen years later, the contrast between "the bland, quiet, rather dull Canadian" on the surface and "the bizarre and passionate life" within.[14] His writing increasingly emphasizes the necessity to liberate the passionate self which he feels the Canadian characteristically conceals.

Davies is sometimes called "old-fashioned," and one of the things that makes him seem so is his optimism. He disparages the current fashion for what he calls "misery plays,"[15] for he does not subscribe to the view that man is imprisoned in a sociological or psychological or existential trap. *Hunting Stuart* first breaks down the barriers to freedom imposed by those who say that a man is determined by his environment; within him, Davies points out, are also all the hereditary factors that make him more than simply a product of his environment. But belief that a man is ultimately determined by his genes can also be a trap, and the Jungian view that we have access to the collective experience of the whole human race is liberating. At the end of *Hunting Stuart* Carol tries to talk her father out of the idea of being royal. She wants to be "just ordinary." Stuart replies, "Well, Kitty, in spite of environment and heredity and all that, I suppose what one is always remains very much a matter of choice. If you really want to be ordinary, I don't suppose anything can stop you" (100). Her ordinariness, though, will be the result of her choice, not of an environmental or genetic trap. Carol's observation that if he went to the Coffin Foundation for research he'd be "a kind of prisoner" (100) prompts the echo in Stuart's last speech, "a kind of prisoner ... well, we'll see about that" (101). What contact with his inner self has given him is a greater awareness of his range of choice, greater freedom. He has felt what it is to give rein to his sexuality and to dominate his mate. He, who has always played second fiddle to everyone else, is able now to assert his own will. He has experienced greatness — that is, for Davies, as for Jung, wholeness — and he is strengthened and freed by the experience.

Surprisingly, at least from the perspective of the eighties, the play aroused a good deal of comment on its "indecency"; apparently Lilian's horror of Stuart's disappearance into the bedroom with Dr. Sobieska was shared by some members of the audience, who were also dismayed by such language of the Chevalier's as his comparison of the Scotch and Coke he is offered to "horse-piss."[16] In reply to letters sent to him personally and calls made to the Crest, Davies wrote to the *Globe and Mail*:

> What the play says is (a) That if we truly desire to know ourselves we must not neglect some realistic consideration of our ancestors.... (b) Love, fully and freely given, is the human emotion which draws us nearest to God. (c) That the human spirit cannot develop one-sidedly, and that where nobility and magnanimity are present, grossness and cruelty will be, at least, latent. (d) That there is nobility and godhead in every man.... I do not write plays to teach, but to entertain; however, I have no ambition to entertain mindlessly, nor can I hope for the approval of those who regard life as a sweet and simple experience.[17]

Of all Davies's plays, *Hunting Stuart* is the most fantastic, dismissd as "nonsense"[18] by one critic of the published play who did not look past the implausibility of its events. Yet even in this light-hearted fantasy, as in all of Davies's comedies, there are serious ideas, for Davies, however fond of fun and theatricality, is a thoughtful man.

Perhaps the very success of the play's humour and theatricality tends to draw one's attention away from its ideas. There is not a dull moment nor a dull character, though Lilian's perpetual distress may become trying. Herbert Whittaker's review of the Crest production suggests that "we would be happier if her points of view were not so consistently in opposition to Mr. Davies's sympathies," for Lilian carries "the whole responsibility for Canadian bourgeois morality," which "proves too unrelenting for us to accept her wholly as a person."[19] Her attitudes are comically contested by every other character in the play at one time or another, and the comedy of a situation is always enhanced by Lilian's vehement disapproval of whatever is at issue: Clemmie's newspaper testimonial, Fred's intimate knowledge of the Stuart family, Stuart's domineering eighteenth-century personality, the attraction between Dr. Sobieska and Stuart. Davies's directions show that he was aware of the dangers of making Lilian simply a comic butt; he more than once specifies that her distress is real and not to be treated farcically. Yet to present her as a convincingly complete person, which is perfectly possible, is to run the risk of allowing her perpetual unhappiness to depress the otherwise ebullient tone of the play. For this reason Lilian's role is the most difficult in the play, and Davies's description of her as a "bewildered"[20] wife is the best guide to a portrayal that can successfully walk the tightrope between farce and depression.

Each of the characters has his or her own distinctive style of speech — except for Carol, whose "distinction" is, by her own choice, her ordinariness — and the dialogue is handled deftly to create light humour throughout, with key scenes highlighted by more emphatic dialogue. Davies's skill as a theatrical craftsman is nowhere more apparent than in this play. Some critics have faulted Davies, even in this play, for loose structure,[21] but this is a valid criticism only if construction is thought to be solely a matter of plot development. Davies is a dramatist — and a novelist — to whom theme and character and emotional impact are more important than plot. Seen in terms of theme and the closely related matter of the characterization that expresses the theme or in terms of emotional effects, *Hunting Stuart* is beautifully constructed. Though the plot is not set in motion until the conclusion of the first act, the act introduces an array of attitudes towards family heredity together with a collection of comic conflicts between the inadequate conceptions of a character and the contradictory reality that has to be dealt with. At the same time it keeps the audience's emotions engaged with comic suspense over the cause of Lilian's indignation with Clemmie, sympathetic amusement as Stuart tries to deal with the squabbling women, the satisfaction of recognizing the irony in Lilian's idealization of family loyalty in her conversation with Fred, and mystification about the scientists' purpose.

The succeeding acts show similar control of structure. Davies's humour resides not just in single lines of wit, though these abound, but in construction and characterization. The same is true of his evocation of emotional responses other than laughter. An example is the sympathetic awe of the climactic scene, which could not be brought about without earlier attention to the loving relationship between Stuart and Clemmie, the slow movement from boisterous humour to a more subdued key provided through dialogue, action, and lighting, and at least a momentary belief in the virtually unlimited human potential which Stuart's role has been designed to provide. To accuse Davies of "a waggish disregard for such playwriting fundamentals as cohesiveness in construction and tightness in development"[22] is to fail to perceive the legitimacy of an approach to playwriting that puts theme and emotional effect before plot.

The only unsatisfying moment in the play is — unfortunately — the final one. The conclusion must show Ben, restored to his twentieth-century personality, enjoying a new sense of freedom and power; consequently he makes the phone call which is not in accord with the wishes of anyone else. It suggests new beginnings, as the conclusion to comedy traditionally does, but because it must bring the play to a close, a feeling of completion is also required. The questions evoked by Stuart's final gesture are too pressing to allow a satisfying sense of completion, and the implication that he will, like Bonnie Prince Charlie before him, launch an attempt to gain the British throne from Scotland is too tightly tied to the specific fantasy of the play to reinforce the general theme of every man's possession of greater resources than he is likely to suspect.

Hunting Stuart opened at the Crest Theatre on 22 November 1955. In Ben Stuart/Bonnie Prince Charlie, Donald Davis had a delightful and exciting role, and he played it, according to Herbert Whittaker, "with genuine artistry" in a "first-rate performance." Barbara Chilcott, fascinating as Benoni in *Jig*, brought "feminine charm and humor"[23] to the part of Dr. Sobieska, and Max Helpmann played Dr. Shrubsole as effectively as he had played Richard Roberts the preceding year. If the play offended some people's sense of decency, it delighted others. The Crest's press representative observed: "It has roused views so diametrically opposed that it is hard to believe that the people expressing them have sat side by side at the same performance."[24]

Reactions to the published play were equally diverse. With the critics, the play's morality has not been an issue, but some have dismissed it on the grounds of triviality, a charge to which comic fantasy is especially subject. Among those who have paid close enough attention to Davies's work to know that it is unwise to dismiss any play of his as trivial just because it is not sombre or realistic, however, *Hunting Stuart* is highly regarded. Herbert Whittaker, who thought it obvious that the play was "not a frivolous work ... or without point," was happy to see the editorial writer in Davies eclipsed by the theatrical magician and hailed *Hunting Stuart* as a "bold step forward" in Davies's development as a playwright.[25] In her book on Davies's drama, Patricia Morley ranks *Hunting Stuart* as Davies's best play. William New, in a review of the 1972 volume of three of Davies's plays, selects *Hunting Stuart* as the best among them. His commendation of the stageworthy form Davies gives his ideas in this play shows the same appreciation of an effective combination of Davies's ideas and his skill as a theatrical craftsman that Whittaker exhibits. New observes that in this play the various subjects of Davies's satire and his general theme of psychic balance are all connected and that "the language — varying from jargon and cliché to contemporary colloquialism and lyrical eighteenth-century formality — sparkles. The fey plot is animated, and the potentially stereotypical characters are given individual vigour."[26] As time passes, the characters' fascination with royalty may seem increasingly antiquated, but the play's sustained comic vigour, its sprightly dialogue, and its effective interweaving of character, situation, theme, and dialogue into a unified whole made *Hunting Stuart* the best comedy yet to come from Davies's pen, surpassing even *At My Heart's Core*.

8

Jung and Casanova: The Artist in Search of Himself in *General Confession*

BUOYED by the success of *A Jig for the Gypsy* and *Hunting Stuart* and relatively secure in his established connection with a professional theatre that was itself now well entrenched, Davies embarked on a new play for the Crest's next season. "Casanova," Davies states in his author's note on the published play, "had long appealed to me as subject for a play, because his *Memoirs*, though full of erotic incident, reveal him as a man of intellect, wit and philosophy, and upon the whole very good-natured, which has never been said of Don Juan. I was interested, also, in his eventual fate; he ended his days as a Librarian to that Count Waldstein who was a friend of Beethoven, and to whom the Waldstein Sonata is dedicated."[1] Davies not only heeds well-founded criticism, he also takes popular taste into account when he can do so without violating his own convictions, so his decision to write a Casanova play in the wake of a flurry of objections to *Hunting Stuart*'s "indecency" is intriguing.

The type of mentality that would charge *Hunting Stuart* with indecency had always been a target of Davies's satire; the members of his audience whose Puritanical aversion to the natural man led them to cry "Foul!" when the royal (and human) imperative overrode social decorum on stage are the Ethels and Lilians of his plays, the Mrs. Bridgetowers and Mrs. Ramsays of his novels. His study of Freud confirmed the conviction that acceptance of one's own sexuality, along with other uncivilized features of the human being, is essential to self-fulfilment. Plays of the forties like *Overlaid* and *King Phoenix* testified to Davies's admiration for those whose sensuality fed their spiritual vitality and his objections to those whose rejection of sensual experience led to warped and stunted spirits. His reading of Jung substantiated the human truths he had grasped in a general, intuitive way earlier and gave him a fuller understanding of their importance.

As confident as he would ever be of his ability to command the attention of the theatre-going public, Davies determined to risk a play whose central character is infamous for his sexual exploits. He would waive the appeal of a Canadian setting and Canadian characters, indulging his own preference for universal themes and characters whose essence is their humanity rather than their Canadianism. He could use a period setting that would accommodate attractive costumes and polished language. In *Hunting Stuart* Davies had found a strikingly imaginative way to enter a period of wit and grace in language even though he set the play in the present. He knew that stage language could never be completely natural even in naturalistic plays, but he knew too that the wit of his own language at its best is not characteristic of twentieth-century talk. He could write effective dramatic dialogue for twentieth-century characters, but *Hunting Stuart* and *At My Heart's Core*, his best plays to date, had given him the opportunity to put his most polished language into the most suitable dialogue: the speeches of cultivated characters of other centuries. The Casanova play would give him the same opportunity to make the most of his talents. In style it would be romantic, theatrical; the Davises had the capacity to act in the heightened, "classic-romantic style" Davies preferred,[2] and he would make the most of their talents. And since the serious theme of *Hunting Stuart* had been for some undetectable in the exuberantly farcical plot, the new play would have no plot other than the drama of a man's search for the meaning of his own life and his discovery of himself.

Casanova's *Memoirs* conveys his own sense of himself as an actor in the drama of life. His life is recalled as a series of dramatic episodes, and he thought of it in terms of a three-act play: "Here closed the first act of my life," Casanova wrote of his affair with La Charpillon.[3] "The second closed when I left Venice in 1783, and probably the third will close here, as I amuse myself by writing these *Memoirs*."[4] Casanova, Davies felt, must have written his memoirs as much out of a need to find order and meaning in his unusual life as out of a desire to relive his erotic and adventurous experiences. "I wondered how he would defend the book, if it had been necessary. Presumably as an artist, shaping life as a work of art. That is how the play developed. Many men have adventures with women. What makes Casanova's adventures with women particularly interesting is that he *thinks* about what he's doing."[5] The last act of such a man's life must be a time for self-analysis, so Davies set his play then, in Casanova's old age as he writes his memoirs.

The play opens on a seduction attempt: Captain Hugo de Grimes has led Count Waldstein's daughter Amalie away from the ball in progress to the seclusion of her father's library. He wants sexual union; she resists his impassioned rhetoric. Suddenly, they are interrupted by a voice from the darkness: Casanova has been listening, and seeing that Hugo has lost the contest, Casanova cannot resist telling him where his technique was faulty. Amalie was unaware that her father's librarian, now known as the Chevalier de Seingault, is the notorious Casanova, and she is eager to hear about his life. She is eager too for a demonstration of his talent as a necromancer, and at the close of the first act, Casanova raises three spirits from the three cabinets where the Count's forbidden books are kept. From the cabinet containing "all the cynical, un-Christian philosophers" (210), the distinguished old Voltaire emerges; from the cabinet of erotic books comes the beautiful and mysterious Marina, the Ideal Beloved; and from the cabinet of magicians and alchemists, "the men who sinned against the light" (210), steps the menacing Cagliostro. Casanova converses briefly with Voltaire. He addresses Marina in the words of Hugo seducing Amalie — but improves on Hugo by laughing with his lady instead of considering her laughter a defeat — and they embrace. In Cagliostro he immediately recognizes an enemy, and a rapid passage of arms leaves each transfixed on the other's sword. They stand, unharmed, staring into each other's faces, as the curtain falls.

Act II develops the relationship between Casanova and each of the three "spirits," and in it the four of them dramatize episodes from Casanova's life in an effort to make Hugo and Amalie understand Casanova's contention that his life has been not indulgence in trivial eroticism but a search for the ideal. In each of the three charades Voltaire plays the role of a friend and adviser, Marina plays the girl who inspires Casanova's love, and Cagliostro plays the man who, in one way or another, ends the love affair. Casanova play his younger self.

The first charade shows Casanova at nineteen in Constantinople, passionately in love with a veiled Mahometan beauty whom he takes to be the Pasha Oman's daughter, promised to him in marriage. Though she has taken the lead in the affair, the youthful Casanova keeps his respectful distance until she makes it clear that he is welcome to her body as long as he does not lift her veil. Just as he grasps the fact that he is free to consummate his love, the Pasha enters, informs Casanova that the woman is not his daughter but one of his wives, still a virgin, and the affair is ended. Casanova is astonished that the girl cared more about her veil than her virginity and he is disappointed to have lost his love, but he is instructed by a friend that there is a lesson here worth learning: "Except in trivial things, life has no rules" (225).

In the second charade, Casanova is shown in Italy as a young man at the height of his powers. He meets Henriette, who is disguised as a young officer and is keeping company with an elderly Hungarian officer, and he swiftly makes her his own companion. She is an accomplished musician, well read, a woman of wit, taste, tact, kindness, and beauty. For three months Casanova knows perfect happiness with her. Then comes a cousin with news that induces Henriette to leave Casanova. The circumstances of her life are a complete mystery to Casanova, and she leaves him striken and bewildered: she seemed so entirely a free spirit; what could make her go? A wise friend reminds him that though lovers feel as if they live in a vacuum, they are part of an ordered world, where there is duty, and responsibility to and for others. There was a point at which Henriette's apparent freedom ended. "The chains which bind the great to their destiny cannot be broken," the friend advises him; "that is why Henriette has gone. The artist, too, is bound to his destiny by chains no less strong. You, I think are an artist. Perhaps from this bitterness you may pluck a piece of wisdom: nothing is so delusive as the notion of freedom" (234).

The third charade shows Casanova in London at forty-five, bewitched by the beauty of Marie-Anne de Charpillion, *"an obvious but very attractive harlot"* (239) of eighteen. Though he is advised by a friend to keep his distance, he pays dearly in money and even more dearly in self-esteem for two weeks of indulging his passion, though she gives no indication of intent to allow him the privilege of monopolizing her charms. Then he finds her *"in the utmost intimacies the stage allows"* (242) with her hairdresser. The ensuing scene humiliates Casanova, as Charpillion leaves no doubt that she feels only contempt for him, that he meant nothing to her but money, that what she gave him was "value for [his] money" (244), and that at his age he is deluding himself to expect his love to inspire a return in kind from her.

Though Voltaire stages the first two episodes at Casanova's request, it is Cagliostro who insists on the third, despite Casanova's protests. At the end of the Charpillion charade, there is no comforting lesson deduced, and Hugo and Amalie, disconcerted by the unpleasant scene, demand from the "spirits" an explanation of their interest in Casanova's affairs. Voltaire's claim that "we are those without whom there could be no Casanova" and Cagliostro's that Casanova has summoned them "from within" himself (245) draw a vehement denial from Casanova; he insists, not for the first time, that he knows himself better than most men do and they are nothing to do with him, but his attempt to dismiss them is fruitless. To the disinterested observers the truth is more apparent than it is to Casanova himself. The corporeal form assumed by each spirit is more or less accidental; though they look like people Casanova has known, their essence is not corporeal. Voltaire, Hugo perceives, is "Casanova's widsom, his better judgement, his philosophy'' (246). Amalie recognizes in Marina Casanova's "ideal of womanhood. You change like shot silk; you seem to be a dozen women, or three hundred, but you are one" (246). And the servant Wenzel identifies Cagliostro as Casanova's "bad luck . . . everything that says 'No' to a man . . . his Contrary Destiny" (247). The curtain closes on Casanova's expression of horror and astonishment as Voltaire congratulates him on a "unique experience in self-recognition" (247).

The driving force of the third act is basically Casanova's fear of madness, his need to come to terms with himself and his life, but Amalie's curiosity and her desire for entertainment keep the action moving, leading to a mock-trial of Casanova. The act opens with a discussion that generalizes the drama before us. Casanova is the Hero who is inspired by his Ideal, counselled by such Wisdom as he possesses, and thwarted by an Enemy which he can recognize only because of the presence within himself of qualities he hates and fears. He is now close to madness: in answer to his agonized question, "What have I done that this horror should come upon me in my old age?" (251), it becomes clear that he is to be judged, and the charge is his life.

Marina is satisfied that Casanova's guilt is nothing more than the guilt of all mankind; Voltaire is only trying to have him know himself; but Cagliostro persists in tormenting him with accusations. Pride, envy, anger, gluttony, sloth, and avarice: one by one Cagliostro or Casanova brings them up, and Casanova accepts each with relative ease. But last comes the most pointed accusation: lechery. In each act, Casanova's record of 300 amatory conquests has been mentioned, and now Amalie voices the question that is the basis of Casanova's inner struggle: "Why so many? If the Chevalier was a lover, a man of sensibility and not a mere collector of scalps, why so many?" (265). Marina's answer, "a search for the Ideal" (266), is the one that Casanova has embraced throughout, and he insists that he is guiltless of lechery. But Cagliostro will not let the charge drop, and the significance of his persistence is that he is a part of Casanova himself. Cagliostro says of Casanova's speech in his own defence: "He speaks well; an audience brings out the best in him. But in the inner chamber of the soul his words have a hollow sound. He is damned in his own eyes — the only damnation that matters" (267).

Casanova finally yields to Cagliostro's assault and sees himself as guilty and damned, but Cagliostro (no longer an enemy, once he is accepted) suggests that a man is judged not on the sum of his mistakes but on the sum of his life. Now Casanova is able at last to see himself as a whole. In a climactic speech, he concludes that he has been as true to himself as possible; he has made the best he could of the character he was born with and the circumstances he chanced upon in view of what he is, and that is the most a man can do. In a gesture of recognition and acceptance of the dark side of himself, the climax of the play, Casanova kneels before Cagliostro, Cagliostro breaks his sword and throws it away, and the two embrace. The acceptance means not that Casanova becomes more evil but that he becomes more whole, at peace with himself, renewed and invigorated. The speech in which he finally can assess his life with confidence is evidence of the benefit of self-acceptance, as is his change of manner:*"From now until the end of the play CASANOVA seems buoyant and exalted"* (270). The spirits from his unconscious, now at peace, retire, and Casanova finds himself, despite — or rather, because of — his ordeal, "strong, happy and very much in want of [his] breakfast" (271). His visitors leave, and the conclusion of the play is a new beginning: Casanova at the start of the play had long retired from the amorous life, but now he finds his Ideal Beloved again, this time in the pretty girl who brings his breakfast tray, and he begins a new amour.

General Confession is a dramatization of one stage in the process of psychic growth towards a whole individual in whom the conscious and unconscious co-exist harmoniously. Casanova is confident that he knows himself better than most men do. The play shows how much of himself he does not know, though he is probably right to believe that few people are any wiser. As in *Hunting Stuart*, the hidden depths of the human personality are revealed. In the opening exchange between Hugo and Amalie, she hesitates to enter the librarian's cabinet, claiming that it is haunted. Her father has told her that "whenever he comes here he is sure he sees. . . himself" (199). Since the room contains the secrets of humanity, represented by the books hidden away in special cabinets, the setting is appropriate for delving into the secrets of the human personality: the stage is set for self-confrontation.

Jung gives an account of the first step of the descent into the unconscious, which Casanova experiences, in "Archetypes of the Collective Unconscious." Casanova's conscious ego is at first identical with his *persona*, the part of himself that he reveals to other people because it is most likely to win public approval. He has been a man in pursuit of ideal love all his life — his life has been a heroic quest for the ideal. The difficulty is that there are parts of his experience which he cannot reconcile with that view of himself, and worse, the part of himself which he represses and refuses to recognize fights back, making him a frustrated and ineffectual person. He is forced into a confrontation with his unconscious and a recognition that he is a being greater and more complex than his conscious ego, the only part of himself he had been aware of.

Casanova, then, is the conscious ego. The elements of his unconscious that appear in the play are not the whole of his unconscious but, Voltaire

quips, "a quorum of the principal shareholders" (249). In Jungian terms —
which Davies does not use in the play — Marina is Casanova's anima, the
archetype of the feminine side of a man that is "the a priori element in his
moods, reactions, impulses and whatever else is spontaneous in psychic
life,"[6] an unrecognized part of himself that he seeks perpetually in real
women. Voltaire is "the enlightener, the master and teacher,"[7] the archetype of the wise old man which Jung also calls the archetype of the spirit,
who symbolizes the meaning hidden in the chaos of life. Cagliostro is
Casanova's shadow, the dark side of himself that is opposite to the persona,
the side of himself that he would prefer not to see. Though the anima and the
wise old man take part in the drama, the basic conflict is between Casanova
and his shadow.

"This confrontation," Jung writes, "is the first test of courage on the
inner way, a test sufficient to frighten off most people, for the meeting with
ourselves belongs to the more unpleasant things that can be avoided so long
as we can project everything negative into the environment."[8] This matter
of projection is the key to Davies's dramatization of a psychic process. The
anima, the wise old man, and the shadow are, Jung points out, archetypes
of a kind that can be directly experienced in personified form";[9] thus, the
playwright can appropriately personify them and place them on the stage.
These elements of the unconscious may appear as people in dreams, or
they may be projected onto people one meets in life. Davies effectively
dramatizes the projection process by having the personified archetypes of
Casanova's unconscious play the roles of people he encountered in life in
each of the three episodes taken from his life. Though Sophia, Henriette,
and La Charpillon were real women, for Casanova they were essentially
projections of his anima. The wisdom of others he recognizes as such only
because of his own intimations of wisdom. The men who crossed him, the
enemies he hated, were projections of his shadow, hated because he saw in
them the characteristics in himself that thwarted his conscious aims. As
long as Casanova could project everything negative outside of himself, he
could avoid the unpleasant confrontation with his shadow.

"The shadow is a living part of the personality," Jung explains, "and
therefore wants to live with it in some form. It cannot be argued out of
existence or rationalized into harmlessness."[10] It makes itself known to
Casanova in the form of tortured self-accusations, self-doubts that will not
leave him alone, reducing him finally to helplessness and ineffectuality.
Jung emphasizes the pain and risk of self-confrontation: "The prudent man
avoids the danger lurking in these depths" (the unconscious), "but he also
throws away the good which a bold but imprudent venture might bring,"[11]
for once the painful encounter with the shadow is accomplished, the way is
open for the powerful collective unconscious to enrich and strengthen him.

Jung is clear that the process of self-confrontation cannot be solely an intellectual experience and that the way is so fraught with psychic hazards that one is safest in the hands of an experienced guide: an analyst. Davies's play is not an intellectual presentation of Jungian theory, but a dramatic portrayal of a man who is experiencing the emotional crisis of self-confrontation. Casanova is an intelligent and sensitive man who has withered not so much from age as from a paralyzing inability to face the dark side of himself. The play begins at the crisis. We are shown the morning, noon, and evening of his life in the three charades, the last of which precipitated a psychic struggle that has gone on submerged in Casanova's unconscious for nearly thirty years and is only now resolving itself in the dark night of his inner being. The action begins at night, and in the course of the night Casanova experiences the ennui of a former player in life and love who is now only an observer, the helplessness of a man who is unable to put his life in order, the fear of losing his mind which mounts to terror and near hysteria as he feels himself possessed by spirits over which he has no control, the humiliation and despair of a man who sees in himself the triviality and bestiality he had for so long struggled to deny. The play concludes at dawn, a dawn of renewed vitality that comes from cessation of the conflict when each side recognizes the validity of the other. The battling conscious and unconscious embrace to form a greater whole, and a newly alive and vigorous Casanova emerges.

Casanova has no analyst; what he has instead is something of what Davies calls elsewhere a "writer's conscience," which is "the writer's inner struggle toward self-knowledge and self-recognition, which he makes manifest through his art."[12] Artists, Davies explains, are not good subjects for psychoanalysis, because they are "continuously psycho-analyzing themselves in their own way, which is through their work, and it is the only way to peace of mind, to integration, open to them." When the play begins, Casanova has produced an enormous manuscript without managing to arrive at satisfactory answers to his questions. Though he believes he knows "pretty much of the truth about himself," he has to admit, "I have written the truth so far as I know it, and what is the result? A long story with little form and no moral" (208). The manuscript, sadly lacking either form or point, represents his life; it fails to satisfy Casanova, it fascinates Amalie, and it repels Hugo, who is comically fearful that Casanova is going to bore them thoroughly by reading "that immense heap of manuscript" (209).

The essence of what follows might be thought of as the process by which a writer struggles towards self-knowledge and self-recognition. In *General Confession*, Davies has said, "is my attempt to explain what an artist is."[13] The writer's conscience demands self-judgment. Davies has more than once referred with approval to Ibsen's lines,

> To live — is a battle with troll-folk
> In the crypts of heart and head;
> To write — is a man's self-judgment
> As Doom shall judge the dead.[14]

The dramatic form dictates a mock-trial in which the roles of prosecutor, counsel for the defence, judge, and so on, are played by other characters, but there is never the slightest doubt that the judgment must be Casanova's own. Before the third-act scene of judgment begins, Voltaire distinguishes among "God's judgement," "the judgement of one's fellow-men, which is essentially trivial," and "every man's judgement upon himself, which in the case of Giovanni Casanova, we could attempt" (251). When Casanova declines to pass judgment on himself, and Amalie, loathe to lose her entertainment for his lack of courage, volunteers to be judge, Voltaire emphasizes that she will only "play at being a judge" (255). And towards the end of the "trial," when Hugo asks Cagliostro, "You are not satisfied, sir?" he replies, "It is not my own satisfaction I seek, for I have none apart from him [Casanova]" (267). It is clear throughout that for Casanova writing his life story entails self-judgment. The other characters are present fundamentally to help dramatize the process.

Davies's play accounts very nicely for the incompleteness of Casanova's *Memoirs*. The revitalized Casanova turns not to his manuscript but to his love life, his true *métier*; reconciled with himself, he can return to living in the brief time he has left and has no further need of writing.

Davies chooses three episodes from *The Memoirs* to dramatize Casanova's life. Apart from inevitable condensation, he leaves the first essentially unaltered with respect to Casanova's character and his relationship with Sophia, the Mahometan beauty, though he makes the girl even more surprising and more of a lost treasure by insisting on her virginity. Some changes are made in this episode and the others simply to clarify the parts played by the wise old man and the shadow in Casanova's life. If an episode in *The Memoirs* does not contain a counsellor and an enemy, Davies creates them, or rather, he alters the peripheral characters of *The Memoirs* to suit his purpose. In the Constantinople episode of *The Memoirs* the same man is both Casanova's close friend and counsellor and also his future father-in-law and husband of his sweetheart. Davies gives the counsellor role to a man who was actually only a casual acquaintance of Casanova's and reduces the complex figure of the friend and husband to a shadow-projection, the indignant husband.

The second episode, though greatly condensed, contains only one change of substance. Davies's Casanova tells his audience that he "contrived to lose the Hungarian Captain" who was Henriette's lover when he met her, and he jocularly remarks to Henriette that they have "un-accountably mislaid" (228) the Captain. *The Memoirs* tells a different story; there, the accommodating Captain, who had never thought of the liaison as anything but temporary, yields Henriette to Casanova's care willingly. Davies has altered the portrayal of a Casanova who was actually only twenty-three, in the direction of what he perceived to be a "tough and opportunist middle age."[15]

The third episode is the one in which Davies makes the most significant changes, and these are obviously germane to his purpose. His Casanova is forty-five, not thirty-eight, when the affair with Charpillon occurs. The Charpillon of *The Memoirs* is a tease and a cheat; Casanova never enjoys her sexual favours, though she obtains a good deal of money from him at various times by giving the impression that she is ready to accommodate him, or that he has really injured her in one of his fits of fury over her behaviour, tricks that he, blinded by passion, falls for repeatedly. Davies makes his Charpillon "honest" in the exchange of sexual favours for money, a striking alteration. In both memoirs and play, the affair is regarded as a turning-point in Casanova's life. In both, he is humiliated almost beyond belief. However, *The Memoirs* shows him bent on suicide, believing that Charpillon is dying as a result of his rage on finding her with her handsome hairdresser. When, in the last stages of despair, prevented from suicide only by the fortuitous intervention of a friend, he sees her dancing and realizes that her "death" is only another trick, the shock releases him from his bondage to her. Though Charpillon is unmistakably indifferent to Casanova's charm in *The Memoirs*, what makes the greatest impression on the reader is his vulnerability and her perfidy.

Davies's version has quite a different effect. His Charpillion is shallow but not perfidious. Her position is defensible: she gives Casanova "value" for his money, and having declined his offer to be her "protector," she has a right to bestow her love elsewhere. After he surprises her with Toby, she rides him about the stage, flogging him with a cane, while Toby trips him up whenever he tries to stand. She calls him "Dobbin," a "worn-out ladies' mount," and when Toby speaks of gelding him, she replies, "Gelding? He's close to that already, from age and hard riding" (242). All of this is of a piece with the change Davies makes in Casanova's age. Well past forty, he has arrived at that second half of life during which, according to Jung, the usual pattern of individual development dictates a shift of focus from one's social role in life to one's own inner being.[16]

Everything about Davies's depiction of the Charpillion episode is a demand for Casanova's self-assessment. Through the eyes of La Char-pillion and Toby (his shadow, whom he sees as a defiling "thing") he sees himself not as a gallant lover, devoted to an ideal, but as a lecher and a fool.

There is no sense of resolution following the Charpillion charade, only Casanova's humiliation and the discomfiture of the others. Casanova is left to question himself, and in the decades between the event and the present he has been drained of all his zest for life by the impasse between the claims of his ego and the counter-claims of his unconscious. For each of the charades a heightened "acting" manner is assumed by the participants to distinguish the charades from the present action, but for the Charpillion charade Davies specifies extreme stylization: *"the acting is grotesque, except in the case of CASANOVA, who seems to be a man moving in a phantasmagoria"* (237). The charade has the impact of a nightmare, which underlines its significance as a psychic experience.

Davies is dazzlingly successful at creating a theatrical experience out of what is essentially a man's soul-searching: dramatic enough for the person who undergoes it, but, one might think, difficult to stage effectively. The charade portraying a scene from Casanova's earlier life is one method by which he achieves dramatic interest. Another is the personification of three elements of Casanova's unconscious. This has the obvious advantage of externalizing the inner struggle and so making it accessible to the audience, and it also has the effect of allowing the audience to share in Casanova's dreams — or nightmares. As in *Hunting Stuart*, the means by which Davies makes the transition from the external world to the inner world is magic. Here Casanova himself is the magician, and he performs a cabbalistic ritual (using candles and a bowl of water as in the Stuart ceremony of the Royal Touch) designed to call forth "a spirit" to satisfy Amalie's desire for entertainment and to allay her scepticism about his powers.

The extent of his success surprises even Casanova. With the advent of the spirits, the texture of reality in the play changes. The first sign is that when Casanova and Cagliostro run each other through with swords, no injury is suffered. Amalie testifies to the change and accepts it without specifying its nature. When the servant Wenzel forgets his place and Hugo rebukes him, Amalie says, "Let him alone, Hugo. Don't you understand? It's all part of it — like being in those Arabian tales where animals suddenly speak. HUGO: All part of what? AMALIE: Whatever this is. Don't interrupt. Let it happen as it will" (219). For the duration of the second act, the spell we are under, the "whatever" Amalie does not attempt to define, seems to be the magic of theatre, as three scenes from Casanova's life are staged. The three spirits and Casanova himself are the actors; Amalie, Hugo, and Wenzel are the audience. At the end of the second act, however, our understanding of the nature of the new reality changes when the audience's bewilderment over the performance leads to the revelation that the three spirits are not the spirits of Voltaire, Cagliostro, and a specific nameless woman at all, but personifications of elements from Casanova's unconscious who just happen to be cast in the shapes of real people who are appropriately wise, menacing, or attractive. Now the spell we are under, the new reality, is that of the unconscious interacting with the conscious, as earlier the world of the theatrical performance was mingled with the world of the audience watching it.

Casanova is himself astonished by the magic he has wrought in raising the spirits. He had intended "the usual thing. Shadows on the wall, chairs toppling over, perhaps a voice speaking in an unknown tongue" (248). But the power of the room full of forbidden things and the power of Casanova's own psychic energy struggling to resolve the conflict within him produce greater wonders than he had counted on. This is consistent with Davies's view — expressed first with emphasis in *A Jig for the Gypsy* — that life is full of surprises and not to be confined or set in rigid patterns. It is also consistent with the picture given in *The Memoirs* of Casanova's powers as a magician. In his study of the occult, Colin Wilson names Casanova (along with Cagliostro) among the three most noted practitioners of magic in the eighteenth century.[17] Though Casanova thought of himself as an imposter, he "possessed a natural 'occult faculty,'" Wilson theorizes. "When some of his absurder prophecies came true, he would experience. . . a moment [of] superstitious awe." Wilson attributes Casanova's amazing luck for the first half of his life to "a 'sixth sense'" that made him say or do the right thing, and notes that "this curious psychic radar began to fail him in his late thirties," when he lost his confidence after the Charpillon affair.[18] Inspired by Amalie, Casanova again sets out to perform magic, and, as of old, he is first pleasantly surprised by his own success, then awed by the mysteries he does not understand; finally, he is frightened by his lack of control over the mysterious powers he has loosed.

Casanova's surprise, his awe, and his fright are appropriate reactions to magic, and equally appropriate reactions to a discovery of the energies of the psyche. By Act III the "magic" world has become the "ordinary" world of a man's mind, and the reality we experience is the reality of a dream, or at least that of consciousness recalling a dream, for we witness interaction between the conscious and unconscious components of Casanova's mind. As early as *At the Gates of the Righteous*, Davies's characters realize that the most important revolutions occur within the individual, and now we are witnessing such a revolution in progress. With the anima figure, the inspiration he finds in women, Casanova is satisfied. "I have sufficed you for a lifetime," remarks Marina near the end of the play. "It is not always so" (269). With the figure of Voltaire and especially with that of Cagliostro, however, there is a reckoning at hand.

Davies's old theme of the limitations of reason and the attractions of other modes of perception, particularly intuition and feeling, is infused with new life here. The wise counsellor of his unconscious, upon whose guidance Casanova depended through much of his life, is cast in the guise of that personification of reason in the Age of Reason, Voltaire. The enemy, the element of his unconscious which Casanova distrusts and fears, is cast in the guise of the sinister and mysterious Cagliostro, a man who was among the very few to wield formidable occult powers in an age when reason was supreme. Casanova's *Memoirs* records meetings with both Voltaire and Cagliostro. Voltaire he greeted with "This is the happiest moment of my life. I have been your pupil for twenty years; and my heart is full of joy to see my master."[19] In Cagliostro's face he found boldness and cynicism. Casanova's aversion to Cagliostro is attributed to the fact that "he usually hates his own kind,"[20] by E. W. Dupee in his introduction to *The Memoirs*, an implicit corroboration of Davies's view that Cagliostro was a figure on whom Casanova projected his own shadow.

Davies alters Jung's wise old man archetype somewhat to emphasize the limitations of reason. Jung's archetypal spirit, often personified as a wise old man in dreams and fairy-tales, helps the hero out of tight spots; he does not just enable him to find out the meaning of his experiences. He represents "knowledge, reflection, insight, wisdom, cleverness, and intuition," and also "moral qualities such as good will and readiness to help,"[21] not simply reason or philosophy. Though Davies never calls this faculty "reason" but usually "wisdom," which is not so limited, its personification as Voltaire suggests reason, and it is reduced by implication to something that resembles reason. "Wisdom" fails Casanova in the Charpillion affair. When Casanova appeals to Voltaire as "the wisest man I have ever known," Voltaire implies that he has allowed Casanova to overvalue him because he enjoyed Casanova's admiration. Cagliostro is contemptuous: "You look for comfort from wisdom, do you? You shall find out what sort of comfort wisdom is" (244-45). Towards the end of the play Casanova says to Voltaire: "You, my spirit of wisdom, my best judgement, could you not have been a better friend to me?" Cagliostro, who takes control of the proceedings with the staging of the Charpillion affair and who reasserts himself periodically (though Casanova never loses control entirely; to do so would mean madness), steps in firmly here: "You have something to learn about wisdom. Its chief desire is not to be helpful but to be in the right. It looks well; it talks well; but — you see what it is worth at last" (269). No one offers a rebuttal to this, and Voltaire himself concurs when he bids Casanova farewell: "I am always at your service, to the best of my ability. But what wisdom is infallible?" (271).

Jung's view of the "wise old man" archetype, expressed in "The Phenomenology of the Spirit in Fairy Tales," is not so limited, but Davies is not violating any of Jung's basic views; he is only making the ideas more accessible in dramatic form. Cagliostro's scornful "you see what it is worth at last" implies that the wisdom Voltaire suggests, the light of reason, is not worth much compared with the darker and more mysterious sources of human truth represented by Cagliostro. Casanova has overvalued the one and undervalued the other, a tendency Jung recognized as typical of modern western thought. If one enlarges Davies's Voltaire figure to equate it with Jung's archetype of the spirit, the recognition of Voltaire's limitations and of Cagliostro's value takes on another meaning, for Jung tells us that the spirit cannot effectively come to the aid of the hero as long as he is divided against himself, as Davies's hero is before Casanova and Cagliostro embrace. Without embracing all of himself, all of his resources, the hero may be unable to act on such wisdom as he possesses, or even to recognize it as wisdom when it suggests itself to him. Davies's deviations from Jung simply make the play accessible to people who are unacquainted with Jung. Davies presents the experience directly, with maximum emotional impact. Though the archetypal figures explain themselves to Casanova and the observers, they make no long intellectual speeches. There is no attempt made to explain why Casanova is so transformed by his acceptance of Cagliostro — with his accusation of lechery — as part of himself; we see only that acknowledging his dark side gives him new life.

Jung offers the explanation: there are both positive and negative sides to every element of the human personality; if the animal side of human nature is frighteningly amoral, it is also a source of vital energy. The anima which inspires Casanova does so without regard to good and evil; she may lead him to a Henriette or to a Charpillion. If he wants to live fully, he must take his chances. "Bodily life as well as psychic life have the impudence to get along much better without conventional morality," Jung remarks, "and they often remain the healthier for it."[22] A bad experience that made Casanova focus on ugliness in himself undermined his psychic health, for in avoiding the ugliness, he also avoided the best in himself. We see and feel this in the play; for an intellectual explanation, we can go to Jung.

Concentrating on wholeness rather than virtue as the ideal for man, and perhaps reflecting on the charges of indecency against *Hunting Stuart*, Davies renewed the attempt made earlier in *Fortune, My Foe* to disabuse his audience of the notion that art should be educational in the sense of incorporating social values. Voltaire objects to Cagliostro's proposal to dramatize the Charpillion affair with the observation that the incident "was certainly unedifying." Hypocrite!" Cagliostro jeers. "Edification is not our object" (237). Certainly Voltaire, with all his wisdom, can make nothing of the affair; yet its emotional impact is indisputable. There is more to life than edification. Casanova makes a clear distinction between "works of art, which deal with life as it is," and "works of edification, which deal with life as the timid think it ought to be" (254), which effectively prevents one from concluding that Davies means a work of art should not embody ideas. Amalie repeatedly indicates that she expects to find not "edification" but "entertainment" in Casanova's life story, by which she evidently does not mean a good laugh. She wants to understand his life with her "understanding heart," emotionally, and in the end this is accomplished, for her and for us.

In the clearest possible form that a "message" can be given in a play, General Confession offers us two: Voltaire's summing up of each of the first two dramatized scenes from Casanova's life. The message from the first charade, "Except in trivial things, life has no rules," is repeated five times (twice with slight variations) by four characters in the space of a page and a half of dialogue. It could hardly be more emphatically delivered. The message of the second charade, "Nothing is so delusive as the notion of freedom," is delivered slightly less emphatically, for we have already been taught by the first charade to look for a message. But the two statements appear to be contradictory; neither, then, can be "the message" of the play. We will, of course, look for the message of the third charade, and Davies's refusal to give us one leads us past the expectation that his play will give us a simply verbalized message. But Casanova cannot drop his attempt to understand his own life, and the audience does not expect the play to end without illumination; he and we have to seek satisfaction in a different way or at a different depth.

A play that contains a play invites a comparison between art and life. In General Confession equations are drawn between Casanova's art and his life. The scenes that are acted out for Amalie, Hugo, and Wenzel are played in response to Casanova's plea to Voltaire: "Help me to make myself understood!" (220) It is not clear whether they are scenes from his life or from his art, The Memoirs. "A love affair," Casanova claims, "is a work of art" (225). Even apart from the scenes staged within the play, theatrical terms are employed. "You make me feel like an actress in a play," Amalie says to Casanova, and he replies, "The most entrancing of plays. . . ," by which he means life (208).

One might expect to find distinctions made between life and art, but what interests Davies here are the similarities. Casanova's Memoirs conveys his sense of himself as an actor in the drama of life, and Jung speaks of life as "the most distinguished and rarest of all the arts."[23] Davies's play presents a man's life as a work of art. The key to fulfilment in both life and art lies in the paradox of the contradictory truths which emerge from the first and second scenes from Casanova's life. If they were applied to art, their meaning would be clear enough: except in trivial things, art has no rules, yet nothing is so delusive as the notion that the artist has perfect freedom. A painter needs paint, something to apply it with and something to apply it to, but what rule of colour or composition or technique has not been discarded in the creation of some great painting? Yet in the creation of a specific work of art the artist has little freedom; each stroke must be in accord with the others if the end is to be indeed a work of art and not a hodgepodge. Similarly, apart from biological basics like the need for food and oxygen, individuals and circumstances vary so greatly that no rule of life is inviolable. Still, a specific individual has his own distinct nature, which determines his destiny in life, and to violate it is to diminish the quality of that life. "Deny destiny," Hugo says, "and life becomes a mere tangle....A jumble of shoddy expediency. It lacks shape" (235).

Casanova's climactic speech, his self-judgment after he has acknowledged guilt in all the seven deadly sins, even lechery, describes his life as a work of art:

> God will know that in all the makeshifts of my life I have loved some things truly, held some things sacred, and that I have striven to give some pattern to the muddle of experience which the moving years have brought me. Where I could, I put a shape on the obstinate granite of circumstance; when it was possible I gave some grace to the insubstantial and often shoddy stuff of my character. The result is no saint, nor yet a vulgar whimpering sinner, but an artist whose work was sometimes good and sometimes bad. God gave me life, and I have lived it, with the gifts and the blemishes he gave me, with as much — (*He searches for the word*) — style, as I could (268).

The pattern, the shape, implies pursuit of his destiny and suggests the form of a work of art. The style is his own distinctive behaviour in particular circumstances, as in literature the style of the language will accord with both the writer's individuality and the matter to be expressed. He was as true to himself as he could be in the unfortunate circumstances of the Charpillion affair; a man can do no more. The facts of his life have not changed, but his perception of himself has; this gives him the sense of fulfilment that is so satisfying when one experiences it in a complete work of art. Finally he achieves the understanding of his life that he has sought, and his audience — in the play and in the theatre — has a share in the satisfaction that the understanding brings.

Though the play's intense focus on Casanova (who as a total personality encompasses four of the seven characters) may make the other three

characters seem extraneous, their contribution is essential. Most obviously, they provide a context for Casanova's self-discovery; they question
him, mock him, wheedle him, disarm him, providing whatever external
stimulus is required at a given moment. Their responses to what they are
witnessing, as varied as their personalities, provide a dramatic means of
conveying information to the audience about the significance of what is
taking place and a great deal of humour as well. Their resemblance to the
characters who make up Casanova's personality provides a resonance
which adds to our impression that the events of the play are archetypal, not
merely particular. Amalie has aspects of Marina; she "fascinates"
Casanova, and she provides the "inspiration" for his conjuration of the
spirits. Wenzel is the lower-class, uneducated equivalent of Voltaire; his is
common-sense wisdom in the vein of Lug or Chilly Jim or Benoni. His
resemblance to Voltaire is suggested most persuasively by the comparison
Amalie makes between Wenzel's surprisingly uninhibited speech and animal speech in fairy-tales. There is no reason to believe that this is meant to
imply contempt for Wenzel. Rather, it suggests Jung's observation that the
spirit archetype, though it most often takes the form of an old man, can also
take the form of a helpful animal. Such animals, often found in fairy-tales,
"act like humans, speak a human language, and display a sagacity and a
knowledge superior to man's."[24] Hugo, who plays the Casanova role in the
attempted seduction of Amalie, fittingly displays aspects of both Casanova
and his shadow, Cagliostro.

Perhaps the most important contribution this trio makes to the play is in
establishing the degree to which Casanova's experience is a universal one,
though of course its details are individual. Hugo, Amalie, and Wenzel
receive with alarm Voltaire's assurance that they too have unconscious
"spirits"; on a minor scale they establish both that everyone is "similarly
equipped" and that this realization is disconcerting. Casanova's emotions
are more powerful because he is experiencing directly what they are only
comprehending intellectually. An even more important step in the
universalizing process is the recognition that the guilt Casanova feels so
personally is universal human guilt, but there is a great difference between
the ease with which we accept the theory of universal guilt and the emotional impact of particular personal guilt. Marina, speaking on behalf of the
accused, breaks up the "trial" with the longest and most impassioned
speech of the play in which she accuses Wenzel, Hugo, and especially
Amalie, who is playing the role of judge, of guilt in very specific terms. She
concludes with "you, Grand Ducal Highness, are slothful in the highest
degree, because wealth and position have made you slothful of mind —
slothful of mind, or you would have seen the trap into which you have fallen
by charging Casanova with no sin worse than that of being a man, with a

man's passions and a man's frailty! All, all are guilty, and where all are guilty, who dares judge?'' (258).

Subtract from the speech its passion — suggested by its rhythms and its effect — and the accusations are not so terrible. But the personal nature of the accusations and the intensity with which they are made make them felt much more strongly than their actual content would seem to warrant. Amalie, Hugo, and Wenzel are thrown into turmoil — yet despite the emotional impact of the accusation, the point that is finally made, comically, is that it amounts to no more than an accusation of humanity. The "outside" trio comes to terms with this first in a comic hubbub, then, in a lower, more intense, and moving key, Casanova, too, painfully, then joyfully accepts his own humanity. The universality of his condition is suggested by Davies's choice of title, by which he apparently means something more than Casanova did when he said his memoirs were meant as a general confession rather than a boast. In Davies's hands, the confession becomes general in that in its essence, if not in its particulars, it could be anyone's.

With its grand theme, its archetypal characters, and its heightened style, which at critical moments has the surrealism of a dream, *General Confession* clearly fulfils Davies's ideal of theatre as a collective dream. A great play, he believes, a great "dream of the tribe," in a good performance for a sympathetic audience "reassures you as to who you are, what you are, what life is. This is noble and this is great, and that's what I want in the theatre." In a good performance of *General Confession* "everybody in the audience is going to be stripped naked like Casanova himself, right down to the basic man, and the basic man isn't so bad. I think that's what's cheerful about the play."[25]

Cheerful it is, as well as very dramatic. The tone of the play is in keeping with both the seriousness of the theme and the cheerfulness of Davies's outlook on humanity. It is not at all a sombre play, but there are few of the satirical thrusts that seem characteristic of Davies's other writing and less farce or "low" humour than in any of his plays since *Hope Deferred*. *General Confession* is high comedy: witty and graceful, amusing and thoughtful, though its powerful emotions place it in the realm of romantic comedy rather than comedy of manners.

The part of Casanova was intended for Donald Davis, Cagliostro for his brother Murray, and the Ideal Beloved for their sister, Barbara Chilcott. The family resemblance would have been especially appropriate to the parts. But the play was never staged, a development Davies cites as an illustration of "the funny life playwrights live." The comment testifies to Davies's ability to find humour even in painful things, or to use humour as a shield against the painful things. More revealing is his admission that "it's the kind of thing which either gives you a strong character or drives you mad.''[26] The Crest Theatre was having its problems, both financial and critical, and a number of factors combined to keep *General Confession* off the stage.[27] J. B. Priestley, a writer at the height of his great reputation, had met the Davises at a dinner party given by Davies. Taken with the striking appearance of the brothers and sister, Priestley offered to write a play especially for the three of them, to receive its world première in Toronto and subsequently to be staged in London. It looked like a wonderful opportunity to gain international recognition for the Crest and it must have eclipsed Davies's play-in-progress, though Priestley's *The Glass Cage*, which opened at the Crest on 5 March 1957, did not turn out to be very successful. On their return from London, the Davises were fighting to keep the Crest alive financially, struggling to fill their 850-seat theatre. A good deal of criticism of the Crest's artistic efforts apparently stemmed from antipathy for the Davis family, who were perceived by many as "too refined and elitist." They were "the enemy class," "the rich upper-class WASP."[28] Davies was another such, and in any case, after the Priestley play to produce a family affair again featuring the Davis brothers and their sister seemed unwise when they needed to widen their base of support both inside and outside the theatre community. Though the Davises did not abandon their efforts to stage Canadian plays in their attempt to fill their large theatre, the few they chose were as "surefire" as possible. Among the twenty-one plays offered by the Crest over the next two seasons, the four new Canadian plays were John Gray's *Bright Sun at Midnight*, a serious drama built around the topical issue of the suicide of Canada's ambassador to Egypt; *The Ottawa Man*, a farce set in nineteenth-century Manitoba adapted by Mavor Moore from Gogol's *The Inspector General*; and two musicals: a revue called *This is Our First Affair* and John Gray's *Ride a Pink Horse*, about the fate of a centaur in modern Canada. Nothing like Davies's high comedy with its eighteenth-century European characters was judged likely to be a success.

All things considered, the Crest's decision not to produce *General Confession* is not surprising. What is surprising is that no one has yet produced it.[29] Never produced, its potential has never been realized. To assess accurately the value of a play from a script is difficult, and few people, even directors or academics whose business it supposedly is, have the time and the ability for it. Even the experienced playwright counts on rehearsals to help him finalize the script; Davies acknowledges that a production of *General Confession* would doubtless entail "quite a lot of cutting and splicing and some reshaping"[30] of the script. Even after it was published in 1972, the play did not generate much excitement. Journal reviews of the volume, which included *Hunting Stuart* and *King Phoenix* as well as *General Confession*, tended simply to describe the three plays in terms of themes. Those who offered opinions of the plays' theatrical merits could not have differed more completely. Of eleven reviews,[31] two were enthusiastic about all the plays, six were generally unimpressed; of those who differentiated among the plays, only one reviewer thought *General Confession* the best, finding it "eminently dramatic."[32] Patricia Morley describes *General Confession* in her book on Davies's plays but makes no attempt to assess it beyond calling it "ingenious." Her equation of Voltaire with the Jungian *self* suggests that she is rather bewildered by the play. Her comment on the Charpillion scene, which she sees "within the context of the entire play" solely as "a dash of lemon which adds a desirable tartness to the piquancy of the romantic comedy,"[33] shows more appreciation of the flavour of the play than most critics display, but not the understanding necessary to a full recognition of its value. Even Patricia Monk, whose study of the Jungian self in Davies's novels should have served her well as a critic of *General Confession*, admits to being uncertain of what the play is about.[34]

General Confession is Davies's dramatic masterpiece, and it may be *the* neglected masterpiece of Canadian theatre. It was written after Davies had accumulated a great deal of practical experience of the stage and had refined his writing skills beautifully. He was writing not only at the peak of his powers, but also at the peak of his confidence as a playwright. The mature writer is very evident in the serious theme, the dramatic unity, the absence of satirical jests for their own sake. *General Confession* embodies the most perfect blend of theme and form of all Davies's plays: the problem, the crisis, and its resolution in Casanova's life are the dramatic problem, the dramatic crisis, and the dramatic resolution of the play. It is one of the great ironies of Canadian theatre history that this play remains unproduced. When Davies finally decided to publish his virgin script in 1972, Canada was firmly in the throes of self-conscious nationalism, and a comparison of Davies's plays with those of younger playwrights such as George Ryga, David French, and David Freeman suggested that while Davies's plays had unmatched "brilliance in theatricality and dialogue," he was less "in touch with the current mood of Canada," writing less "distinctive Canadian drama."[35] Moreover, Davies's recent publication of *Fifth Business* and *The Manticore* resulted in an inclination on the part of some reviewers to underrate his "old" plays in comparing them with his new novels.

General Confession is not set in Canada, it is neither sombre nor farcical, and it is not about the trapped and limited twentieth-century everyman who apparently defines and reflects the limits of human aspiration today; accordingly, its style is not restrained, but flamboyant. These are all sins against current fashion, not against the criteria for a dramatic masterpiece. Davies, evidently his own best critic, declares *General Confession* "my best play and my favorite,"[36] and the fact that it has not found its way to the stage must be a significant factor in his conclusion that his taste is out of step with current taste in Canadian theatre. Perhaps *General Confession*'s day will come, but it certainly did not come when it was written. It was his best play, and it was not to be produced. This was a turning point in Davies's playwriting career.

9

A Novel for Broadway: *Leaven of Malice*

IN THE THIRTEEN YEARS from 1944 through 1956, Davies had written five one-act plays, a masque, and seven full-length plays. He had registered some gratifying triumphs in playwriting competitions and the Dominion Drama Festival, and as Canada's professional theatre grew, his opportunities as a playwright seemed to grow with it. But that changed after the mid-fifties. Certainly he was disappointed about the Crest's failure to produce *General Confession*. He had prepared a free adaptation of Ben Jonson's *Bartholomew Fair* for the Stratford Festival's 1956 season, but when Michael Langham replaced Tyrone Guthrie as artistic director, he decided against producing the play,[1] though the "Lost Scene from the Merry Wives of Windsor" which Davies wrote was included in the Stratford production of that play the same season. Davies's enthusiastic support of the Stratford Festival continued unabated, as did his friendship with the Davises, but he may well have felt that the kind of playwriting he wanted to do, exemplified by *General Confession*, was not compatible with opportunities for production.

During the seventeen years after *General Confession* was written, Davies's dramatic writing consisted of an adaptation from one of his novels, another masque, a centennial spectacle and part of a centennial play written by five authors. There was little progress in his work as a dramatist and no sparkling success to fuel his passion for playwriting. Though he wrote a play now and again for a special occasion, there was little reward for his efforts. By comparison with the frustrations of trying to get one of his plays performed by people capable of doing it well, getting a novel published must have seemed simple, and for his second effort, *Leaven of Malice*, he had received the Stephen Leacock Memorial Medal for humour in 1955. After he wrote *General Confession* he set to work on a third novel, *Mixture of Frailties*. Its theme of wholeness, developed by depicting the acquisition of a full and balanced personality in one central character, relates it more nearly to *General Confession* than to the first two novels. The grotesqueness of Revelstoke's death is reminiscent of the Charpillion scene in *General Confession* and quite unlike anything in the first two novels. For the first time, the main line of Davies's development as a writer seemed to be through a novel rather than a play, and reviews showed some appreciation of Davies's progress as a novelist, noting the wisdom added to his humour and the more convincing humanity of his characters in "his first serious novel."[2]

Davies's next dramatic project was an adaptation of *Leaven of Malice* for the stage. This was an uncharacteristic step, partly because he was moving backward to old ideas for a new play, and partly because he is quite definite about the inherent distinction between an idea that can be suitably developed into a novel and one that is appropriate for a play: "As a general rule, a play has a plot that is more simply dealt with than the plot of a novel. The content of a play is not simple, but it should, in its unfolding, follow a simpler line than the plot of most novels, which may have ramifications and by-concerns that would muddle the action of a play. This is why dramatizations of novels such as *Don Quixote* or *David Copperfield* deal only with a few incidents from the whole work, and often leave us unsatisfied. The totality of a play and the totality of a novel are different in kind."[3] But Tyrone Guthrie offered to direct a dramatization of *Leaven of Malice* for the New York Theatre Guild, and Davies felt that he "would have been a fool to turn down the chance" of a Broadway production directed by Guthrie.[4] Though it is full of lively scenes and interesting characters, *Leaven of Malice* lacks focus; it is not as good a play as *Hunting Stuart*, and it does not come close to *General Confession*. However, it is particularly interesting as a means for considering the relationship between Davies's work as a novelist and his work as a playwright. And though a close study of the story in both its forms reinforces some commonly held suspicions about the difficulties of adapting novelistic material for the stage, it also provides some interesting insights into means of getting such material onto the stage, occasionally even in a way which improves on the original. Davies's inventiveness is as evident in this adaptation as it is in his other writing.

The play, "the first truly native Canadian play to be produced by a New York theatre group,"[5] was called *Love and Libel* so as not to puzzle a New York audience with the biblical reference of the original title. Guthrie took it on tour for a month, beginning at Toronto's Royal Alexandra Theatre on 2

November 1960, where it earned five curtain calls, and ending in New York, where it opened on 7 December and ran for only a few days. Reviews there were unenthusiastic; *Theatre Arts* reported "two tolerably cheerful notices" among the seven daily New York papers.[6] Tyrone Guthrie and Dennis King, the star attraction, got more notice than Davies did. Individual players, particularly King as the madcap organist Humphrey Cobbler, and individual scenes, particularly the one in which Humphrey, his wife Molly, and their friend Solly Bridgetower all climb into bed to keep warm as they converse about Solly's troubles, won praise. But as a whole, the play was not a success. Toronto reviews reflected awareness that Toronto was the first stop on the tour and there was yet time for repairs. Herbert Whittaker's review ends with "It's all a dazzlement of good and familiar things that needs sorting out a bit more at the moment."[7] Nathan Cohen concludes, "There are enough good things in it to make me believe that with the right changes, it can be made to work. And the first and most important change is to give the play a more disciplined and less elaborate shape."[8] A Detroit reviewer too found the play "hodge-podge and episodical," "far too long," despite "many ludicrous scenes, many laughable bits of business."[9]

Davies calls the play "an extravaganza"; the elaborate and episodical shape was part of his design, and he made no attempt to achieve a streamlined structure. However, he did a good deal of rewriting during the tour, mostly to meet the demands of the show's star, Dennis King, who wanted his part expanded. New bits were generated furiously and tried out during the tour, which no doubt contributed considerably to the "hodge-podge" effect. Davies recalls one night when King walked on stage, forgot the lines for a new scene, and turned around and walked off again, leaving Tony Van Bridge on stage to ad lib his way through the gap in the play. The tour, theoretically an opportunity to improve the play and set the production before it got to New York, seems only to have widened the rift between Davies's perception of the play and the New York Theatre Guild's notions of what would make a Broadway hit. Davies thinks of it as an ensemble play and believes that trying to put a star into it was the first big mistake.[10]

In the end, Davies was unhappy with the version of his play which was performed in New York, and all the changes which had been insisted upon by management, director, and star did not create a hit. Tyrone Guthrie's official biographer, James Forsyth, gives him more blame than credit for the production, though Guthrie meant well by Davies, who had been a close friend for many years and a strong supporter of his work at Stratford. He was caught in the middle between Davies and the New York management, and he was not strong enough to steer his way through the conflicts successfully. He had suffered a heart attack early in the year. Recovering, he produced Gilbert and Sullivan's *H.M.S. Pinafore*, after which, Forsyth says,

> this distinguished heart patient went straight on to produce the new
> play of his old friend of Old Vic and Canada, Robertson Davies' *Love
> and Libel*. That he made a proper botch of it, all agreed. It was an
> unwise undertaking, to do a new play when the prognostication had
> been that he would not be fit enough to do one old one. Rob Davies had
> been of great assistance in all the Stratford ventures and Tony Guthrie
> probably felt he owed it to him. But the play and the playwright
> suffered.[11]

While *Love and Libel* fared no worse than a number of other plays on
Broadway at about the same time, its reception did nothing to ensure
Davies's fame as a playwright.

The play was shelved for a dozen years until it was produced as *Leaven
of Malice* at Hart House Theatre in 1973 and again at the Niagara-on-the-
Lake Shaw Festival in 1975. For these productions Davies's original script
was used. The director of the Shaw Festival production, Tony Van Bridge,
had acted in Tyrone Guthrie's production, and his decision to revive the
play was testimony that Davies's play was better than Guthrie's production
suggested. Van Bridge says of the Guthrie show, "All I can remember
about it is that it was chaos." Nevertheless, he decided to do the play in
1975, because he thought it was "one of the best Canadian comedies
around," "a first-class Canadian play."[12] Still, *Leaven of Malice* in both
his production and Martin Hunter's at Hart House got mixed reviews, with
high praise for various scenes and characters, but not for the play as a
whole. The reason is at least partly the difficulty of adaptation from novel to
play. The most obvious challenge in adapting a novel for the stage is to
condense the material to what can be played in little more than two hours. It
is clear that unless a novel is dreadfully diffuse, something of value — minor
characters, episodes which are not essential for the development of plot or
character, and authorial musings on the inner lives of characters or the
abstract implications of speeches or events — must be cut out in the
process of adaptation.

Davies may have felt equal to the challenge of adapting his novel simply
because its plot is not essentially complex. "As a general rule a play has a
plot that is more simply dealt with than the plot of a novel," Davies
observed. What could be simpler than the plot of *Leaven of Malice*?
Someone puts a false engagement notice in the local newspaper. Its effects
on all concerned are explored; in particular, the two young people linked in
the announcement find each other and the strength to stand up to their

parents. Finally, the culprit is found and his motives discovered. It would seem that the only necessity for dealing with this plot in the scope of a play would be to limit the implications of the "effects on all concerned." Reduce the number of characters affected by the engagement notice, and the plot is instantly simplified.

Those characters most essentially concerned are few. Gloster Ridley, editor of *The Bellman*, in which the engagement notice appears, is technically responsible for the notice; he is not only embarrassed by the fact that somehow the notice managed to slip by his staff without the signature of the person who submitted it, but he is afraid that the ensuing fuss, including a threatened libel suit, may cost him the honorary doctorate from the local university that he hopes for. Pearl Vambrace and Solly Bridgetower are the two young people named in the engagement notice. In fact, they are only slightly acquainted, and Pearl is aware that Solly has long been the suitor of another young lady. Solly's mother, Mrs. Bridgetower, and Pearl's father, Professor Vambrace, are both eccentric and demanding parents. The Professor, nursing an old grudge against Solly's father, now deceased, is outraged to have Solly named as Pearl's fiancé. He would probably be outraged at the idea of losing his daughter to any young man, and having no idea who has perpetrated the hoax or why — except to annoy and embarrass him — he vents his wrath on Ridley, Pearl, and Solly. Mrs. Bridgetower is concerned primarily with keeping a stranglehold on Solly, ridden with anxiety that some young lady may win him away from her. Humphrey Cobbler, a Bohemian musician, is involved as the prime suspect in the minds of a few meddlers who believe him capable of anything because he is unconventional in behaviour, appearance, and outlook on life.

First thoughts about the novel suggest that only one other character is essential; Bevill Higgin, an Irish newcomer to the town who is attempting to establish himself as a teacher of singing and elocution, proves to be responsible for the engagement notice, motivated by malice because he had been snubbed at one time or another by Gloster Ridley, Solly Bridgetower, and someone he mistakenly took for Pearl Vambrace. This comes to only seven characters, a manageable number for a stage production. At first, then, it is a surprise to find that the play retains a number of minor characters from the novel who do not seem to be central to the plot. George and Kitten Morphew are still scuffling and nuzzling on stage; Norm and Dutchy Yarrow are still inflicting awful party games on their guests and congratulating themselves on how normal they are. Altogether, the play includes sixteen characters plus a number of supernumeraries, a larger cast than in any of Davies's earlier plays except *A Masque of Aesop*, which was designed to include as many boys as possible.

Guthrie saw the dramatization from the beginning in terms of an extravaganza, but there are at least three additional reasons for the large number of characters and the consequent complexity of the play. The first is that the real subject of *Leaven of Malice* is not the couple named in the engagement notice; it is small-town mentality. Because this involves ancient disputes, gossip, social pride, and petty malice, the subject could hardly be effectively treated through just a few characters. The Yarrows, for instance, epitomize the well-meaning meddlers who are motivated by good intentions but limited by insensitivity and overconfidence in their own perceptions and values. They appear in three scenes. In the first, Dutchy Yarrow is inspired by the engagement announcement in the paper to force Pearl and Solly into embarrassing intimacy in a party game, and they are unable to explain their predicament in the face of the effusive congratulations and sentimental speeches of their hosts. The second scene expands the characterization of Norm and Dutchy as tiresomely conscious of how well-adjusted and determinedly normal they are; this scene prepares for the third, in which Norm, in his capacity as a guidance counsellor, carries out his campaign to smooth Pearl's path to wedded bliss by having a heart-to-heart talk with her father, a professor of classics, about the Oedipus Complex, which he takes to be the root of Professor Vambrace's agitation about the engagement announcement.

This scene is a comic triumph. In addition, it brings the background of the townspeople's gossip about the Vambraces' affairs into the foreground; Norm exposes the ugly face of Rumour with his reference to the episode in which Vambrace broke his stick over Solly's car: "Now about Pearlie.... They say you were walloping her with a pretty big stick...."[13] Yarrow's interview with Vambrace is also the best opportunity in the play for providing depth to Vambrace's character; his emotional intensity, intellect, and eccentricity are shown to good advantage in contrast with ultra-normal Norm's fatuous professionalism. The Yarrows are well-meaning onlookers who add greatly to the discomfiture of the central characters; they may not contribute much to the plot, but without such people, the "leaven of malice" on which the play comments could not work so effectively.

A second reason for the large number of characters becomes evident in a consideration of Davies's purpose for including George and Kitten Morphew in the play. They and Kitten's sister, Edith Little, contribute to the depth of the characterization of the town as a whole. But, more importantly, they provide a context in which to develop the character of Bevill Higgin, the outsider who struggles to market his limited talents under the impression that he is bringing "culture" to Canada. Part of the play's point is that such a small thing as a false engagement notice affects a variety of otherwise unrelated people in the town. Pearl and Solly hardly know each other; Gloster Ridley, the newspaper editor, is unconnected with either the Vambraces or the Bridgetowers; Humphrey Cobbler, though he happens to be a friend of Solly's, is affected primarily because his natural prankishness makes those who fail to distinguish between highjinks and malicious mischief suspect him of being responsible for the engagement notice. All can come to life only with a context to operate in, which means the introduction of additional characters. Higgin, the true culprit in the case, has only very brief scenes with Ridley and Solly and one in the library with Tessie Forgie, whom he mistakes for Pearl Vambrace. He is hardly given a second thought by those chiefly affected by the false notice; it is important that he have little connection with them. For us to understand who and what he is, then, he must be given life in another context: the home shared by the Morphews and Edith Little, where he is a boarder. There his seductive charm, his ambitions, and his mediocrity are shown. There we see the irony of his crowning triumph in bringing culture to Salterton: the ribald songs in which he has coached George Morphew are a hit at George's club.

In addition to bringing small-town mentality to life and providing a context for important characters to function in, there is a third reason for the inclusion of so many characters in the play. One of Davies's greatest strengths in writing both novels and plays is the characters he creates. The real interest of *Leaven of Malice* is not in the plot but in the characters. Having peopled his novel with so many successful creations, Davies may well have wanted to see them come to life on the stage. There is, of course, a limit to the number of characters which can be fully realized in the scope of a play. Since there are so many, one might assume that they would be quite insubstantially characterized in comparison with their novelistic counterparts. Indeed, old Swithin Shillito, whose immense pride in his nineteenth-century journalistic style and whose determination to stay on as resident pest at *The Bellman* until he "drops in harness" makes him the bane of Ridley's existence, suffers greatly in the transition from novel to play, and Ridley too is regrettably reduced. Dean Knapp, dean of the church where Humphrey Cobbler is organist, is a less significant but unmistakable victim of condensation. The surprise is that all others come to life as completely in the play as they do in the novel, and at least one, Professor Vambrace, is a marked improvement on the original.

Characterization, accomplished in the novel in part by omniscient narration, must in dramatic presentation rely wholly on action and dialogue. Or almost wholly — Davies introduces a dream scene in which a montage of five characters' dreams accomplishes very economically characterization which in the novel can be lingered over and gradually introduced through authorial commentary. Enacted when Molly and Humphrey Cobbler and Solly fall asleep after huddling together in bed to keep warm during their late-night conversation, the scene spotlights a series of five characters talking in their sleep.

Mrs. Bridgetower's dream accounts for the iron grip in which she attempts to hold her son Solly. She dreams of his wedding to Louisa Hanson (her maiden name), sighing happily, "What a lovely bride!/ . . . /A mysterious girl, I seem to know her face/Yet I do not know her/ . . . /But I can trust *her*/With my dear son's peace" (160). Gloster Ridley dreams of the distinction he will attain with a honorary doctorate, the cherished hope that is threatened by the repercussions of the false engagement notice published in his paper. Higgin's dream of himself in his youth as a choirboy shows us the peak of his lifetime's accomplishment and conveys the fact that all his life since has been a futile struggle to regain the bliss of his childhood success. Professor Vambrace's dream about Pearl in part parallels Mrs. Bridgetower's about Solly, but it also shows his yearning to be above and beyond and secure from the mob of humanity which mocks him while he attempts to keep aloof and maintain his dignity. The final dream is Molly Cobbler's, extolling the love she and her husband share and establishing her real happiness, despite the oddities of life with an eccentric musician. The farcical effect of Molly reaching for Humphrey in her sleep is that Solly is pushed out of bed, which wakens them all and provides a natural ending to the dream sequence.

The dream scene is one of three especially designed to convey economically on stage information which is provided at greater leisure in the novel. Another, which contains a rapid succession of six telephone calls, encompasses a number of scenes from the novel. It moves the plot along efficiently and conveys a sense of waves of interaction among the people of Salterton peaking as the climax approaches. The third is a comic choral scene in which Ridley, Shillito, Dean Knapp, and Tessie Forgie provide many of the novel's reflections on small-town mentality, focusing on the newspaper and what it means to the townspeople.

Ridley by himself is a choral figure in the play, opening the first and second acts and closing the third with direct addresses to the audience. In the novel Ridley and his newspaper, *The Bellman*, are central, and many pages are devoted to the work of the newspaper staff and the role of the newspaper in the life of Salterton. Ridley's viewpoint comes naturally from Davies's long experience as editor of the *Peterborough Examiner*. Little of this newspaper motif is found in the play; it disappeared after the first draft Davies wrote, in which, he says, "Gloster Ridley...led the characters through the plot in a much more direct and economical way than was subsequently possible. Tyrone Guthrie's immediate response was, 'That won't do, nobody is in the least interested in newspaper editors.' " This, Davies suspects, was more an indication of their relationship — "He seemed to feel that it was part of his duty to keep me humble'' — than of the original draft's shortcomings, but Guthrie wanted less focus on the newspaper editor and more of an extravaganza, with lots of characters and satiric scenery.[14]

Still, in the completed play *The Bellman* remains the medium through which Higgin works his mischief, and Ridley, as its editor, remains one of the victims of Higgin's malice. The general function of the newspaper in the lives of the townspeople and the particular effect of the engagement notice which appears in its pages are developed in the choral scene, with Dean Knapp and Tessie Forgie, a minor character even in the novel, together with Swithin Shillito and Gloster Ridley acting as voices of the townspeople and the newspapermen. *"They speak,"* Davies directs, *"in the stricken tones of a verse-speaking choir"* (149). The solemn rhythm and tone of the others' speeches are punctuated by Tessie's refrain:

> O nosey, nosey under the wood
> O nosey, nosey over the lea;
> But nosey, nosey to nobody's good:
> That's what news means
> To Nosey Me (150).

The gist of the choral statement, comically couched in poetic lines and elevated diction, is that newspapermen's daily concern is to pry into other people's business, and newspaper readers are more interested in the business of their next-door neighbours than in the news of the Great World. Moreover, who put the notice in the paper is of less interest than the ensuing fuss and the embarrassment of the victims. All conclude together:

> Perhaps it may sometimes be true that the world loves a lover;
> And in moments of crisis mankind may achieve magnanimity;
> But most of the time, beneath our external good-fellowship
> Flows a quiet, deep stream of irony, mingled with malice (151).

Higgin may be the chief culprit, but the nosiness of others, their great concern about personal embarrassment, and their eagerness to discomfit one another exacerbate what was initially simply an erroneous announcement in the newspaper. Higgin could rely on these aspects of human nature; without them, his "joke" would have had little effect. These ideas are dramatized in characters' speeches and actions, but the choral scene sums them up and gives them emphasis.

The choral scene, the dream sequence, and the telephoning scene are inventive means of condensing and dramatizing many pages of the novel.

The other scenes are all taken more or less directly from the novel, with some changes of locale for convenience, occasional collapsing of two scenes into one for efficiency, and some functions of characters in the novel who do not appear in the play transferred to other characters. Mrs. Bridgetower, for instance, absorbs the role of the novel's Miss Pottinger, and Molly Cobbler speaks some lines which originally belonged to Mrs. Fielding. A close comparative examination of parallel scenes from novel and play helps to show how Davies met the challenge of adaptation, and it also points up the highly dramatic quality of the novel. With the exception of a very few passages, such as the opening about the appearance of the engagement announcement and a discussion of the quirks of newspaper readers, the novel is constructed entirely of distinct scenes in specific locales. Of course there are far too many of these to allow a simple transition to the stage, but the difficulty for Davies was primarily the need to condense rather than to dramatize what was not dramatic in conception. Ideas come to him, he has said, primarily in terms of character and dialogue, rather than as abstractions;[15] this appears to be true of his novels as well as his plays. Large segments of a scene in the novel consist of dialogue, often direct exchanges unbroken by so much as "he said" or "she replied."

The bulk of the scene between Norm Yarrow and Professor Vambrace in the novel, for instance, consists of five pages of dialogue in which are imbedded only six and a half sentences of description. The scene is adapted for the stage almost without alteration. Some of the looks, actions, and feelings reported in the novel would be conveyed directly by the actions and expressions of characters on stage. Some are incorporated into dialogue: the novel's "Norm beamed. As he always said to Dutchie, they were easier to deal with when they had some brains, and didn't weep, or shout at you"[16] in the play becomes Norm's line, "I'm glad you're going to take it like that, Professor. It's always easier in these problems of Relationship Engineering when we have to deal with a man of intelligence" (166). A few changes in the dialogue are introduced in the play to make the presumptuousness and superficiality of Norm's assault on Professor Vambrace more apparent, an impression which is conveyed in the novel in part by a narrative description of the intellectual poverty of Norm's professional training.

Another change is the addition of eight speeches to do the work of the next scene in the novel, omitted from the play, in which Professor Vambrace asks Pearl why she talked to Yarrow about her family, and she replies, "I must talk to someone occasionally" (212). The Professor's grief at his alienation from his daughter is established in this separate scene in the novel; in the play, Vambrace asks Norm why Pearl discussed her family affairs with him. Norm's "Pearlie couldn't talk very frankly to you, I don't suppose?" (167) hits home, and the Professor admits that he and Pearl have not spoken to each other at all for three days. After Norm leaves, the scene closes on Vambrace, with the stage directions, *"His rage is spent, and now a terrible unhappiness sweeps over him, and we are conscious of the sudden ebb and flow of emotion that makes him what he is. Before we take leave of him, tears are running down his face, and perhaps, under his breath, we hear him say, 'Pearl'"* (169). With minimal alteration from the novel then, this scene transferred easily to the stage and was noted by reviewers as a particularly successful part of the play.

Another scene play reviewers picked out for its success is the bedroom scene between Solly and Mrs. Bridgetower, in which the comic focus is her change into nightclothes with Solly's assistance. The stage directions read, *"Under cover of a vast bedgown Mrs. Bridgetower removes various intimate garments which she hands to Solly, who hangs them up or puts them away; it is all extremely decent, but achieved only with much bulging, rucking up, accordian-like expansion and contraction, and modest fuss"* (147).

Again, the seven pages of the corresponding scene in the novel consist primarily of dialogue, though there are four paragraphs of description. This scene is more extensively condensed and reordered that the Yarrow-Vambrace scene. One long argument over Higgin is replaced by Solly's brief statement: "You know, Mother, I'd think a long time, if I were you, before I tried to push Higgin into the Cathedral. He strikes me as rather second-rate" (147). Another long exchange focusing on Puss Pottinger, who is omitted from the play, is eliminated. The central point of that passage and of the entire preceding scene in the novel depicting Mrs. Bridgetower's "At-Home," also omitted from the play, is summarized in one line: "Several people this afternoon thought it was that fool Humphrey Cobbler [who was responsible for the engagement notice]" (147). Other passages are rearranged and bits of dialogue added to effect natural transitions.

The only substantial addition to this scene in the play is its concluding seven speeches. In response to unexpected resistance from Solly when she brings Pearl into the discussion, Mrs. Bridgetower lapses grotesquely into baby talk: "Has Mummy been a baddy Mummy? Does Tolly want to pank Mummums 'tuz she wants to keep the howwid dirls away and have her Tolly all for her own self?" (149). This revealing speech tells a great deal about Mrs. Bridgetower's desire to keep Solly entirely devoted to her as he was in his childhood; the baby talk is partly to cover her embarrassment at such a direct revelation of herself and partly to recreate that eminently satisfactory past. When Solly announces that he is going out, she tries, none too subtly, and unsuccessfully, to get him to report his destination and then makes one more attempt to keep him tied to her: "You won't be late?

You know how Mother worries when you are out in your car'' (149). This addition firmly establishes the nature of Solly's relationship with his mother. In fact, this scene, together with Mrs. Bridgetower's dream in the dream sequence and a discussion of filial loyalty between Pearl and Solly which is expanded in the play, combine to establish Solly and Mrs. Bridgetower's relationship even more clearly in the play than in the novel.

A type of scene which is rewritten entirely for the stage is the memory scene which is simply interior monologue in the novel but is dramatized in the play. Some scenes are presented directly, in sequence, in the novel but occur in the play as flashbacks: the Yarrow party, for instance. Others, such as Higgin's encounters with Ridley and Solly, are introduced in the novel simply as memories of Ridley and Solly. In the play, these two episodes are introduced as memories but then acted out directly, like the scenes in Arthur Miller's *Death of a Salesman* which are dramatizations of Willy Loman's memories. In the novel, Ridley's recollection of his interview with Higgin is immersed in his ruminations on the problem of dealing with Shillito. In a long paragraph, the primary subject of which is Shillito, Ridley's refusal to publish a series of articles that Higgin has designed to advertise his services is presented in eight sentences. Davies deliberately obscures its significance by presenting it from the point of view of Ridley, who attaches little importance to it. In the play, however, Shillito presents himself to the audience and explains his relationship with Ridley. During this speech, Ridley's office is set onstage, and then Higgin, Shillito, and Ridley act out the interview. The dialogue is new, and the scene, witnessed directly and occupying two full pages of script, makes a much greater impression on the play's audience than its counterpart makes on the reader of the novel. In particular, Higgin's closing line directs our attention to the significance of the scene: ''I wonder,'' he says to Shillito after Ridley leaves, ''if that man has ever been humiliated as he's humiliated me today!'' (136). The other two scenes in which Higgin is snubbed — by Solly in his office and by Tessie Forgie sitting at a desk with Pearl Vambrace's name on it — are also acted out in the play and thus have greater impact than do corresponding passages in the novel. In fact, in the novel Higgin's motive for making Pearl as well as Solly and Ridley a victim of his malicious joke is revealed only at the very end of the story.

The necessity to dramatize the incidents which motivate Higgin to retaliate with the engagement notice meant that Davies would have been hard put to make a success of retaining the ''whodunit'' approach of the novel. It is clear that he recognized this and decided to take a different approach in the play, making use of dramatic irony instead of suspense. In the play Davies emphasizes the importance of the snubs to Higgin instead of glossing over them. The first act ends after the scene in which Higgin is curtly refused university library privileges by Tessie Forgie and some concluding dialogue between Higgin and the Morphews in which Kitten comments on Higgin's malice: "We don't want to get on the wrong side of this fella" (142). The second act opens with Ridley's direct address to the audience: "Who did it? You know, I'm sure, but it is still a mystery to us" (142).

The play is memorable for individual characters and individual scenes. Characterization, more than function, accounts for the prominence of such characters as Mrs. Bridgetower and Professor Vambrace and, in particular, Humphrey Cobbler. Cobbler is an extraordinary character in both novel and play: raffish, capricious, warm, and exuberant, an eccentric whose rumpled appearance and harmless pranks earn him the disapproval of such upright citizens as Mrs. Bridgetower, who considers him an unsatisfactory church organist, despite his musical distinction, because of his levity. In Guthrie's 1960 production, Cobbler's part was played by the star attraction, who insisted on having the part expanded and won praise for his performance, as any competent actor would, because it is a glorious role. Part of the drawback to allowing Cobbler to steal the show, however, is that he has little to do with the plot; he functions primarily as a red herring in the effort to identify the author of the engagement notice, and inflating his part throws the play out of balance. Davies's intention, surely, was to contrast Cobbler's harmless Hallowe'en escapade in the cathedral with Higgin's spiteful action, using Cobbler as foil to Higgin to show the difference between spur-of-the-moment highjinks and maliciousness, and to point out the mistake other characters make in equating the two. Cobbler's musical virtuosity contrasts with Higgin's "second-rate" pretensions to culture, and his cheerful disregard of propriety contrasts with Higgin's pitiful struggle to break into Salterton society. The size of Cobbler's part exactly balances the size of Higgin's in the published play, which indicates that Davies intended the two to be parallel characters.

Although play and novel have some similar strengths, the different genres dictate differences. Davies has commented on the difference between the part dialogue plays in a novel and its function in a play:

In a novel a whole important scene can be confined to a few lines of dialogue assisted by some descriptive writing; in a play the dialogue must do it all. Dialogue in a play should be economical; audiences quickly tire of talk that moves too slowly. On the other hand, too much economy may be a mistake, because your dialogue may become telegraphic, and the audience will miss something important. A great part of the playwright's art lies in establishing the right tone and pace in his dialogue. It is at the farthest extreme from reporting ordinary speech.[17]

Davies's ability to make dialogue in the play do the work of some descriptive passages in the novel is evident, but of course the dialogue does not "do it all," because a play can convey directly information which a novel can only describe. Davies's witty commentary on characters and mores is a delightful feature of the novel version of *Leaven of Malice*, and it can be transferred to stage dialogue only when such a comment can appropriately be made by a character, though in the choral scene and the dream scene Davies incorporates a sort of commentary which passes the limitations of verisimilitude. The play version of *Leaven of Malice*, though it lacks the authorial commentary, makes good use of the visual element: sets, props, costumes, lighting, and action. In addition, music and the vocal inflections of the actors do some of the work of the novel's descriptive passages. Davies does not employ stage directions as extensively as many modern playwrights do, but those he does include, together with cues in the dialogue, show that his practical experience in the theatre has given him a firm grasp of the importance of the visual and aural ingredients of drama.

The engagement announcement which launches the action would have relatively little effect if it were simply read aloud. To ensure maximum impact, it is presented visually, not once but twice. In the second scene of the play, as Pearl reads the notice in the paper aloud to her father, a large sign bearing the notice is carried on by masked stagehands. At the end of Act I, as Higgin reads the notice, retrieved from the bottom of the Morphews's birdcage, it is projected, complete with bird droppings, on a screen. We are reminded again of the engagement announcement when, in the dream scene at the end of Act II, Mrs. Bridgetower's dream is accented by a large engraved wedding invitation announcing the marriage of herself and her son Solly, again carried on by masked stagehands. Action which departs completely from verisimilitude is used to convey abstract concepts. Rumour is depicted by a dumb show in the first scene. Curiosity and the contribution made to it by the local newspaper are indicated by the choral scene in which each of the four characters carries a copy of *The Bellman*. Many pages of the novel are devoted to characterizing Shillito as a bore and a nuisance; in the play this is deftly accomplished by a brief bit of action during which Shillito settles himself for a rambling address to the audience, though other characters are clearly ready to begin the next scene. Finally the masked stagehands pick Shillito up and carry him offstage in mid-speech.

Costume is a visual ingredient of the play which contributes to characterization. Ridley opens the play in his doctoral gown, but because he is really a newspaperman, not an academic, he steps forward out of the gown to address the audience, and the gown, supported by masked stagehands, stands independently. In the dream scene the gown, worn by a stagehand, resumes its separate existence to convey that for Ridley it is merely a trapping and cannot make him a better man, though it can make him seem so. Thus, much of the novel's exploration of Ridley's aspiration to an honorary doctorate is concentrated in a visual device in the play.

A combination of sight and sound gives some scenes more impact on stage than they have in the novel. The early scene of Cobbler's Hallowe'en escapade in the cathedral uses costume, dancing, and music to give us at once Cobbler's *joie de vivre*, his irrepressible spirit and musical *panache*. In a later scene between Solly, Pearl, and Vambrace, Solly actually drives his little car onstage. The crash of Vambrace's stick on Solly's car is accompanied by the tinkle of broken glass and the sounding of the horn, both to maximize the effect of Vambrace's rage and to impress on us the truth of the episode so that we recognize as rumour the later allegation that Vambrace has broken his stick on Pearl.

All the visual and aural possibilities of theatre cannot entirely accomplish the necessary condensation in adapting a novel to the stage, however. This "extravaganza" is a structurally complex collage of sixteen scenes in three acts, and one scene may contain many discrete parts. The last scene of the first act is the most complex; it opens with Ridley's address to the audience, followed by a short exchange between Ridley and Edith Little, then moves to Solly and Pearl in his car after the Yarrows' party. There is then a flashback to the party, followed by the altercation between Vambrace, Solly, and Pearl. Shillito enters to give his version of that episode, which leads into the dramatization of the encounter between Ridley, Shillito, and Higgin in Ridley's office. The comic bit of action in which Shillito is removed from the stage effects a transition to the Morphews's living room, where a conversation among the Morphews, Edith, and Higgin, with the insertion of the exchange between Higgin and Tessie Forgie in the library, concludes the scene. The extravaganza incorporates fantasy and memory scenes into present action, at times moving rapidly through a succession of short scenes, at other times lingering over a fuller portrayal of interaction between two or three characters. The rapid succession of scenes requires much ingenuity in staging, and Davies's script shows that he has given careful attention to the physical problems involved, though reviewers seem inclined to give to directors and designers the entire credit for the fluidity of productions.

Condensation of the novel for the stage results in some diminution of character development, which is unfortunate but perhaps inevitable. All Ridley's plans to give "the Old Mess," Shillito, "the silken sack" are omitted from the play, as is almost all exploration of that large part of Ridley's character which is absorbed in overcoming his guilt about his insane wife. The result is that in the play Shillito seems to be an extraneous character, useful only mechanically for starting the rumour that Vambrace broke his stick over Pearl and for discovering the incriminating receipt for the engagement announcement in Higgin's scrapbook. The two references to Ridley's wife in the play are simply puzzling. In Ridley's dream scene, his statement that "we must never mention the title 'Doctor' to Mrs. Ridley. It would alarm her to think of me as any sort of Doctor" (161) is bewildering. The only other reference to her in the play illuminates the first statement, but introduces further difficulties. Higgin explains to Edith that Ridley has a wife who is confined to an insane asylum, but how he, a newcomer to the town, should have stumbled onto this information is not explained, and because its relationship to Ridley's yen for the honorary doctorate is never clarified, the opening scene with Ridley in his doctoral gown becomes nothing more than a rather clumsy device for introducing the main action of the play as an incident which "very nearly kept [Ridley] from getting what [he] so much wanted" (119). *Why* he wanted it so much the play's audience is unlikely to discern without reading the novel.

Pearl is another character whose development is curtailed in the play, but in this case the play's characterization is perfectly adequate. In the novel, we witness a change in Pearl from a helpless, mousy girl, wallowing in self-pity, to a more independent, determined, self-assured young lady. The play does not show us this marked change in Pearl. In this respect the characterization of the novel is richer, but the play considered on its own merits does not suffer, for Pearl is a consistent and credible character whose role is well defined.

The condensation necessary for the play does not necessarily impoverish its characters, however. While the characters of Shillito and Ridley suffer in the play, Pearl emerges whole, Solly's change of character is efficiently and effectively presented, and Vambrace becomes more credible. In a new bit of dialogue in the play, Cobbler tells Solly that his trouble lies in his own self-image, that "for everybody who privately regards himself as a prince, there is somebody who thinks he is a frog .... You think of yourself as a toad under the harrow" (159). Solly picks up this observation in a later scene with Pearl. After their first kiss, he announces, "I don't think I'm quite ready to be a failure; it's always attractive, mind you — a nice, tear-sodden tunnel of failure — but suddenly I don't *feel* like a failure. I'm sick of being a toad under the harrow...I'm going to have a try at being the Frog Prince. Nor really wretched you know. Just rather unfortunately enchanted" (172-73). The metaphor of transformation, linked with Solly and Pearl's discovery of each other, marks a clear and quite credible change in Solly's outlook. In the novel the change is manifested in Solly's decision to become a creator of literature rather than "an embalmer" — a critic — but the play's metaphor of a toad under the harrow becoming a Frog Prince economically and convincingly encompasses a change in Solly which affects his whole character.

The same scene between Pearl and Solly introduces dialogue which does a good deal to explain and soften Vambrace's character. Solly admits that Vambrace seems a monster to him, as he does, perhaps, to the audience, judging him by his frenzied actions and raging speeches. Pearl replies:

> He isn't like that all the time. That's what's so unjust. He's a great man, really; a wonderful scholar and ... well, never mind. But his standards and ideals are so different from those of most people. There isn't a drop of compromising blood in him. And it sometimes makes him seem so odd that — it's terribly unjust....When I was younger it was embarrassing that Father was always in rows about things — things that other people didn't understand or care about. But I know him better now, and the more I know him, the better I understand his worth (170).

Pearl's understanding of her father, lacking in the original character of the novel, assists the audience in understanding the eccentric Vambrace as well, making him a more credible and sympathetic character. The necessity to condense sometimes had adverse effects on characters, but at other times it inspired Davies to extremely effective dialogue, economical yet packed with information and emotion which contribute to character portrayal.

Leaven of Malice is a play in which most of the individual scenes and characters are delightful, but the parts are more memorable than the whole. Urjo Kareda, reviewing the Hart House production in 1973, was especially enthusiastic about the scenes of fantasy, such as the choral scene and the dream scene: "The play has odd, chilling intrusions of mystery, of masques, dances, dreams, fantastic visions. Balanced with Davies' wit and satiric thrust, the hallucinatory sequences reveal a world of fascinating obsessions beneath the comic conventions."[18] But even Kareda, who thought the play "delicious," found it overcrowded and unwieldy.[19] Herbert Whittaker's suggestion that it might make a good television series[20] sheds light on both the strengths and the weaknesses of the play. It is long, requiring close to three hours of playing time, and complex in structure and dramatic technique, but still it is less successful than the novel in conveying the mentality of Salterton, representative of small-town Canada. Since this was Davies's larger objective, not just exploring the effects of Higgin's particular malicious act, his material really was better suited to novelistic development, as he recognized in the first place.

Would he attempt another adaptation of one of his novels for the stage? "No," he says, "I don't think adaptations make any sense at all....I wouldn't want to try it again."[21] The adaptation was not a move forward in his work as an original dramatist, but it did stretch his ingenuity and increase his versatility in stagecraft techniques. Whatever the gains to his versatility as a dramatist may have been, however, they cannot have seemed worth the anguish by the end of 1960, when the Broadway production folded.

Davies described the experience of rewriting during rehearsals and on tour in two of the weekly pieces for his syndicated column, "A Writer's Diary," the first cheerful, the second more subdued, and in a distinctly cheerless letter to Herbert Whittaker. He started rehearsals in October full of confidence in his ability to work productively with the director and actors. Guthrie wanted him at all the rehearsals, and at first Davies found this work on the spot "a life-enhancing experience." He did not resent making cuts: "What reads well is not necessarily what acts well, and it is stupid to keep 10 words to express something which the actor can make clear by a tone of voice or a gesture." On the other hand, actors' suggestions are often made with a view to their own roles only, so they do not necessarily improve the play as a whole. "Such suggestions must be met with much friendly head-nodding, followed by masterly inaction." This first column contains much praise of the professionalism of actors and others involved in the production and a clear view of his own ideal role: the author has "certain powers of veto, which he cherishes, but which he abuses at his peril. His job is to see that the main purpose of his play is not distorted....He rewrites, with good humor if his head is screwed on straight, but only when he agrees that re-writing will improve matters."[22]

By the time the play opened in Toronto, its first stop on the pre-Broadway tour, it was clear that predicting what would improve matters was none too simple and that the rewriting process did not necessarily end with opening night. In a column that appeared a few weeks after the first, Davies observes that "nobody, however experienced or intuitive, can tell just how a play will strike an audience. The scenes which seemed so telling in the rehearsal room may somehow fail to impress in the theatre. Then they have to be altered, and tried on an audience again." He likens playwriting to clockmaking: a lot of tinkering is necessary to get a play running smoothly. And he describes the loneliness of the playwright on opening night: "He does not mingle with the audience at intermission time, asking people how they like his piece; he wants to know, but he would rather die than ask ....He watches the audience with the intensity of a cannibal surveying a missionary conference." Drained afterwards, he goes to bed. "But not to sleep. To think of cuts, of expansions, of tinkering that may improve the play."[23]

In the letter to Whittaker, written from Detroit, the next stop on the tour, he sounds quite desperate: "Like T G [Tyrone Guthrie] said, every audience is like pushing a freight train up a steep grade. I could add, with your eyeballs." He despaired of the more "inventive" actors who felt no obligation to stick to the text, among them Dennis King: "If he should die during one of those inventions, his fate Above will be worse than if he had a thrombosis at the peak of an adultery. God is an author, and Job is no mean drama; God will not see the playwright unavenged."[24] But even vengeance would probably not have consoled Davies for the New York reviews. Walter Kerr described the play as "a curious series of oddball musings... which have never been assembled into anything resembling an intelligible narrative structure,"[25] and Howard Taubman thought it "played as if it were the dusty comic relief accumulated in the lecture notes of a professor with a complacent opinion of his own wit."[26] Of the major critics, only Harold Clurman was kind; in a review written after the play closed, he called it "well written and not without humor and charm" but observed that it needed an intimate audience to share its quality of fun and was quite out of place in a big New York theatre.[27]

Working alone,[28] guided only by his own sense of what a good play should be, Davies wrote *General Confession*, and no one produced it. Working in accord with Guthrie's ideas for a hit at every stage of writing[29] the dramatic version of *Leaven of Malice*, he got maximum exposure for a play that was not his best, and suddenly he was "just one of those people who had failed in New York."[30] The effect of these two experiences was to reduce the flame of Davies's passion for playwriting to a wavering flicker.

10

Punch, Demonic Humour, and *The Black Art*

THE 1960s were fallow years for both Davies the novelist and Davies the playwright. In this decade he published no new novels and only one new play, *A Masque of Mr. Punch*, written in 1962 for Upper Canada College. This was hardly a period of inactivity for him, however, and his pen must rarely have been still.[1] He looks back on the decade as a time when he was too busy for an extended piece of creative writing (though he always managed to find time for such work when he really wanted to). He wrote play reviews for *Saturday Night* and the *Peterborough Examiner*, book reviews for *The New York Times Book Review* and *Saturday Night*. He wrote for and about book lovers: "A Writer's Diary," his weekly column for the *Toronto Star* and eleven other papers, ran from January 1959 until June 1962. The book lover spoke too in *A Voice from the Attic*, published in 1960, and in articles for *The Saturday Evening Post* and *Holiday*. When he made trips to Saltzburg or London or Vienna he wrote about their culture in articles for the *Peterborough Examiner*. He published articles in drama journals, literary journals, even journals of architecture and medicine. And in 1960 he began a new academic career at the University of Toronto.

Davies was appointed as a visiting professor of English at Trinity College from 1960 to 1962, at University College from 1961 to 1962, and in 1964 he was appointed the first Edgar Stone Lecturer in Dramatic Literature. In 1961 he was appointed the first Master of Massey College, which opened its doors to graduate students in the fall of 1963, when he and his family took up residence in the Master's Lodge. There he had a role to play in students' affairs, and he continued teaching as a member of the Graduate Department of English until his retirement in 1981. He did not stop writing for newspapers and popular magazines, but as well he began to write articles for *The Varsity Graduate* and the *University of Toronto Graduate*, book reviews for the *University of Toronto Quarterly*, articles on education for *The Times (London) Educational Supplement* and *Atlantic Monthly*, and scholarly pieces on Stephen Leacock's work. His work as writer and educator, as humorist and humanist was recognized with a trickle of honourary degrees from Canadian universities beginning in 1957. The trickle became a flood in the seventies.

The demands of his work as a professor and his disillusionment with his work as a dramatist did not prevent Davies from again obliging Upper Canada College with a new masque for the boys to perform in 1962. With the delights of *A Masque of Aesop* fresh in his mind from its most recent performance in December 1961,[2] Headmaster Stephens suggested that a new play for the school's sixtieth anniversary would be very welcome. An indication of real appreciation for his talents as a playwright was enough to encourage Davies to put his dramatic skills to work, though it was to be a long time before he again put all his creative powers to dramatic use.

Like *A Masque of Aesop*, *A Masque of Mr. Punch* provides a good deal of fun as well as some learning in a play about conflicts between the artist (or the exceptional man) and the world that does not want him. In both masques the art, Aesop's fables and the Punch and Judy show, is generally thought of as entertainment for children, though Davies does not treat it as such. In the second masque Davies's hero is not a man of wisdom but a man of spirit: Punch.

The masque opens on journalists and television people waiting to interview a visitor to Canada. A public relations man tries to prepare them for the interview, but they have no notion who Punch and his wife are; the description of an old and famous actor with "an astounding personality" and "long-standing literary associations"[3] travelling with his wife has the media people ready to depict them "walking into the sunset of life, courageously, hand-in-hand, upheld by a great love that has ripened in the sun like a beautiful tomato —" (6). This misconception is immediately and comically contrasted with the reality of Punch and Judy, who are heard quarrelling offstage; their entrance is preceded by Baby's, flung across the stage to strike the scenery with a thud. Punch revives Baby by swinging it by its feet in a circle, then hands it to Pretty Polly, so he and Judy can charm the reporters. Is there a place in Canada for Punch's show? The media people are dubious — he is not "what we'd call contemporary" (10) — so he and Judy summon an audience with trumpet and drum and perform a play for an enthusiastic crowd and the sceptical critics.

Punch tricks Harlequin's dog Toby into eating a pepper sandwich; Toby drags Punch around the stage by his nose. Punch and Harlequin fight with a slapstick and an oversize club. Exasperated with his howling baby, Punch flings it up into the sky and sets out to seduce its governess, Pretty Polly. From time to time, a piece of Baby's clothing floats down. Judy discovers Punch and Polly dancing and singing together; Polly runs off and Judy beats Punch thoroughly. His call for a doctor is answered, but the doctor's tranquilizer obviously has no effect on Punch, and when Punch retaliates with the doctor's syringe, the doctor dies of his own medicine. The policeman who comes to arrest Punch for killing his baby is stopped by Punch's offer to buy one of the officer's seventeen children as a replacement. When a hangman comes for Punch, Punch hangs him instead. Then Baby falls out of the sky, Judy catches it, and she and Punch dance and sing about their model married life. At the end of the song a devil comes for Punch; they fight, and Punch beats the devil to great applause from the spectators — but the end of Punch's play brings only embarrassing silence from the reporters, who are unable to say what they think of the play until the adjudicator has spoken.

The rest of the masque is a series of responses to Punch's show. The adjudicator from the Dominion Drama Festival pontificates at length about the show as "a not very happy excursion into the Theatre of the Absurd" (35). Swanee River, an American playwright modelled on Tennessee Williams, offers to rewrite Punch's play along the lines of American Southern Decadence: Punch will be a down-and-out southern belle — beautiful and ladylike but a heavy drinker and dope-user, finally pulled to pieces and eaten by a group of underprivileged children. Samuel Bucket, a European playwright modelled on Beckett, offers to rewrite it as Drama of Nothingness, with Punch playing a blind deaf-mute in a garbage can with the lid wired down attempting to communicate with another garbage can that contains no one. Then a professor representing the Stratford Festival's Board of Governors claims that Punch's show is a distorted version of a lost play of Shakespeare's. What follows is a performance of Punch's show in the form of a Shakespearean tragedy. King Punch finds his glory blighted by his envy of his infant son: he lusts for the rattle of Prince Omlet. Paulina reminds him of the curse on anyone who might take the rattle from the prince, but King Punch kills Queen Judy and the prince to seize the rattle, and he kills Paulina to silence her railing. Harlequin and Toby clown to pass time until King Punch re-enters, wracked with guilt, soliloquizing in Macbeth's vein and visited by the ghosts of his victims, à la Richard III. He repudiates conscience, but a devil enters and beats him in combat.

Punch goes mad and dies, leaving the devil and ghosts to recite the moral epilogue.

The masque concludes with the critics' decision that there is no place in modern theatre for Punch: "The theatre has become thoughtful, and what have you to do with thought?" (54). But Mephistopheles enters to point out that humanity cannot spare Punch. "If we let you go, it will be no time at all before the whole human race is living on government pensions and Canada Council grants....You are the Spirit of Unregenerate Man....the Old Adam; and without you, the human race would cease to be human" (55). Punch is currently out of fashion in the theatre, but his day will come again, and meanwhile the obvious place for him is politics, a world "full of Judys to be bullied, Tobys to be bribed and coaxed to jump through hoops, doctors to be given doses of their own medicine, officers to be swindled, and hangmen to be tricked" (56). The masque ends with all singing of the world as Punch's oyster; the spectators carry him off in triumph while the critics scribble furiously and Mephistopheles helps the television people capture Punch's exit.

This is Punch's second appearance in Davies's drama, for in *Fortune, My Foe* Punch was the only puppet Franz Szabo brought with him to Canada, so important to Szabo that he cannot bear to have anyone else handle it. Punch, like Don Quixote, represents the indomitable spirit of the true artist in that play, and in the later masque, his irrepressible vitality is again his essence. This time he represents not so much the artist as a basic element in human nature without which man cannot hope to thrive. What is it? Punch is elemental, emotional man, without conscience or respect for others. Davies describes him as "a perfectly free and natural man. If he doesn't like somebody, he hits him over the head."[4] He is vindictive, passionate, mischievous, violent. He is also irrepressible, indomitable, unbeatable. "The whole point of Punch's Show is that nobody beats Punch" (53), he tells the professor who wants to turn the show into an Elizabethan tragedy that ends with Punch's defeat by the devil. *General Confession* tells us that Casanova's vitality is inextricably bound up with his lechery. Punch personifies the vital energy of elemental human passions.

Punch's opponent, the object of Davies's satire, is not the common man as in *A Masque of Aesop*, but the professional critic. At least, the critic is the most obvious target. But since a substantial part of the masque is given to absurd suggestions for rewriting Punch's material in the popular veins of Samuel Beckett and Tennessee Williams and even in the mode of Davies's beloved Stratford Festival, the larger target of the satire is modern taste. Its limitations are shown by satirizing the most influential arbiters of modern taste in theatre: media critics, professors, adjudicators at drama festivals, and highly regarded dramatists. Davies, of course, was feeling that contemporary theatre seemed to have no place for him, and he sensed that it should have, because something that he could provide was lacking in the theatrical fare that dominated the stage. Reflected in *Mr. Punch* are his suspicion that he was out of step with the times and also his conviction that audiences enjoyed his plays even when those who made the important decisions in the theatrical world were unreceptive. Yet his sense of personal injury suffered in the Battle of Broadway comes to the surface of the masque only once, when the Television Woman approves of Punch's declaration that he does not memorize lines, he makes them up: "That's really contemporary. Gets rid of the author, which is always an important beginning to any serious work in the theatre" (11).

Davies's introduction to the published masque begins with the observation that critics are always interested in detectable "influences" on a writer's work, and so he acknowledges Punch's influence on him, dating back to his first experience of a Punch play as a boy. He disclaims any sense of identification with Punch, though he admires some of his characteristics: "Though I have never aspired to be like him (for my knowledge of my limitations is one of my chief defects as an artist), I have often wondered what he would do in some situations that have confronted me. I have admired and coveted his gaiety, his masterful way with physical and metaphysical enemies, and his freedom from remorse" (xi). Though Davies here dissociates himself from Punch, there is unquestionably an element of Punch in Davies: the irrepressible spirit, the ebullience, the sense that natural man should not be entirely repressed, because without him life becomes a grim affair. Davies ends his introduction as he began it, with tongue in cheek, as he considers a way in which he might yet impress critics: maybe one of the boys for whom he wrote *Mr. Punch* will grow up to write a "great philosophic drama about Punch." "Then I should be an 'influence,' which is an honourable — indeed, an enviable — literary achievement" (xii). Certainly, however, he would prefer recognition for his own dramatic creations.

A measure of the Punch in Davies is the number of characters he creates who display Punch's zest for life and resistance to civilized restraint: Pop, Aunt Clemmie, Jack the Poacher, and Humphrey Cobbler, among others. Such characters do violence only to the small spirits of the conventionally respectable; their violence is not physical as Punch's is. Davies's Punch is less violent than the early nineteenth-century Punch that was his source,[5] but he is hardly a nice guy. His violence is perfectly evident, but Davies defuses it sufficiently so that his twentieth-century audience will not reject Punch.

The media people are foils for Punch, who is vulgar but vital. When Punch wants an audience for his show, he gives the drum and trumpet to two of the media people, but they are utterly ineffectual. *"MORNING-PAPER CRITIC taps the drum in a very gentlemanly manner and looks about, half-ashamed, as he says*: Ah ... would anyone be interested in a little play? I don't suppose anybody wants to see a play do they? I mean, I guarantee nothing, but —" When Punch protests that he'll never attract paying customers that way, the critic objects, "Your whole notion of theatre is vulgar." " 'Course it's vulgar," Punch agrees. "And *I'm* vulgar! Gimme that there drum! I'll show you how to bring 'em in!" (12-13). As soon as he and Judy take over the drum and trumpet, an interested crowd begins to gather, and the chorus of the song Punch sings emphasizes the nature of his entertainment's appeal:

> He'll make you laugh,
> He'll make you cry,
> He'll make you scream and yell-O! (13-14).

No gentility here; Punch offers basic human emotion.

Throughout, Punch has the enthusiastic support of the crowd, the "real" people, whom he distinguishes from the effete critics. When he requires an audience for his show and a critic asks, "Aren't we audience enough?" Punch hoots: "Do you take me for a fool? Do a show for nothing but critics? It'd be the death of me. No, get me some people — real people" (12). With Punch's song, "the character of the entertainment changes greatly." Spectators, attracted by Punch's high spirits, gather; *"they laugh and become excited."* By contrast, the reaction of the critics to Punch's prologue is a protest that it is out of step with current theatrical fashion: "Oh, but *you* can't speak the prologue. The leading actor musn't appear till later on. But don't worry, we'll rewrite it for you according to modern ideas" (15). The spectators, already under Punch's spell, shush the critic. At the end of Punch's show, the spectators applaud vigorously, but the critics are silent, awaiting the Adjudicator's pronouncement. Punch is puzzled, obviously "terribly out of touch with the theatre as we know it in Canada. The Adjudicator," he is informed, "is the man who tells us what to think" (35). Davies had long been critical of the undiscriminating awe accorded the Dominion Drama Festival adjudicators. Now he satirizes both the rambling, pretentious pronouncement of the adjudicator and the assumption of his hearers that his is the last word.

The adjudicator's long speech is the key to Davies's reservations about the fashion of modern theatre, and it shows too why in this masque, unlike the earlier one, and rather uncharacteristically, Davies does not choose the ordinary man as his primary satirical target. The adjudicator expounds on the Theatre of the Absurd as the standard for modern theatre: "It is rooted in the despair which every intelligent playgoer feels about the future, the past, and the present. We are all agreed, I am sure, that everything is bad and is rapidly getting worse — that there is, in fact, No Hope. [*There is applause from the REPORTERS.*] Against this overpowering and omnipresent Nullity, Man opposes his feeble spirit; but we all recognize that man hasn't a chance. Man is done for, and life is a mess. [*More applause, and a few cheers.*]" He analyses Punch's play in terms of "the fragmented home," "the Freudian jealousy," "the sadism," "the mockery of established institutions — the incompetent law enforcement and the brutality of capital punishment," and judges its beginning promising. "But the denouement — the death of the Devil — is utterly unacceptable." To make the play appropriate for modern theatre, it must be rewritten with the Devil as the hero. "Let me assure the author that we shall not build an indigenous Canadian theatre on plays with happy endings. We are miserable or we are nothing. Hope is out of fashion" (36). This credo is exactly opposed to Davies's optimistic assessment of man's potential. The "misery play" may be fashionable, but it is not to his taste, and he was concerned that the fashion for it was crowding his own high-spirited plays off the stage. The spectators in *Mr. Punch*, left to themselves, respond with enthusiasm to the fundamental appeal of Punch. But they are easily led, and the adjudicator's pronouncement wins their applause, as does the performance of the tragic Elizabethan *Punch*.

Punch epitomizes for Davies what is missing from fashionable theatre in a number of important ways. First, he is basic emotion. Theatre of the absurd, represented in the masque by Beckett, Davies sees as theatre for the intellect. Second, he is indomitable human vitality. The masque opens with lights up three-quarters. They come on full with Punch's entrance. He is light and hope, as opposed to the decadence of Williams, the meaninglessness of Beckett, the defeat — however noble — of Elizabethan tragedy. Third, he is humour.

Davies, largely supportive of Punch, is fascinatingly and honestly ambivalent about him, as he is about humour. Both clearly have their daemonic aspects. In *Masque of Aesop*, Aesop is supported and defended by the god Apollo, but Punch's supporter and defender is Mephistopheles, a devil who regards Punch as "an old friend." Only he recognizes Punch's significance as "The Spirit of Unregenerate Man," "the old Adam," without whom "the human race would cease to be human." "If they've kicked you out of the theatre, they'll have to ask you back" (56), Mephistopheles assures Punch, but until they do, there is plenty of room for him in the real world; "the spirit of Punch flourishes" (56) in politics, if not in theatre. Punch, whom Davies acknowledges as a "demonic" influence,[6] is undeniably at work in the world, for better and for worse. The theatre had better recognize him.

Davies has a chapter in *A Voice from the Attic* (1960) on humour which he begins and ends by resisting the temptation to pin humour down to a theory or a definition. "What little I know of it," he ventures, "suggests that it is not something which a man possesses, but rather something which possess him; it is constantly in operation, it has a dark as well as a light aspect, and its function is by no means that of keeping its possessor in a fit of chuckles; it is daemonic in character, and, like a daemon, it is most respected by those who best know it. Like a daemon, also, it resents all attempts to put it in chains."[7] Punch and humour are both fundamental constituents of human character — Punch of the race, humour of individuals, for though not everyone possesses humour (or is possessed by it), those who have a sense of humour are born with it, Davies believes.[8] Punch is without conscience; Davies contends that "as the tragic writer rids us of what is petty and ignoble in our character, so also the humorist rids us of what is cautious, calculating and priggish — about half of our social conscience, indeed."[9] He cites Freud's point in *Wit and Its Relation to the Unconscious* that the humorist's object is "to strip away, momentarily, the heavy intellectual and moral trappings of adult life, including so many things that we regard as virtues" and to restore us to that state when "we did not have to make allowances for the limitations or misfortunes of others: when we dared to call a thing or a person stupid if they seemed stupid to us."[10] This is the aspect of humour that makes its position — like Punch's — insecure on the modern stage, Davies believes: our age is Puritanical about human rights. "Nowadays if you're funny at anybody's expense they run to the U.N. and say, 'I must have an ombudsman to protect me.' You hardly dare have a shrewd perception about anybody." Still, he is convinced that Punch — and humour — must ultimately prevail: "Any group that becomes too serious about itself, and this means most minorities, needs reminding about the humanity that encompasses us all."[11]

Davies's observations about humour sometimes seem inconsistent, which is only another way of saying what he admits, that he knows of no theory that encompasses all humour. He says that "humour is a thing of the intellect," for instance, "a civilizing element,"[12] which does not seem to accord with his view of its daemonic aspect. He is perfectly consistent, however, in his view that humour is anything but kindly; in his book on Stephen Leacock he insists that Leacock was deluding himself to think of humour as kindly: "He must have known, in his heart of hearts, that humour is a razor, and even in the most skilled hand it sometimes cuts." "Leacock is violent as Charlie Chaplin is violent; under the clowning works a vigorous, turbulent spirit, whose mellowest productions leave always on the palate a hint of the basic brimstone."[13] The razor edge of humour he perceives as a weapon, whether it is used defensively or aggressively. Like Dunstan Ramsay in *Fifth Business* he uses wit to conceal painful sensitivity, as a diversion, "a distancing thing," "to keep things at bay." He uses it also to attack; "the narrow outlook, and limited sympathies, and want of charity" provoke in him the desire "to blast them like an Old Testament prophet"; instead he just "swat[s] them around with the jester's bladder. But the impulse is the same."[14] Despite his perception of humour as a personal weapon, its general value is evident to him. In the book on Leacock, he speaks of the humorist's desire to present things which appear intolerable in another light, "the light of truth," and he compares the humorist to the writer of tragedy in "his ability to see beneath the surface of life and to see what other men do not see."[15]

Davies's fascination with humour and his uncertainty about its sources and effects make it a topic for discussion by some of the more thoughtful and sophisticated characters of his later novels. Its demonic character, implied in *Mr. Punch* and stated in *A Voice from the Attic*, is expounded by Ramsay in *World of Wonders*: "This notion that nobody can explain humour, or even talk sensibly about it, is one of humour's greatest cover-ups .... I have been wondering if humour isn't one of the most brilliant inventions of the Devil....It diminishes the horrors of the past, and it veils the horrors of the present, and therefore it prevents us from seeing straight, and perhaps from learning things we ought to know....Only the Devil could devise such a subtle agency and persuade mankind to value it." Liesl counters, "Humour is quite as often the pointer to truth as it is a cloud over truth,"[16] and she recounts — or invents — a legend that when God displayed his creation, Man, to the Heavenly Host, only the Devil was so tactless as to joke about him. He was thrown out of Heaven along with others who laughed. She doesn't deny that a sense of humour is diabolical, but she does imply that the Devil may possess a significant portion of the truth. Of course, Liesl is herself something of a demonic character, the path to Ramsay's discovery in *Fifth Business* that intimacy with the devil is necessary if one is to hold one's own against him — a view suggested in Punch's friendship with the devil.

A Masque of Mr. Punch was for Davies a means of assuaging the hurt he felt over failure in the world of theatre — a defensive use of humour — and it was also a means of exposing truths about current fashions in theatre. For the boys of U.C.C., it was probably both as entertaining and as educational in its way as *A Masque of Aesop* had been, though the point of *Aesop* can hardly be missed, while *Mr. Punch*, though it is delightful scene by scene, is more obscure as to the relationships among the scenes and the point of the whole. This is especially true because the parody of Elizabethan tragedy, though great fun in itself, is not clearly related to modern drama or clearly contrasted with Punch's show, except in its conclusion. Critics who reviewed the published *Mr. Punch* all praised its high spirits and the ingenuity of its various parts without apparently making much sense of the whole. More recent criticism shows more perception about the whole: Elspeth Buitenhuis [Cameron] makes a provocative statement about Punch's role in art, that he is "the wellspring of creativity itself,"[17] though she does not comment on the implication that there is no place for him on the modern stage, and Rota Lister observes that "Davies is juggling the traditions of literary and folk drama to comment on each other."[18] Even in a short play written for juveniles, though the sheer delight of Davies's humour is most striking, in his hands humour does more than amuse; it is also a means for exposing truths that are not obvious to most observers.

Davies did no more writing for the stage for another four years, until Canada's impending centennial celebration inspired efforts to produce appropriate dramatic entertainment. Then he launched two dramatic projects, one with reluctance, the other with more enthusiasm. The former was a group project, called *The Centennial Play*. The idea was to have playwrights from different regions of the country each provide a chunk of script. In addition to writing the Ontario scene, Davies provided the continuity with a prologue and epilogue featuring Nanabozho as the great spirit of Canada (which sometimes lies dormant), Fox as a lesser god — a Trickster figure — and a series of settlers. The theme of the Canadian imbalance between material and spiritual things that was featured in *At My Heart's Core* and earlier plays figures again in *The Centennial Play*.

In the prologue Susanna Moodie sniffs, "I owe precious little to Canada, but as things have worked out, Canada owes quite a lot to me." Nanabozho and Fox comment on her bitterness, and she replies: "I produced poetry and ideas. When has Canada ever had a daily or even a yearly need for those?...You've got the money and the electric wiring for a culture. Now all you need is a few thousand people like me — or better. Your mistake, Fox, is to confuse a high standard of living with a high standard of thinking and feeling."[19] The Ontario scene is set in a nineteenth-century schoolroom where children are "learning" by rote. They can reel off the kings of England, though the names and the sequence have no real meaning for them; the premiers of Ontario, however, they are not taught at all.

The construct did not allow much scope for the imagination, and despite the dramatic talent involved — Eric Nicol, W. O. Mitchell, Yves Thériault, and Arthur L. Murphy in addition to Davies — the result was a rather wooden patchwork. The various centres across Canada that might have performed it did not want it in the end. "I undertook to arrange for the writing of the group play because it was put to me as a patriotic obligation in 1966," Davies says. "I thought it was a bad idea and said so but was persuaded to try it. It never worked." The play was produced in Lindsay, Ontario, on 6 October 1966 and again by the Ottawa Little Theatre on 11 January 1967, revamped by the director "to make it a P.L.Q. piece of work … a travesty of the original," Davies thought.[20]

The other centennial project, *The Centennial Spectacle*, was written by Davies alone. It was conceived as a spectacle on the grandest scale, with a cast of 950 from different parts of Canada. Since it was to be performed for a large audience comprised of both anglophones and francophones, there would be little dependence on the spoken word; the effects were to be primarily visual and musical. The intention was to depict symbolically the outline of historical, geographical, and political facts leading up to Confederation, and then to reflect generally the current state of Canadian affairs. The production was to be prefabricated, with separable geographical blocks to be rehearsed independently and then assembled in Ottawa.[21]

In the first part of the spectacle, people place maps of their provinces on stage, acting out conflicts and distinctive activities; then they get together in confederation while Britannia and La Belle France (who have been directing activities — notably a tug-of-war — in Ontario and Quebec) are shoved out east in rowboats. But then a huge Uncle Sam directs a swarm of little Uncle Sams into every province, passing money in but taking more money back. The unsatisfactory situation provokes a move into the second part, which depicts Canada's shift from nature to technology. Eventually, the scientists get out of hand, beginning to move on the Universe, which means disaster. Finally Cosmic Order is re-established, with forest and city life brought into harmony. The few bits of dialogue in Davies's fourteen-page draft are in simple language; part was to be in French and part in English. Commentary between the two parts reflects what was for Davies the dominant theme of Canadian history: the settlers "have worked so hard with their hands that they have had little time to think and feel …. They have done their chores. Now it is time for other tasks." Voices at the conclusion of the spectacle say hopefully, "Perhaps they are learning to accept the Natural Order." "Perhaps they are learning to move in harmony with Nature." "And with themselves."

Tyrone Guthrie was, to direct the spectacle, with music by Louis Applebaum, designs by Murray Laufer and Marie Day. "This was all arranged and the work was under way when it was cancelled by the Department of Public Works on the grounds that if, by any remote chance, the Queen were to come to Canada the grandstands in front of the Parliament Buildings would be in the way," Davies explains.[22] The reason given for cancelling the production sounds far-fetched — though not impossible, bureaucracy being what it is — but he has a more plausible conjecture: "I think they were resentful of Guthrie's high-handed treatment of them, as they were surly Quebecois and he made jokes about them."[23]

Davies may have felt rewarded for his patriotic efforts by his election in 1967 as a Fellow of the Royal Society of Canada, but certainly there were no rewards for him as a dramatist. During the next six years he seemed to consider himself a "former dramatist."[24] He published a third Marchbanks volume, a short book about Stephen Leacock, and two more novels, but his interest in theatre was confined to his teaching and such scholarly work as his history of the drama in English from 1750 to 1880,[25] his Stratford Seminar Lecture, "Ben Jonson and Alchemy,"[26] and his reviews in scholarly journals of books about theatre.

In the early seventies there occurred what Herbert Whittaker called an "upsurge of conscience concerning the country's drama as part of the seasonal search for Canadian identity,"[27] The national identity crisis was felt everywhere, and the urge for expression of the national identity through the arts affected publishers, theatre managements, and television programmers. Their response brought the dramatist in Davies out of hibernation. The success of *Fifth Business* and *The Manticore*, published in 1970 and 1972, brought him more public attention that ever, and this helped to resurrect interest in his plays. In 1972 New Press published *Hunting Stuart and Other Plays*, following volumes of plays by George Ryga and James Reaney, as part of an effort to get more Canadian plays into print. The following year *A Jig for the Gypsy* was revived at the Lennoxville Festival, and *Leaven of Malice* (returned to its original title and form) was revived at Hart House. This production, directed by Martin Hunter, must have heartened Davies sufficiently to allow Tony Van Bridge to produce *Leaven of Malice* at the Shaw Festival in 1975, since he had two or three years earlier refused requests by both the Lennoxville Festival and the St. Lawrence Centre to perform it.

The stir about his old plays was accompanied by temptations to write new ones. Would he do it, in the midst of his success as a novelist and despite the injuries he had sustained from his forays into writing for the theatre over the past seventeen years? His old friend Whittaker summed up the situation in the spring of 1973: "The old disappointment is still there, the old rejection still felt, but the old hope still springs eternal .... No matter what Macmillan, The Book of the Month Club, The Literary Guild, even the Governor-General ... might dictate, in Robertson Davies ... the old love of theatre persists, and he would rather see his name on a playbill than even the glossy dust jacket of another best-seller."[28]

Davies's first new piece was a short play for television. CBC wanted one-hour Canadian plays for a series in the 1973-74 season, and Davies's

Brothers in the Black Art was produced 14 February 1974. The black art was printing, which had been his father's trade in his youth. His father's stories about printers in Canada around the turn of the century were the inspiration for the play, which is about three friends who worked together in the printing trade. It unfolds as reminiscences of one of them, Jesse, during an interview occasioned by the death of another, Griff, who had become a very important man. Jesse is an old man remembering the lives and loves of the three "brothers." Their friendship was grounded in pride in their trade, a craft which provided its practitioners with an education as they set type.

The story centres on the third "brother," Phil, who falls passionately in love with a very young and very beautiful girl whose essential mediocrity he does not recognize. Evvy is everything to Phil, and though Jesse and Griff's girls have reservations about Evvy, they are kind to her. Phil and Evvy marry in spite of family opposition, and there is a touching scene in which their four friends, despite their fears for the marriage, do their best to create an appropriate celebration with music, small gifts, and a cake. Three months later, Griff and Jesse discover a recent photo of Evvy and a young buck named Harrison at a nude bathing party. After a week during which they worry about how to tell Phil that his wife is up to no good, Phil's body is found in the shop urinal, the face "stone-white," and the mouth "a ruinous black hole":[29] he has swallowed lye. The scene is very grim; the gruesomeness of the death Phil has suffered is emphasized, and the black humour of management's practical perspective on the episode only increases the shock of Phil's fate. Evvy disappears, but Jesse learns the rest of the story when he encounters her accidentally nineteen years later. Phil discovered Evvy and Harrison in bed, and obsessed with his worship of Evvy, it did not occur to him to blame her. Harrison was the villain, and in the fight between them, Phil was thoroughly beaten. Bleeding, crying, his last words as Evvy reports them were, "I'm unworthy of you; I can't defend you" (39).

Evvy tells her story while munching sweets, chuckling at the memory of Harrison in the black tie he bought to make her laugh after they heard of Phil's death. Her story is a small masterpiece of characterization and a triumph in presenting the comedy and tragedy of life side-by-side. Evvy liked a good time with Harrison, but she married Phil because "he was sweet" and "nobody'd ever said they loved me before." "I liked being courted and treated as if I'd break if I ran into anything hard" (38). But she soon found being adored "dull work"; bed with Phil was like "High Mass on Easter Sunday....Too much reverence, and not a laugh whatever you did" (38-39). Her recollection of the fight is grotesque: Harrison "wiped the floor with Phil. He really beat him up pretty bad. I tried to stop him, and I guess you'd have had to laugh to see the pair of us, hopping around in our birthday suits and Phil bleeding a lot and trying to keep everything on a high line. Till he was laying there and couldn't get up no more. Got another of those Chinese Chews?'' (39) she interrupts herself to ask Jesse. She is not totally unaffected by the events; though she claims to have "wiped out the past" (41), a chance remark as she is leaving Jesse reveals that she has named the son of her second marriage after Phil. She knows she treated Phil badly, "but you can't brood on that. Everybody does badly by somebody, some time. He didn't do so hot by me, come to that" (40). Jesse's concluding speech puts Evvy and Phil in perspective: "How can you believe that a really beautiful girl is just a very ordinary person? It goes against nature. You can't believe she's a mediocrity, and responds to mediocrity. That would be tragedy if it weren't so common. I suppose that was poor Phil's trouble. And we Brothers in the Black Art wanted a lot from life. We weren't content with the minimum. We were proud" (41).

The story of Evvy and Phil and their sharply contrasting ways of seeing themselves and their lives is set off by the black and white symbolism of the printer's trade. The black mark made by ink is temporary, but the whiteness of the hands that use lye to wash down the formes and type is permanent after a year or so. Whiteness, purity, honour — and death — are associated with the lye. Though black and white suggest a stark contrast between good and evil, the use of the lye works against that suggestion, for appropriately used, it produces only purity and snow-white hands, but used without discretion, it causes a "ruinous black hole" and death. Phil's sense of honour did him credit, but when he injudiciously tied his honour to Evvy, who had no understanding of it at all, the very strength of his sense of honour destroyed him. There is nothing simple about good and evil in human life; the symbolism and the structure of the play emphasize the inadequacy of any such assumption. The simplicity of black-and-white associations is complicated by the manner of Phil's death, and the simplicity of our first impression of Evvy as villainess and Phil as victim is complicated by further light shed on the relationship at the end of the play. Phil's fate is dreadful, but it is not tragic, only ironic: the tone is that of black comedy. This is because at the same time we learn the full story of Phil's end, we learn too of the magnitude of his folly in overvaluing Evvy. The events leading to his death are told from her perspective, which trivializes them. His fate, at first just sad and shocking, when it is explained more fully, partakes of bad luck and misjudgment as well as betrayal, and the explanation reveals a character that is shown at the same time as both noble and foolish.

Phil's fate is contrasted with the fates of the other two brothers in the black art. Simply summarized, while Phil's fate is Death, Jesse's is Love, and Griff's is Success. The differences seem to be at least as much due to luck as to character; specifically, to luck in love. "Girls," Jesse reflects, "that's a subject on which every young chap thinks he's an expert. Though it's luck mostly." He repeats it: "Yes, mostly luck, and I was lucky" (11). His own luck in love is the motif for his character; though Bess dies young, their love lasts him his lifetime, and he doesn't seem to need much else. Griff's girl, Lou, is a New Woman with "a lot of Views of Matters of Moment" (12), as Jesse puts it. She does not have Evvy's beauty and shallowness nor Bess's warmth and spirit, but she has drive and tenacity, and she is a great help to Griff "in everything that looked like success" (31).

The greatest problem with *Brothers in the Black Art* is that its themes cannot be satisfactorily developed in an hour less time for commercials. The title suggests that the play is about all three men, but though Jesse's character is well developed in the course of his narrative commentary, his story is left sketchy, so it is difficult to contrast his life effectively with the others. "One or two things happened that killed any ambitions I might have had" (32), he says, and that is all about that, so the relationship, if any, between Bess as the centre of his existence and his station in life is not explored for contrast between him and Griff. The interview occasioned by Griff's death suggests some focus on Griff, but his story is only vaguely suggested. Jesse says that Griff was happy — "it's all rubbish to say that success and wealth can't be reconciled with happiness" — and that their failure to meet frequently in later life was due simply to the fact that they "took different roads" (31). The photograph of Griff as a senator inscribed "To Jesse from Griff — Brothers in the Black Art" (3) suggests that Griff has not forgotten his old friends. Evvy implies that because Griff has gone "up" and Jesse has not, Griff finds it convenient to overlook his former friend, but Evvy is "sour," as Jesse observes, though she also speaks some home truths. (Her reply to Jesse's question, "You know what happened to Phil, of course?" is "I know what Phil *did*. It didn't 'happen to him' ") (39-40). Davies's intention concerning Griff would not be clear without his prefatory note to the published play, which denies that Griff is to be identified with Davies's father, despite the many superficial resemblances: "My father was a very much nicer man than Griff, and never forgot an old friend." Apparently, we are meant to see that Jesse is too generous a person to recognize the shortcomings in his friends; Evvy provides a contrasting perspective. But all else being equal, we are bound to choose Jesse's view over Evvy's because of his dominant role as narrator and because he is a more sympathetic character. The case against Griff comes down finally to one statement made by Jesse, which carries relatively little weight because it is not dramatized. After Jesse asserts that Griff is both successful and happy, he adds, "He stopped singing, though" (31-32).

   This observation is significant in connection with the theme of *Brothers in the Black Art*, which is introduced fairly early and reiterated in Jesse's closing speech: "We may tell much — perhaps everything — about a man's character if we observe in what guise he invites Beauty to touch his life" (12). This is perhaps a justification for Davies's failure to characterize Phil and Griff very distinctly, and it seems to take the fate of the three men out of the realm of luck after all — only Jesse, whose character leads him to make a valid choice of a form of Beauty in Bess and remain true to it, modestly perceives it as a matter of luck. Phil chooses Evvy, whose beauty is only skin-deep. Griff, we are shown and told, invites Beauty to touch his life in the form of music. We must assume, then, that when he stops singing, his life is impoverished, despite Jesse's belief that he is happy. The difficulty is that we see nothing of Griff after he begins his climb to success; the full implications of the theme cannot be dramatized in the time alloted for the play. If they were, the conclusion would be ironically effective instead of seeming like a lame attempt to shift the focus of the play at the conclusion from Phil to Griff, the subject of the interview. For Griff, Jesse concludes, the guise in which Beauty was invited to touch his life "was music and he's going out with a band. He'll like that. He'll like that very much" (41). The irony is that the opening speech of the play, about "those amazing winter funerals Canada seems to manage especially for her great men," includes the observations that inevitably Chopin's funeral march is played, which is "not a band piece, really. Written for the piano," and that "the band is always a bit out of tune because the instruments are cold" (1). If Jesse is right that Griff would love it, it is because he would value the glory of the tribute, not the beauty of the music. *The Manticore* and *Fifth Business* can perhaps tell us through Boy Staunton and his second wife Denyse something of the story of Griff and Lou that we do not see in *Brothers in the Black Art*; the play itself lacks the scope to fulfil its potential. It can properly treat within its limits only the brief story of Evvy and Phil.
   Brothers in the Black Art was a minor effort, written in about a week,[30] but it signalled a renewal of dramatic creativity in Davies. The middle seventies was a period of greater dramatic creativity than any time since the middle fifties, not just in terms of quantity of production but also in terms of fresh ideas and dramatic techniques.

11

The Politician in Search of Himself:
Question Time

Even as Davies was writing *Brothers in the Black Art* for television and the third novel of his Deptford trilogy, *World of Wonders*, he was tantalized by Leon Major's request for a new full-length stage play for the St. Lawrence Centre. The temptation to write a new play for a theatre that could afford to spend lavishly[1] proved irresistible. The play, *Question Time*, combined Davies's theme from the plays of the fifties (and the novels of the seventies), a search for the self, with the national pastime of the early seventies, a search for the Canadian identity.

Davies's sense of the urgent need for modern man to cultivate an awareness of his innermost self, fostered by his reading of Jung, is evident in many of his talks to graduating classes and other groups, as well as in his creative writing. A talk he gave to the Ontario Welfare Council in 1966 outlines as a general hazard to all professionals exactly what he depicts in *Question Time* as the trap into which his central character has fallen: losing oneself in the process of endeavouring to serve others. "The danger of a busy professional life," he told the social workers, "is that it will eat you up. The more thoroughly and committedly you become a professional person, the greater is the danger that you will cease to be a private person .... What is the basic thing, and potentially the best thing you offer?" he asked. "Is it not yourself?" Preaching selfishness, he advocated "an intelligent regard for the preservation and nourishment of the Self....We never seem to take time to feed it, clothe it, encourage it, love it, and forgive it....Unless you bring a well developed, strong, resilient personal Self to your work, you are nothing," he insisted. "You are working for mankind, are you? Well, the best thing you can do for mankind is to devote your best energies to making the best possible job of yourself; then you will have something to give mankind that will really rouse its attention.''[2] In *Question Time*, Davies dramatizes this modern malaise in the character of Peter Macadam. Peter, son of Adam, it has frequently been observed, is Everyman. He is also Prime Minister of Canada, and in exploring the relationship between his public self and his private self, Davies depicts the identity crisis not only of a man but also of a country. In fact, though *Question Time* does not make a point of it, Davies shares Jung's view that the loss of the private self in the resignation of individual responsibilities to the state is ''the chief failure and disease'' of the whole of Western civilization, as he states in his review of Jung's *The Undiscovered Self*.[3]

Set in the Arctic Mountains, *Question Time* opens with a plane crash that kills everyone aboard except the Prime Minister. Macadam is found in a coma by aliens who are snooping in the Canadian Arctic for undiscovered natural resources and brought to an Eskimo Shaman for treatment. The Shaman explains that in shock Macadam has ''gone inside himself,''[4] and his inner exploration will determine whether he lives or dies. The play is Macadam's self-exploration under the Shaman's guidance, set against the reactions of the outside world to news of his condition. The remote Arctic setting becomes a metaphor for Macadam's own personal arctic, his ''terra incognita,'' and as he wanders in his mind, seeking his true self, he is seen wandering the icy slopes of Les Montagnes de Glace, searching. In the first act, televised news reports are interspersed with Macadam's conversations with the Shaman and Arnak, an Eskimo nurse who is made to represent his dominant quality, intellect; with his wife, Sarah, who suddenly appears at his side on the mountain; and with La Sorcière des Montagnes de Glace, a figure who represents both the essence of the Canadian land and the lost essence of Macadam himself. Also shown are the activities in Ottawa of the Minister for External Affairs, the Secretary of State, and other highly placed civil servants, as well as Sarah, a pair of ''ordinary Canadians,'' Tim and Marge, and a representative of the Canadian Medical Association, as they all respond to news of Macadam's situation.

Macadam witnesses and comments on the behaviour of all of them, and the distinction between objective and subjective reality is blurred by the Shaman's explanation at one point that what Macadam sees is his ''own truth,'' ''life seen through the spectacles of [his] temperament'' (11), and his assurance at another point that what Macadam sees ''down there'' (as opposed to on the mountain) ''is real enough'' (36). The televised news reports, of which Macadam seems unaware, appear to be objectively real, but the televised interview with Sarah is of central concern to him in his inner exploration. The Shaman's role in the proceedings also works against a distinction between objective and subjective reality, since his personality is unchanged between his role as an Eskimo doctor and his role as part of Macadam's fantasy, the voice of Macadam's own doubts. In both roles, he acts as the guide on Macadam's journey to recovery.

The first act establishes the essence of Macadam's problem, the loss of his private self in his life as a public figure. A man of great intellect and chilly temperament, his emotional, instinctive side is starved, and as Prime Minister, he believes firmly that concern for the public good must take precedence over concern for his own good. His objective is to improve life for all Canadians, yet he cannot say whether he is happy himself. The Shaman observes that he speaks as though he "had no reality except what exists in the eyes of others" (9), and when he witnesses people's responses to the news that he is at the brink of death, he finds that none but Sarah is concerned with the possible loss of Peter Macadam; the others react in trivial ways to the possible loss of a Prime Minister. Even Sarah seems much absorbed in consideration of the public evaluation of the dress and demeanour of the Prime Minister's wife in a time of personal crisis.

Act I contains two important stages in the development of Macadam's recognition of his own inadequacy. The first gives him a detached look at his own intelligence, projected in Arnak who carries a jester's bauble, used "to knock an opponent cold, or let the wind out of him" (20). Illustrations of the political effectiveness of his wit are enacted, but the Shaman emphasizes the inadequacy of intellect as a source of inner strength and wisdom. He explains the primitive belief in totem animals that can be called upon for greater strength and wisdom than the conscious self possesses, activating the animal part of man. Macadam's intellect can choose nothing less for himself than the polar bear, but when he puts on the Shaman's bearskin and "becomes" the bear, his expression changes from incredulity to perplexity to agony as he is engulfed by this terribly alien mode of being. His instinctive, primitive self is so underdeveloped that to experience its full power for more than a few moments is beyond his capacity. He emerges from the experience ready to die, feeling that he lacks the spirit, the heart, the courage that the Shaman urges him to draw upon. Seeing his intelligence as a "feminine intelligence" that is "part of his charisma" draws from him a protest against the "eternal cadging for popularity" (30) that democratic politics necessitates.

This brings us to the role of the media in modern politics, and the second stage in Macadam's recognition of what is wrong with his life begins with a television interview of Sarah. Hurt and angry in the knowledge that what the interviewer wants is a public exposure of her private emotion, she calls his "a squalid art" (34), leaving Macadam to experience the inner conflict between his sympathy with his wife's feelings and his knowledge that her shot will cost him support from the media. Sarah then appears beside him to explain her role as part of "the Macadam Complex," those whose efforts combine to create Macadam's public image. Though she claims real affection for him, the primary reason she gives for never having thought seriously of leaving him is that "it wouldn't be fair to the Complex" — to "Peter Macadam as the world knows him" (38); it would destroy his public image.

Macadam has relied on his intellect and the strength of his marriage, and now his confidence in both has been undermined. Views of the Minister for External Affairs and Secretary of State show their callous acceptance of Macadam's probable death, and the Shaman urges him to make a decision: for life or for death. The first act closes on Macadam's enthusiasm for the method by which he has "made every important decision of [his] public career" (41); the second act is staged as a Parliamentary debate.

In Act II, the ice mountain is changed to "*a fantastic evocation of the Commons Chamber*" (43). The Minister for External Affairs, the Secretary of State, and Arnak are on the government's side of the House; Tim, Marge, and Sarah are on the opposition side. The procession of the Speaker — the Shaman, "*fantastically dressed in robes that parody those of the Speaker of the Commons*" — with Sergeant-at-Arms and Speaker's Clerks is "*a grotesque elaboration of the reality, frightening in effect*" (43). It is Question Time in the Parliament of Macadam's Terra Incognita, and the question is: will he live or die? The Prime Minister and the Leader of the Opposition are both Peter Macadam, played by the same actor, with a faceless double taking the place of the one who is not speaking. The Prime Minister is "*accomplished, assured, and shrewdly political, in contrast to the intense manner of the Leader of the Opposition*" (49), who opens the debate by asking, "To decide, must we not know who the Prime Minister is?" (45). Spokesmen for the government side, including the Prime Minister, reply entirely in terms of his political function — it seems a stupid question. Their speeches are interrupted and the scene enlivened by wrangles between Tim and Marge, duels between Arnak and Sarah, and general hubbub in response to sensational speeches.

The second act debate is in three sections, each introduced with a question asked by the Leader of the Opposition (designated in the script as PM_2). Commenting that the response to his first question indicated that the Prime Minister is no more than an appendage of a country, PM_2 launches the second section of the debate by asking: "What sort of country are we talking about? ... What are we?" (52). The discussion develops in three parts, the first reintroducing the two snoopers who found Macadam at the crash site to demonstrate that "if we do not love the land for what it is, there are others who love it in a very different way for what it has" (53). The second part introduces Canada's heritage in the person of an old Herald, symbolically dressed to represent as many countries as possible. His function, he explains, is to "remind you of what you were, so that you may have a clearer idea of what you are, and can therefore decide intelligently what you may become" (54). Tim (the average Canadian) rejects him as irrelevent, but the Herald begs to be accepted "as a nourishing, romantic legend" (55).

The third part of the discussion of national identity centres on totem figures. When the subject is broached, PM_2 quickly advises caution, to the delight of the Shaman, who realized that Macadam is learning from his inner exploration; his experience as the Great Bear has made a lasting impression. The Beaver appears as an obvious candidate for a Canadian totem, though the Herald protests that "no country can hope to rise above mediocrity if it lacks a mystique of the courage, the humour, and also the cunning and roguery of its people" (57). The Beaver is conservatively dressed, his hair beautifully brushed. He has short legs, heavy hips, prominent upper front teeth, and almost no forehead, but "*his smile speaks of unlimited self-satisfaction*" (57). He has industry and morality (mating monogamously and coddling the kits) to recommend him, but when the discussion turns to international relations on the Beaver Formula, the Herald voices his dismay at the suggestion of the Beaver for a national totem. According to medieval legend, he explains, a threat from a larger animal causes the Beaver, which lacks a strong voice and can produce only a feeble whistle, to put his policy of appeasement — the Beaver Formula — into effect: he bites off and offers up his own testicles! When rejection of the Beaver as a national totem mounts to an uproar, the desperate creature, whistling pitifully, produces a large pair of scissors and falls on his back "*in an obliging position*" (61); he is dragged offstage by the clerks.

PM_2, dissatisfied with the answer to his second question, asks a third: "Why does anybody want to be Prime Minister?" (62). PM_1 promptly dismisses the question as frivolous, but Sarah has puzzled over the question herself. Why would anyone want to pay the terrible price of high office: self-estrangement? PM_1 protests against pursuing the debate on such a personal level, provoking Sarah to the climactic arguments of the play. Everything, she tells him, comes finally from the personal level. "The Prime Minister cannot rise above the level of Peter Macadam, and the party cannot rise above the level of the Prime Minister. What is a man that other men should exalt him if he is not someone whose life on the personal level — on the deepest bedrock of the personal level — is of worth, and colour and substance and splendour that makes him a man in whom other men see something of what is best in themselves?" (64). She insists that his determination to serve his people without concern for himself is lunatic, because such a person is "a man without a core" (65). Though he claims that the world which has been his concern has served him well in return, she questions the ultimate value of his life: "We are debating whether you shall live or die, and you have no opinion to offer. Poor Peter!" (65). PM$_1$ thinks that she merely wants him to elevate his love for her above his public service, and she is left at a loss for a clear explanation of what it is in himself he should value.

To speak for her, the Herald suggests the Queen, la Sorcière des Montagnes de Glace. "She is the final reality: she is ourselves, our for-bears, and our children; she is this land — so old it makes all monarchies seem like passing shadows on her face, and all forms of power like games children tire of" (67). PM$_1$ is exasperated by this "Parliament of Irration-ality," but the Shaman insists that irrationality is the bedrock at which "every man is his own Prime Minister, holding office under the queen" (67), and strength in the rational world of government that Macadam thinks of as "reality" depends on success at this level, where defeat means loss of self. Demanding a dissolution of the House and told that only the Queen can dissolve it, Macadam agrees to an audience with her.

He speaks first as PM$_1$, and their conversation emphasizes his pride in his intellect and his deficiency in feeling. He still does not care whether he lives or dies, and she explains this indifference as "want of understanding for yourself; want of knowledge of yourself; want of compassion for your-self." She describes him "posturing as a strong man, posturing as one who lives, who leads, who serves a whole people, but without any true, humble love for the creature he should cherish most" (69). As she speaks, PM$_1$'s defiance wanes, and when she calls him "child," he answers as PM$_2$. She calls him both her child and her lover and reproves him for seeking another way when he could find everything in her. When each tells the other "Never turn your face from me again" (70), the question of Question Time in the Parliament of the Terra Incognita is answered.

Macadam's homage and submission to the power of his inmost, irra-tional self and the power of his land means new life, and the play closes with the televised announcement that Macadam has been found alive and well, followed by a brief exchange between Macadam and the pilot of the rescue plane, who, concerned about taking off with any significant weight aboard asks, "Got anything to take out with you?" "More than I brought," replies Macadam. "Nothing too heavy, I hope?" "No, no; I was joking. Only myself." "That'll be enough though, eh?" (70) concludes the pilot, think-ing that rescue is all-important, but to Macadam what matters is that the self he has now is much more than the self he had at the beginning of his ordeal.

Question Time is more complex in conception than any of the earlier plays, because it combines the exploration of the depths of a personality featured in *Hunting Stuart* and *General Confession* of the fifties with the depiction of a nation that was the object of the centennial plays of the sixties. The complexity of the staging techniques in Act I, which combines action featuring Macadam on the mountain with action in Ottawa on the forestage and televised scenes projected on a large screen, comes naturally from Davies's steadily increasing awareness of the flexibility of the stage, particularly after working with Guthrie to translate *Leaven of Malice* to the stage and on the centennial spectacle which demanded visual ingenuity in place of reliance on the spoken word. The device in Act II of doubling Macadam is unique among Davies's plays, though his very early play *The King Who Could Not Dream* calls for an actor to play one role in Acts I and III and another in Act II to suggest an essential equivalence between the characters, despite their striking differences. Doubling is also an important feature of the novel that Davies was working on as he wrote *Question Time*. In *World of Wonders* (1975) the simple and common technique of using one actor to double for another is given an added psychological dimension when young Magnus Eisengrim doubles for Sir John Tresize. In *Question Time*, the psychological dimension is central; the inner debate is conducted between parts of one personality, so both roles are fittingly played by the same actor. The technical difficulty is to create diversions which cover the exchange of places between the actor and his double on three occasions and to fill in the opposite side of the argument with other appropriate speakers when Macadam cannot answer himself. Davies manages both smoothly.

The complexity of *Question Time* accounts for some of the bewilderment of its audience and the dissatisfaction of its critics. Because it operates on multiple levels, it is easy to become absorbed in one of these and find other parts of the play irrelevant or confusing. In an article on "cultural redemption" in Davies's writing, Richard Plant comments on the double theme that Davies describes in the preface to *Question Time* as "the relationship of the Canadian people to their soil, and ... the relationship of man to his soul": "this binocular vision, at least in part and quite understandably, made the play confusing in performance. Audiences found that Macadam's dual role as representative of Canadians and of mankind at large was overpowered by the political implications of his office and his nominal resemblance to Pierre Trudeau. What is primarily a metaphysical drama became a political character play."[5] Certainly, given Davies's satiric bent, a significant ingredient of political satire in the play was inevitable. Macadam's cool intellect and charisma invite the comparison with Trudeau, though there is little of Margaret Trudeau in Sarah, and the mannerisms of Kenneth Pogue in the leading role were more suggestive of Lester Pearson than of Trudeau.[6] The political satire is more general than specific; its object, as in *A Jig for the Gypsy*, is the limited mentality that can grasp nothing of reality beyond immediate political advantage.

The primary vehicle for this satire is the Minister for External Affairs, who steps into the Prime Minister's place in his absence, though the Secretary of State, who is absorbed in the most superficial aspects of the funeral arrangements, carries part of the weight. The Minister is an opportunist who cares nothing about the fate of Macadam except as it affects himself. Macadam, he claims, has "allowed the party to slip badly. The old trouble. I've said it to his face; 'You're too much the statesman; not enough the party man.' That's a mistake I'm not going to make and it's not too early to start changing a few things" (10). Later, when it is known that Macadam has been found alive, though in a coma, the Minister's primary concern with his own personal power shows through the facade of good will towards Macadam: "He's alive, it appears, though that can't go on forever. He may still make it. A great leader. When have I ever denied it? But there's a good chance — I mean a possibility, which we must never lose sight of — that he won't return" (40). The Minister plans to make the most of this "good chance." The petty concerns of Davies's politicians contrast with the creative force of the Shaman as he guides Macadam towards discovery of the true sources of power and meaning in life, as in *A Jig for the Gypsy* the politicians' world contrasts with Benoni's. The politicians in *Question Time* are children at play, with no conception of the ultimate realities of life the Shaman points to. These are embodied in the Queen, La Sorcière des Montagnes de Glace, who makes "all forms of power [seem] like games children tire of."

The single feature of *Question Time* that excites most universal comment is the Beaver. On the one hand, this is a measure of Davies's success in giving humorous, concrete dramatic form to abstract features of national identity. But on the other, it is indicative of the difficulty of getting past the most entertaining specifics of Davies's dramatic creation to the underlying concepts that inform it. Davies's problem is reminiscent of G. B. Shaw's with *Man and Superman*, his "dramatic parable of Creative Evolution." Shaw reflected twenty years after it was written that he had "decorated it too brilliantly and lavishly .... The effect was so vertiginous, apparently, that nobody noticed the new religion in the centre of the intellectual whirlpool."[7] In *Question Time*, Davies presents his political satire and the concrete embodiments of his ideas about the essence of personal and national identity with such flair that one tends to focus on individual scenes, losing sight of the connections among them that constitute the total meaning of the play. The Beaver is usually considered an "amusing digression," and even Davies seems to acknowledge the validity of this criticism with his admission that he "cannot bear to throw away" something that is really amusing, even if it does not "push the play forward." He cites the Beaver specifically, contrasting his view as a playwright who wants to entertain audiences with the view of the critic who wants "a naughty superfluity" removed for the sake of a perfectly shaped play.[8]

The Beaver is amusing, but he is not superfluous. If Davies's jokes were irrelevant to the themes of his plays, they might be dismissed as naughty superfluities, but they are among the means by which he explores his subject. A play worth something more than two hours of amusement must do more than move the plot forward; it also explores character and theme. In *Question Time*, the character of a nation is at issue because Macadam defines his worth in terms of his service to the nation, and Davies's contention is that neither the nation's nor the individual's best interests can be served when either is cut off from the source of essential strength. A nation's strength must come at least in part from the individuals who comprise it; Macadam represents this source of strength as a citizen, and even more as the head of the national government. He must love and understand the nation before he can serve it at all; he must love and understand himself before he can summon the strength to serve it well. By resurrecting the medieval myth that the beaver offers up its own testicles to an intimidating opponent, Davies comments sardonically on Canada's policy of appeasement in international relations, but this element of political satire is not the major significance of the Beaver's emblematic role.

More importantly, he depicts the disastrous policy of cutting oneself off from one's own ultimate strength, for "when the orbs are gone, the scepter is unavailing" (61). The Beaver's physical gesture is equivalent to Macadam's psychic self-gelding by cutting himself off from his own inner self in the process of accommodating demands from those outside himself: the people he serves. In response to the Secretary of State's contention that most people in public life are sincere and "really do speak and act from the best that's in them," Sarah protests, "But it isn't their best! The best is lost and trampled in the scramble." She is not citing the cliché that power corrupts; she believes "it is losing touch with the source of power that corrupts" (64). The plot of *Question Time* is Macadam's struggle to accept this truth and renew his contact with that source of power. To the extent that perceiving the Beaver's inadequacy as a national emblem moves Macadam towards a recognition of his own inadequacy, then, the Beaver is not even extraneous to the plot. Only if he is seen as nothing other than a comment on Canada's international relations does he seem superfluous.

In characterizing Canada, Davies presents both its weaknesses and its strengths. The danger that a democratic system poses in terms of levelling to the mediocre in all respects is one that has always been a concern of Davies's; this shows up in the Marchbanks persona, and, particularly in connection with the nation's cultural life, it is the basis of *Fortune, My Foe*. In *Question Time* the problem is explored not specifically in terms of culture but more generally in terms of the nation's leaders, whose ideas are not necessarily in line with popular opinion. "Oh...to be one's best self...!" yearns Macadam in the first act. "To do what one knows to be right without having to persuade every good, dull supporter and provide an answer for every dull, envious detractor" (35).

In the second act, the Secretary of State explains that "the Hero is absolute for victory; he must maintain his chosen course and his opinions come ruin, come exile, come death. But not the democratic leader. He is — he must be — a party man." She accepts the fact that "Heroes are out .... It's part of the price we pay for a communal, democratic life....Every democratic realist knows that part of the cost of democracy is the gelding of the Hero" (47). This stand is opposed by Macadam's intelligence, portrayed by Arnak, who vociferously supports the Hero. Both the Secretary and Arnak are on the government side of the House, the side of PM_1, so neither is likely to speak for Davies. The problem is not directly resolved, but the desirable compromise is implied by Macadam's eventual acceptance of the importance of his inner self and by the lack of any indication that he intends to give up his political work (unlike Richard Roberts in *A Jig for the Gypsy*, who turns away from public concerns to concentrate on self-improvement). The ideal leader will have to act in accord with the promptings of his inner self, but part of his job is to persuade others — to teach the truths he finds.

Canada's strength in Davies's view is largely potential, lying dormant and waiting to be activated, as he suggested in the image of the sleeping Nanabozho in *The Centennial Play*. In *Question Time*, there are two figures that embody untapped strength. The minor one is the Herald, who represents Canada's heritage — all the wisdom and romance of all the old countries from which Canadians came. He is shabby and dusty, *"with perhaps even a cobweb or two"* (54), suggesting not that he is no longer useful but that he is no longer used. His value is popularly overlooked, as Tim's rejection of him suggests. The Herald offers Canada the collective wisdom of civilization, but he is less important as a source of national strength than the uncivilized, instinctive wisdom of nature, embodied partly in the Bear but most of all in La Sorcière.

Man is not separate from nature; though civilized man may make the mistake of thinking himself apart from or even opposed to the natural world, he is part of it. La Sorcière represents nature both in man's inner being and in the external world. In a symposium sponsored by the

Association for Canadian Studies in the United States in 1977, Davies concluded his talk on "The Canada of Myth and Reality" with a comment on Douglas LePan's poem, "Coureurs de bois," in which LePan turns from the subject of exploring the wilderness of the continent to "the desperate wilderness behind your eyes, / So full of falls and glooms and desolations...." "The Canadian," Davies said,

> is a coureur de bois who must understand — understand, not tame — the savage land. And is it the savage land of rocks and forests only penetrable by the patient explorer? Only in the sense that this is a metaphor for that equally savage land of the spirit .... In our time, when men have journeyed to the Moon, and returned quite unchanged and only scientifically enlightened, the dangerous voyage is the voyage into man's spirit, our knowledge of which is still very much at the point that geographical knowledge had reached when Magellan, Vasco de Gama, and Columbus dared greatly and enlarged the world of man.[9]

La Sorcière, whom Macadam must embrace before he can find the best in himself and serve the nation truly, is the untamed wilderness of both Canada's north and Macadam's — everyone's — inner self.

Question Time has frequently been criticized for a purely formal and unconvincing happy ending[10] in which Macadam suddenly submits to La Sorcière and comes back to life. To so evaluate the ending is to ignore the perfectly clear premise of the play: that *all* the action and the arguments of *all* the characters constitute Macadam's inner struggle to come to terms with himself. Though there is some difference between characters who are presented strictly as parts of himself — Arnak in her role as his intelligence, and the Leader of the Opposition, who plagues the Prime Minister with questions that he would prefer to think are irrelevant — and others, who are presented as he perceives them, even the others, such as Sarah, are saying things that he would have heard them say before. Her views trouble him, and he has to come to terms with them; otherwise they would not be part of the play, which is his search for a life worth living. The plane crash in all-but-inaccessible terrain and the days in coma constitute a respite from his busy public life which permits the deeply troubled man to turn inside himself for once in an attempt to resolve his problems. The ending is no more sudden than Casanova's acceptance of his shadow in *General Confession*; it is the natural culmination of the entire action of the play. The formerly dominant part of Macadam's personality yields to the pressure of the formerly unacknowledged part, accepts its worth, and Macadam is revitalized by the strength of the newly integrated whole.

In *General Confession* the archetypes represented by Voltaire, Cagliostro, and Marina were quite specific; each was a clearly defined part of Casanova. *Question Time* is also profoundly influenced by Davies's reading of Jung, but the character relationships are less precisely systematized than in *General Confession*. Only Arnak is defined as a specific part of Macadam's personality: his quick, incisive — and shallow — intellect.

The Shaman, who dominates the first act, is more like a Jungian analyst than a particular part of Macadam's personality. Like David Staunton's analyst in *The Manticore*, he knows both the modern, civilized world in terms of which the protagonist defines himself and the primitive, elemental world which is the source of modern man's problems and also the key to their solution. *Question Time* is developed largely in terms of contrast between the civilized world and the primitive, and Davies uses the Shaman very effectively to contrast the two at the beginning of the play. Our introduction to him is both comic and instructive. The comedy is in the contrast between the solemn assurance — heard twice — that Macadam is to have "the best medical attention available" and the vision of "*the best medical attention in full shriek*": "*The Shaman is a terrifying figure, rigged out in skins of Polar Bear and necklaces of bear's teeth; he hops, crouches, and bounds hither and thither, uttering horrible moans and cries; he shakes a rattle and now and then whacks a small drum*" (3). The instructive twist is that this *is* the best medical attention. The Shaman has received medical training in Edinburgh; he has the regulation neat black bag of modern medical equipment and can perform the routine examination, peering into mouth and eyes, checking heartbeat, respiration, temperature, and blood pressure. But all this he dismisses as "white man's magic." His modern medical kit is his "lesser bag," in contrast with "a skin pouch of incalculable age and filthiness" (4). His Edinburgh medicine gives him no useful information about Macadam's state that he does not possess intuitively, but his Arctic medicine understands the coma as a state in which a person withdraws to deal with inner problems. The Shaman's noisy routine is an attempt to "talk" with the patient on the irrational level which he currently inhabits; rational, civilized medicine has no means of doing this.

The Shaman is a complete man, because he knows both the primitive and the civilized worlds and understands the connections between them. Macadam wants to dismiss the whole primitive side of life. The world in which he is wandering is unfamiliar and uncomfortable; "it doesn't make sense." It is merely "a world of fantasies," he protests.

SHAMAN: Fantasies is one of your dismissive words. Call it the inner world, and fully as real as that other, where you walk so proudly.

PM: A world of unreality.

SHAMAN: No: a world of another reality. And the farther you explore it the more significant the fantasies become for the world you think of as reality....Free trade between the world of fantasy and the world of reality is what gives dimension to life. But...you've put a big tarriff-wall between the two worlds, and you look for self-sufficiency in your world of reality. It can't be done, man. Not with safety (24-25).

What the Shaman gets from his contact with the primitive he can explain without hesitation: "Fullness of life even at its worst. A union with my fellow-creatures — human and not human — which is sustaining when life is hard. A never-failing sense of the colour and savour of things great and small" (17). What Macadam gets out of his one-sided life he cannot say.

The Shaman's modern, civilized counterpart, the President of the Canadian Medical Association, is ruthlessly satirized for narrowmindedness, as he totally dismisses the possibility that anyone who is not "a properly qualified member of the Canadian Medical Association" might have any medical competence. All others are "bootleg quacks" (28). (He, of course, would not think of leaving the comforts of civilization to practise in the Arctic.) Davies sets up other oppositions between the primitive and the civilized in images. As Sarah talks on the phone, we see on the mountain La Sorcière. When Macadam speaks of the army of civilization, we see a great bear prowling the mountain slopes. The apparently haphazard structure of the first act is in fact designed to provide counterpoint between the two worlds. One critic complains of the play's unevenness, accusing Davies (as many have) of being unable to resist "what he considers a good, entertaining joke. That the action can shift from a superficial and pointless sendup of the Canadian Medical Association directly to Macadam's harrowing experience as his totem animal is but one instance of the play's unevenness."[11] Actually, the satire of the overcivilized physician is placed between Macadam's experience as the bear and his subsequent despairing response to the experience; Davies purposefully contrasts the superficiality of the civilized world with the depth of emotion experienced in contact with the primitive world.

At the end of the first act, Macadam is still unwilling to accept the value of the irrational world, but he has recognized the inadequacy of his personal life. He feels despair — a leaning towards death — but he is not a quitter, and he is reluctant to give his political colleagues the satisfaction that his death would bring. Thus, with Act II, he takes the lead in his own self-analysis, choosing a parliamentary style of debate on the question of whether he should live or die. This personal style of decision-making is reminiscent of David Staunton's method in *The Manticore*. He is a lawyer who argues his case "in court," acting as prosecutor, defence, and judge himself. Macadam is a parliamentarian; he will be the leaders of both side of the House that argues the question. Because Macadam has taken the lead, the Shaman's part in Act II is less prominent, but he is Speaker of the House, because it is a Parliament of the Irrational, not run by rational parliamentary procedure. Now the cool, rational intellect of Peter Macadam (PM_1) squares off against the intense voice of his own doubts (PM_2), with supportive arguments on both sides from the familiar inhabitants of his everyday world. PM_2 questions insistently; PM_1 parries the questions with the rapier of his polished wit. But pressed by Sarah's support of PM_2, PM_1 backs away from the confrontation when he cannot maintain it on a rational, impersonal level. However, Macadam's resistance against his own deepest feelings, the irrational side of himself, has been weakening during the course of the play.

This weakening is shown by the contrast between the scene in Act I between Macadam and La Sorcière and the parallel scene in Act II, the climax of the play. In Act I, Macadam speaks; the Queen's words are secondary, an echo of his. Davies makes the echo effect in both scenes astonishingly versatile, contriving significant conversation by selective use of the echo and varying intonation. In this he surpasses even John Webster's use of the voice of the dead Duchess in *The Duchess of Malfi*, whose echoes of her husband's speech are used for irony and emphasis, as well as to create a sense of her spiritual presence. The first-act exchange between Macadam and the Queen comes very early, before any conversation between Macadam and the Shaman. He does not see her, only hears her voice. Her identity as part of himself is established:

> PM: Who's that? Who are you?
> LA SORCIÈRE: Who are *you*?
> PM: I am Peter Macadam. Who are you?
> LA SORCIÈRE: You.

He doesn't understand, of course, and persists on the obvious level: "Peter Macadam. Head of State. Apart from the Queen." "Apart from the Queen," she echoes sadly, a succinct statement of the source of his problem. He does not understand what she means by "the Queen": "A purely symbolic figure, you understand — the Queen." "Understand the Queen ... the Queen ... the Queen ...," she pleads, offering the solution to his problem. He feels stupid, playing like a child with an echo, but he is wishing he were "not so much alone." "Not so much alone," she reassures him (7-8). She is always with him, part of him, waiting to be acknowledged, and at that moment the Shaman joins him, his guide on the journey to discover a part of himself, the Queen.

The climactic scene is the completion of that journey. Macadam's progress is indicated by the fact that La Sorcière's voice is now dominant; Macadam's is the echo and he is no longer uncomprehending. Though he is at first defiant and stubborn, this is the last gasp of his resistance to the source of inner strength that is his own irrational self. In the last phase of his self-integration, he speaks as PM_2, the self that Macadam saw on the mountain but made no contact with in Act I, the self he has debated with throughout Act II. Now the double who is PM_1 *"begins to fade before our eyes"* (69): he is no longer divided in a struggle against himself. Macadam is now able to accept the Queen, the anima figure who is mother and lover, the complementary side of Macadam's rational self. Acceptance means that he is finally able to understand, to know, to feel compassion for himself — all of himself, the irrational with the rational, the emotional with the intellectual. He can now return to his life, strengthened and deepened by making contact with what is most vital in himself.

Critical reaction to *Question Time* has ranged from qualified admiration to total condemnation. All recognized the play as an ambitious undertaking, but assessment of Davies's success in achieving his goals ran the gamut from Scott Young's assertion that this is a "first-rate" play that "will be played the length and breadth of the country, always to fascination"[12] to Urjo Kareda's estimation of the play as "a very grand, ambitious and idiosyncratic disaster," "a failure with a master's signature on it."[13] Reviewers of the production found it above all entertaining, if flawed in one respect or another. Singled out for special praise were Ken Pogue's depiction of Macadam's experience as the great bear and Jennifer Phipps's of Sarah being interviewed on television. Commentators on the published play, without the benefit of *Question Time*'s theatrical impact, tended to be less enthusiastic.[14] The critical prejudice that emerged in response to the publication of *Hunting Stuart & Other Plays* in 1972, when Davies had become in the public mind a novelist rather than a playwright, was still evident: one reviewer stated flatly that Davies was "not a playwright," regarding him as a "dabbler" in theatre who ought to stick to his academic and novelistic pursuits.[15] Critical consensus seemed to be that the depth of Macadam is not convincingly established, that the question of national identity is not clearly related to the question of Macadam's personal identity, and that the play's ending is perfunctory.[16]

That Macadam's dominant characteristic is cool intellect does minimize his emotional range, especially as PM_1 in Act II; Kareda accused Davies of giving "poor Kenneth Pogue...nothing to act but a rhetorical manner."[17] But the claim that Macadam's worth is not demonstrated is simply invalid.

Macadam is Prime Minister of Canada. As such, he is accorded the automatic stature that came with kingship in classical drama. Oedipus appears hot-headed and closed-minded, Lear appears childish and selfish — yet their personal worth is established through the loyalty of people close to them and the knowledge that they have ruled successfully for many years. Peter Macadam appears shallow (if one disregards the contribution of his various inner voices) and stubborn, but his stature is established by his wife's conviction of his essential worth and by our knowledge that a man who lacks character is unlikely to become Prime Minister.

The other criticisms hinge, I believe, on the mythic figure of La Sorcière. Close attention to Davies's work is rewarded with a clear perception of her function. Patricia Monk, for example, points out in a discussion of Davies's allegorical use of names that Les Montagnes des Glace are both Ice Mountains, Canada's northern wilderness, and "the Mirror Mountains or the Mountains of Reflection...among which Macadam wanders, his vision reflected or turned back into his inner world." La Sorcière, she notes, is in some versions of the Tarot deck — with which Davies is obviously familiar, as his use of it in *The Rebel Angels* shows — the name of the card that represents "the incarnate manifestation of intuitive feminine wisdom."[18] But the more superficial — and more common — view sees La Sorcière solely as an ice queen, the spirit of the land. From this perspective, the ending is indeed unsatisfactory and the connection between the question of national identity and individual self-discovery is indeed obscure. Even the apparent contention that Canada's identity is fundamentally rooted in the far north, which has in fact little effect on most Canadians, must seem questionable. Without an understanding of La Sorcière as the bedrock of both individual and national character, the fundamental, natural basis of both human being and country that remains unaffected by the civilizing process, the play seems to fall apart.

Scott Young's prediction that *Question Time* would be played "the length and breadth of the country" has not been borne out. Davies at first seemed pleased with the St. Lawrence Centre's production: "It looked splendid, and it was well acted," he said in 1976.[19] But disappointment that the play has received no further productions inclines him more to criticism of the St. Lawrence production. "It was absurdly cast," he said in 1981. "I was told an actor who was small, wiry, alert would be playing the lead; instead an entirely different type was cast. Similarly with the Spirit of the Far North. The result was a bloodbath." Davies claimed too that the director, Leon Major, had "misunderstood" the play, that he wouldn't "attack" it, so that it wasn't cut and "finely honed" as it should have been.[20] (Major said that he and Davies did a lot of rewriting before rehearsals, though not much later and added that he "never regretted" asking

Davies to write a play for the St. Lawrence Centre, though he felt that the second act of *Question Time* was less dramatic than the first.[21])

Certainly *Question Time* is generally misunderstood, which is doubtless one reason why the play has not been revived. Another is the financial factor that tempted Davies to write the play for the St. Lawrence Centre in the first place: with its large cast and elaborate set, the play is expensive to produce. Whatever the reasons, the failure of the play to command a more permanent place on the Canadian stage is a disappointment to those who appreciate the depth of Davies's work as well as its entertainment value. *Question Time* is in many ways the culmination of Davies's work as a playwright. In it, he unites the myth of *King Phoenix*, the modern satire of *Fortune, My Foe*, the magic of *Hunting Stuart*, the Jungian integration of *General Confession*, the contrast between primitive and civilized modes of perception of *A Jig for the Gypsy*. In a way, it is the obverse of *At My Heart's Core*, set in the forest wilderness of nineteenth-century Canada. There, the wilderness dominates and the best of civilization is beyond reach. In *Question Time*, the setting is the only wilderness left in modern Canada; elsewhere civilization has triumphed, and the rewards of primitive life have been lost in the process. This shift of emphasis from the rewards of civilization — or culture — to the rewards of the primitive side of life and the techniques he employed to dramatize his theme are the strongest evidence that in his sixties, Davies was still developing as a writer not only of novels but also of plays.

12

The Innermost Heart:
Theatre in the Courtroom in *Pontiac*

QUESTION TIME put Davies back into the frame of mind of an active playwright; after *World of Wonders* was published, he was planning another play for the St. Lawrence Centre.[1] That play never materialized; instead, he was drawn into the Hart House Theatre staff's plans in 1976 for the University of Toronto's sesquicentennial celebration the following year. David Gardner had suggested producing one of the earliest known plays about Canada in English, *Ponteach*, published anonymously in London in 1766, but like eighteenth-century theatre managers before him, Artistic Director Martin Hunter decided the play did not merit production. Ronald Bryden, once dramaturge for the Royal Shakespeare Company and now visiting professor at the Drama Centre and Hart House Literary Consultant, identified Major Robert Rogers as the probable author of the play. Rogers, leader of Rogers' Rangers, hero of the Indian wars and friend of the Ottawa chief, Pontiac, seemed a promising subject for a play which could provide a context for excerpts from Rogers's play.[2] Hunter, who had talked Davies into letting him direct at Hart House in 1973 the first production of *Leaven of Malice* Davies permitted after its failure on Broadway, asked Davies to write a new play about Rogers with excerpts from *Ponteach* for which Derek Holman would compose music. Davies was enthusiastic about collaborating with the Music Faculty to produce a piece of "Real Theatre," in which he would be "free to do all kinds of things that are not dictated by the necessities and realities of life."[3] The result was *Pontiac and the Green Man*, a play whose title tends to mystify those who think first of Pontiac as a car rather than an Indian chief and who do not know that Rogers' Rangers were experts in Indian warfare who wore forest green instead of the usual scarlet uniform. The play was produced jointly by the University of Toronto's Graduate Centre for Study of Drama and Faculty of Music from 26 October to 5 November 1977, directed by Martin Hunter and starring David Gardner as Major Robert Rogers.

Rogers was accused at a court martial in Montreal in 1768 of stirring up the Indians against the British, of exceeding his authority as Commandant of Fort Michilimackinac by spending too lavishly on presents for the Indians, of corresponding with enemies of King George in Spain, and of planning to desert to the French. He was acquitted, but because of the disapprobation of his superiors, the rest of his life was spent under a cloud of suspicion, burdened by the debts that his superiors refused to discharge. Davies's play is set at the conclusion of the court martial when Rogers is about to be acquitted. Davies uses his artistic licence to introduce "further evidence"; *Pontiac and the Green Man* is an imaginary extension of the historical court martial. In Davies's play, Rogers's play, *Ponteach*, is introduced as evidence of Rogers's sympathy with the Indians' grievance against the English. To save Rogers's judges the trouble of reading the play, a troupe of actors has been engaged to perform those portions of *Ponteach* that are requested as the trial proceeds.

Though Rogers at first declines to acknowledge his authorship, it soon becomes evident that he has written the play in collaboration with his wife, Elizabeth, and his secretary, the Reverend Nathaniel Potter, both of whom are present at Davies's version of the court martial. The authors' eagerness to see their work performed, the court's obligation to determine whether *Ponteach* is treasonable, and later the judges' growing fascination with the character of Pontiac himself lead to the performance of substantial portions of *Ponteach*; over a quarter of *Pontiac and the Green Man* is excerpts from *Ponteach*.[4] The first three segments of the play within the play depict abuse of the Indians by traders, hunters, and the military; the next four show Pontiac's determination not to be victimized: he will lead the Indians in revolt against the British. At Elizabeth's insistence, her romantic scene between a son of Pontiac and the daughter of another chief is played, followed by one of Potter's composition in which a Catholic priest attempts to ravish the Indian maiden. Rogers insists on a scene in which the Indians torture a white hunter to death to establish that he has not whitewashed the Indians. The play within the play concludes with Pontiac's heroic speech after his sons have died and his rebellion has been put down: he is defeated, but his spirit is unconquered.

The plot of *Pontiac and the Green Man* is very simple, partly, no doubt, because the complexity of *Question Time* bewildered its audience.

Rogers's innocence is established when the court is persuaded that his vision of North America and his actions that stem from it are original, but not traitorous. His surprising revelation at the end of the play that he alone of those present has sworn his allegiance to King George personally and that the King himself heard and approved Rogers's views on North America and suggested he write a play to popularize them clinches his case. He might have made this statement at any time, but his judges would have been unlikely to credit it before they had shared his vision by means of the performance of *Ponteach*. Rogers does make a move to explain his special commission from the King at the end of Act I, but he is interrupted with the announcement of luncheon and told that whatever he has to say will have to wait. When Act II opens, the action develops from Elizabeth's insistence during luncheon on having her irrelevant scene of Indian courtship performed, and Rogers's pending revelation is forgotten for the time being.

By the end of the play, dramatic interest centres on the character of Rogers, but he seems a surprisingly minor figure through much of the play. The characters of the Judge Advocate and the three judges of the Court Martial and of Elizabeth Rogers and Nathaniel Potter provide at least as much interest during the first three-quarters of the play as Rogers's character does, and most of the many comic moments grow out of the incongruity of a theatrical performance in a courtroom. The judges react variously but vigorously to the demolition of court routine by the intrusion of art into law, and the pride and jealousies of the acting troupe provide humour, as does the proprietary interest of the three authors in the proceedings and the need to press some of the court officials and witnesses into theatrical service. Rogers is on trial not only as a soldier, but also as a dramatist, as evidenced by a panel of three critics who damn his play, though the court judges declare his innocence of the military charges. Rogers's play dramatizes the feelings that have got him into trouble with higher authority, and during most of *Pontiac and the Green Man* Rogers's play, rather than Rogers himself, is spotlighted. Drama is as much the subject of Davies's play as heroism; artistic expression is compared with heroic action as means of sharing an original outlook with an intransigent society.

For the historical background of the play Davies consulted Francis Parkman's *The Conspiracy of Pontiac* and the Dictionary of National Biography. Others involved in the production read John R. Cuneo's *Robert Rogers of the Rangers*. In addition, Kenneth Roberts's novel *Northwest Passage* may have had some influence,[5] since, like Roberts, Davies emphasizes Rogers's incompatibility with his wife, while Cuneo depicts an affectionate relationship on the evidence of their letters, and Parkman does not mention her at all. The suggesion that Potter had a particular interest in drama and even some acting experience is also in *Northwest Passage*. Both

the novel and Cuneo's biography suggest Potter as a likely collaborator in
Ponteach, though the suggestion that Elizabeth had a hand in it and that
there was a particular affinity between Elizabeth and Potter are Davies's
inventions. Davies's programme note observes that "the roots of this play
are history, but the branches are not" and emphasizes both the freedom
with which he alters historical fact and the essential truth of his characterization of Rogers:

> *Pontiac and the Green Man* treats history light-heartedly, offering
> Rogers and his Indian hero as the principal characters in what is, in
> effect, an extended ballad, taking the ballad's liberty of showing possi-
> bilities, rather than historical facts. Rogers himself was indeed a hero;
> he formed the first guerilla force on this continent. His vision of North
> America, and his sympathy with the Indians, make him a man far in
> advance of his time. Unluckily for him, like many heroes he was a
> nuisance to his superiors, and as a man of letters he followed an equally
> independent and unfortunate course.

The effect of a ballad about a hero is created when the play opens with
"The Ballad of the Green Man," comparing Rogers to such legendary
heroes as Hercules and Hector. The ballad contrasts Rogers's knowledge
of the Indians with his lack of knowledge of his countrymen, which
accounts for the court martial. The opening speech by Judge Advocate
Cramaché states that the court's examination of the charges against
Rogers, which he recites, has produced "no satisfactory proof" of the
charges. Rogers thanks that Court and happily anticipates liberty, and
Davies immediately emphasizes, albeit comically, the rigidity of the trial
structure, which is set against the freedom of imagination once *Ponteach* is
introduced. Captain De Peyster, the youngest and most zealous of the
judges, frostily proclaims Rogers "sadly ignorant of Court Procedures" in
assuming that he is about to be freed, because the Court has not yet
declared him Not Guilty. He then introduces as new evidence the
assurance of Rogers's former secretary, Potter, that the play *Ponteach* was
written by Rogers and is treasonable. Colonel Jones, an aristocrat who
presides over the Court, is contemptuous of evidence produced by Potter,
"who has already made himself absurd with his direct accusations and his
sneaking references against the prisoner," but the third judge of the court
martial, Colonel Prevost is a lover of drama who has read the play. Whether
it is treasonous "depends on how you look at it. And you'd better look at
it," he advises the others.

Accusations and counter-accusations between Elizabeth, who defends
Potter for "toilsome nights. . . spent regularizing those rough verses,"

Rogers, who remembers Elizabeth and Potter working closely together in "touching scenes" to improve his play, and Potter, who tells Rogers that "if your play was ever to have a chance of appearing on the London stage some polishing by an educated hand was very necessary," establish economically and comically the personal and authorial relationship of the three. Prevost persuades Jones and Cramaché to see the performance De Peyster has arranged, despite their conviction that it will make the Court ridiculous, and the players enter.

Noteworthy among the players are the manager, Mrs. Bellimperia Egerton, somewhat worn but still imposing, her son, the juvenile lead, and the leading man, Bartlemy Bengough, who has the role of Pontiac. Mrs. Egerton speaks briefly of the hardships of artists in the New World in a manner reminiscent of Davies's treatment of the theme in earlier plays, from *Hope Deferred* to *At My Heart's Core*, and certainly her experience in the court martial does nothing to alleviate her feelings, for Cramaché, Jones, and De Peyster are all contemptuous of the theatre, and she is not paid for her troupe's work, only invited to send her account to the Paymaster-General and await the next quarterly settlement.

The treatment of Rogers's play and discussions of drama prompted by its performance reflect a good deal of Davies's view of drama. He plays up the shortcomings of both the play and the performance for comic effect, yet truth and passion are also conveyed. In his presentation of the play within the play he runs the gamut from the ludicrous to the profound. The ludicrous spotlights theatrical violation of artistic truth, a preference for trite convention over forceful originality. Admittedly, the company's performance is given on extremely short notice, and there is no time to prepare appropriate effects. In consequence, a setting meant to depict Ponteach's encampment in the wilderness is "*a wooded glade, startlingly unlike any wilderness nearer than Twickenham*," and a war dance is presented as a sedate caper to the tune of "Over the Hills and Far Away."

The play *Ponteach* itself is condemned for similar violations of artistic integrity; for this Davies blames Potter and Elizabeth's interference in Rogers's work. To Elizabeth are attributed "passages of tenderness," without which, she insists, "a tragedy is nothing." Prevost acknowledges the regrettable fact of this dramatic convention: "The Drama's laws the Drama's patrons give, and one of their unremitting demands is that Love must come sneaking into a play, in season and out." Davies underscores the boring, conventional lines of the courtship scene by having Elizabeth happily beat time to the rhythm, but he relieves the boredom with a squabble among the actors about whether Mrs. Egerton should replace the ingénue in the part of the Indian princess, admonitions to the ingénue to speak up, and Jones's obvious relish for the ingénue's charms.

The laughable deficiencies of Roger's play, which Davies has called *"awful,"*[6] are emphasized less towards the end of *Pontiac and the Green Man* than in the middle, and even then the inadequacy of the critics who pronounce upon it is at least as evident as the inadequacy of the play. Act II is introduced with a continuation of "The Ballad of the Green Man," which concludes, "Rogers, whom Red Man never slew/ Is in the playhouse slain." A Prologue on the Theatre delivered by Mrs. Egerton's son, who feels he was given insufficient scope to display his talents earlier, leads up to the entrance of three critics: "From Grub Street, University and Salon,/ They come with cudgel, poison bowl and talon." The three pronounce smugly on the faults of the play, oblivious to the fact that they contradict each other on every detail. One finds a lack of plot; another finds the play plot-ridden. One claims that "the Tragedy is heavily fraught with Feeling, which has not been refined by Reflection, and is therefore uncouth in its force"; another asserts that the "Tragedy possesses everything that is needful, save Feeling, without which Tragedy is impossible." They agree only that the play is a failure. The critics withdraw, the Prologue concludes with a request for audience support for the players if not the play, and the Ballad ends, "In bloody playhouse warfare/ Where fledgling playwrights fall,/ The Forest King, the Green Man,/ Is the greenest man of all." Davies evidently feels that a hero would do better to stick to action and leave art to the artists. A clear distinction is drawn between the hero and the artistic portrayal of the hero early in the play, when Rogers offers to read the part of Pontiac and is told he would not do. His trade is "Heroism"; the actor's is "inspiring belief" in heroism.

Even an inferior play, however, may have the ability to evoke feelings in a way that rigid courtroom routine does not. The play and the players, whose business is to arouse emotions, challenge the dispassionate, logical procedures of the court. Towards the end of Act I, passion takes over, as Jones and Rogers quarrel about what an authentic war dance is and the French Catholic Judge Advocate Cramaché attacks Potter with a law book in his outrage at Potter's portrayal of a scheming French priest. "Damn the theatre and all that belongs to it!" explodes Jones. "Here we have His Majesty's court martial turned into a bear-garden, and everyone — myself among the rest — capering and hallooing and tossed hither and thither by storms of passion. . . . Major Rogers, I venture to say that if you had not meddled with the theatre we should have found you innocent an hour ago, whereas now we are in Pandemonium, Sir, in Pandemonium." Yet Davies's point is that the whole truth emerges more clearly as a result of art's intrusion in the court. When in Act II the court again breaks up in furious quarrels and Jones regrets having admitted the players, Prevost attempts to reassure him: "See how much we have already learned from this play. The dull intellect finds pleasure in the fable, whereas the profound philosopher may grapple with the depths of its implication. Drama is the noblest, because it is the most inclusive of the arts." Elizabeth argues for the nobility of "divine Music," but Prevost observes that unlike drama, music "cannot encompass mind." Begging Jones's patience, Prevost offers an earnest justification for the introduction of theatre into the courtroom, and his argument suggests a reason for Davies's central dramatic device that is less readily apparent than its obvious comic value: "Justice seems all thought, all calculation, all reason: art seems to be all feeling, all improvisation, all done in passion. Whereas the precise contrary is the case." This he acknowledges to be paradoxical, but "bidden, or unbidden, paradox will find its way into our lives. One of life's great principles is that truth is a wedding of opposites." Certainly the hidden passions at work in the courtroom have been exposed by the intrusion of drama; now it is the job of the judges to find in the drama the thought embedded in it, the mind and the "inmost heart" of its author, beneath the surface passions of the play's characters.

We are reminded again of the liberating effect of introducing drama into the court procedures when, after Rogers regrets letting his wife and secretary add their "scenes of trashy gallantry" and "bibble-babble about religion and the lickerish French" to his "honest play [that] spoke honestly of this land as I find it...," he offers to speak of what he wanted to say in his play. De Peyster attempts to quash him with typical court rigidity: "You have spoken all that is proper for an officer before a court martial." Jones, however, acknowledges Rogers's right to speak to the new evidence — his play — and Rogers opens up: "Why does a man write a play?" Not to teach a lesson, which is better done from a pulpit, or to posture as an author, which is better done with poetry. "No, no; he writes his play to persuade people to feel as he does." The feeling Rogers wants to share is his conviction that there is something worthwhile, something noble and honest, in the Indian way of life that civilized people would do well to understand. Drama can range from trivial artificiality to profound reality, and *Ponteach* runs the gamut. Davies's intent in his selection and arrangement of scenes from *Ponteach* was to build from silly passages to those that have real impact.[7] The accompanying music reinforces this impression; he notes that the scene of the priest's attempt on the Indian Princess's virtue, for instance, is played to "*Melodrama Music: Virtue in Danger*," while in the later "blood-red" scene of Indian retribution against the white hunter, the music builds "*in cruel intensity until the end of the scene when it breaks out in uttermost savagery – real, not 18th century*." This scene affects its audience strongly, as does the concluding one, Pontiac in defeat, when the music moves from "defeat and despair" to "nobility and courage" as

Pontiac looks to the future with determination, despite the bitter blows he has suffered, blows which would have crushed most men.

Rogers's heroism is established in two ways: by contrasts between him and all the other characters who participate in the court martial and by his identification with the hero of his play. None of the judges nor Rogers's wife nor his former secretary is part of Rogers's world: the North American wilderness. All are thoroughly conditioned by their Old World inheritance; in their interests, ambitions, and values there is nothing to differentiate them from Old World inhabitants. Davies observed of the ladies he wrote about in *At My Heart's Core* that they were "transplanted English and Irish people, grappling courageously with a new country, but they brought their intellectual furniture with them, and they never changed it."[8] Those who surround Rogers are similarly encumbered with their old intellectual furniture. The single sign of interest among them in the ways of the New World is Jones's amateur enthusiasm for Indian dances. He has made them his particular study, he claims, but the "war dance" he shows the acting troupe Rogers identifies as a dance to avert hail. Their dispute is comic, but it also points up the contrast between Rogers, who has the understanding of one who has taken part in Indian life, and Jones, who has only the impressions of an outsider. All but Rogers have minds closed to the possibility of acquiring new ways of seeing and being from the new world that surrounds them. Some are more sympathetic to Rogers, some less; only Prevost seems really to appreciate Rogers's original outlook, and even he shows no inclination to follow Rogers's lead. In *At My Heart's Core* Davies emphasized the unfortunate but inescapable necessity for the settlers to put their privations into perspective, but in *Pontiac* the emphasis is on people's inability to embrace new truths while they are restricted to old ways of seeing the world. Only Rogers frees himself of the old intellectual furniture.

Rogers's identification with the hero of his play is declared towards the end, when he admits, "I see now that tragedies should be written by poets, not by their protagonists." Elizabeth protests, "The protagonist is Pontiac," and Rogers replies, "My dear, you have never seen that I am Pontiac. . . . A creature of this continent, one of the very first of a new sort of being." This suggestion was planted much earlier by Prevost, after the scene from *Ponteach* in which Pontiac tells of a dream in which he saw "a lordly Elk" attacked by various beasts of prey. ". . .he unmov'd amidst their Clamours stood,/ Trampled and spurn'd them with his Hoofs and Horns,/ Till all dispers'd in wild Disorder fled,/ And left him Master of th' extended Plain." De Peyster, the most unimaginative and unsympathetic of Rogers's judges, does not see "what anybody's dreams have to do with anything whatsoever," and Prevost explains (anticipating Jung): "Dreams

are the windows through which we peep at the landscape of a man's soul."
De Peyster has no interest in peeping "at any Indian's soul," and Prevost
reminds him — and us — why *Ponteach* is on view: "Dear boy, you are not
looking at an Indian's soul, but at the author's soul. And what do you see?
No, don't reply, because you don't see anything. But I see a man who
dreams of great empire, and dreams nobly."

In some respects, Pontiac is an historical figure with his own distinct
features: his determination to make war on the English, for instance, is not
an aspect of the author's soul, or the charge of treason against Rogers
would be justified. Similarly, Rogers himself is an historical figure, not
entirely an aspect of Davies's soul. Yet, in each author's play, the view
offered of the hero's heart and mind, his feelings and motivations, is indeed
an image of the author's soul rather than the hero's. Rogers is to be seen in
his view of Pontiac in *Ponteach*; Davies is equally visible in his view of
Rogers in *Pontiac and the Green Man*.

By identifying the love scene in *Ponteach* as Elizabeth's and the scenes
involving the French priest as Potter's, Davies enriches his characterization of these two. Elizabeth sees herself as the soul of delicacy, sorely tried
by the rough and blunt character of her husband. Her delicacy is made
ridiculous when she begs Cramaché to remove from the court record an
allusion "to a portion of my person by a coarse expression." (A soldier who
drove her away from the window of Rogers's prison threatened to "kick
[her] arse away from there.") Later when she expresses horror at the
vicious words of an early scene from *Ponteach*, Rogers reminds us that this
is public posturing, since she is well acquainted with the play: "There is
worse to come and well you know it." Her portrayal of the Indian Princess,
chastely worshipped by her lover, is a projection of her own prissy self,
under assault by the coarse world of reality (in the form of the lascivious
English soldier the Princess tells about and later the French priest), but
nonetheless pristine. Similarly, Potter, himself a Protestant clergyman
whose character is far from the Christian ideal, projects his character in the
scheming and hypocritical French priest, displacing the dregs of himself
into one of another nationality and another religion.

At many points in the portrayal of Pontiac, there is something to be found
of Rogers's own character and dilemma. The first scene in which Pontiac
appears shows him as an idealist, a leader and hero with real concern for the
spiritual as well as the material welfare of his followers, while the English
officer is contemptuous of Indians and satisfied that they should be taken
advantage of simply because they are Indians. Rogers too is concerned with
morality, with the Indians' right to respect and fair play. The second scene
establishes Pontaic's good will towards the English king: "With Pleasure
I wou'd call their King my Friend, Yea, honour and obey him as my

Father" — but he is not willing to give up his land, nor "To be a Vassal to his low Commanders,/ Treated with disrespect and public Scorn/ By Knaves, by Miscreants, Creatures of his Power." Rogers too is loyal to his king, but misunderstood and abused by those who wield the power of the king in the new land. In the scene of Indian vengeance against the white hunter, Pontiac decides to spare the hunter's wife and children, not because he would not kill women and children, but because they are harmless and their powerful friends will pay for their release, while their deaths would bring severe retribution. His is a politic decision; he acts out of neither blood-thirstiness nor squeamishness — like Rogers, who has explained the authentic method of scalping, which he admits he knows from experience. But though Rogers has fought against Indians, he prefers to work with them to their mutual profit.

The great elk of Pontiac's dream who defends his realm against all attackers is of course Pontiac himself, but the dream is also Rogers's; he hopes to awaken the New World to its full potential without allowing Old World vultures to despoil it. Indians work for survival and sleep the rest of the time, Rogers claims, while the European "keeps his eyes open and his wits about him for sixteen hours out of twenty-four. This is what begets government, industry and art. . . . Until the white man came, this whole great land was asleep." As Commandant of Fort Michilimackinac, Rogers found himself "at the very navel of this new World. . . . There I dream of awakening the New World to such bounteous life as no man can conceive who has not trod where I have trod or seen what I have seen. I desire this great New World, in all its opulent grandeur, for my King."

Rogers's unambivalent loyalty to his king is made possible and probable in terms of Davies's characterization of his hero solely because the king is depicted as the ideal, fairy-tale ruler whose wisdom enables him to embrace Rogers's original view of the New World as others cannot. The king has Rogers's loyalty because he is of one mind with Rogers. "Never in my life was I listened to so attentively," says Rogers, describing his audience with the king, and in response to Rogers's criticism of those representatives of the king who rule in the New World without ever really knowing it, the king "agreed. He agreed in every detail." What earns Rogers the king's appro-bation is just that which makes him a Davies hero: "Wherever you go," the king said at the end of their conversation, "my great goodwill goes with you, for I have not many men in my service who have not silenced the promptings that come from the innermost heart." What makes Rogers a hero is his originality; he is receptive to his own, individual perceptions, and he acts on them instead of yielding to the current of popular opinion. Davies goes out of his way to establish his hero's complete originality when Jones accuses Rogers of having "gone Indian" and seeing "with Indian eyes," and Elizabeth interjects, "When we were at Michilimackinac the Indians did not take him to themselves. My husband was a stranger to them as he is a stranger among his own people." He is wholly of neither one culture nor the other, but "one of the first of a new sort of being," a man who can combine the best of both.

In their concluding conversation, Jones grants Rogers some "devilish interesting" ideas but observes that Rogers "would do better out of the service. You are not well-suited to it. You have not the mind of a colonial officer." Rogers reminds Jones of "a fellow. . . all hung about with drums and cymbals and rattles and whistles [who] called himself a One-Man Band. He could play tunes, astonishingly, but of course he was not a real band. The colonial service, Major, is a damn'd fine-tuned military band, and it plays very well." "Plays all the best-known tunes," Rogers counters. "Never heard a new tune from it yet." Jones exits, displeased with Rogers's reply, and Prevost underscores the image: "He called you a One-Man Band and so you are. It's another way of avoiding the embarrassment of saying that you are also an original. We are marching toward the world of the well-drilled military band, with never a toot or thump of originality about it." As long as Rogers pursues a life of action, he remains an original, true to "the promptings of his innermost heart"; he betrays them only when he turns to another mode of expression: playwriting. In this, he defers to the opinions of Potter and Elizabeth, ending with one of those potpourris that Prevost calls the worst of all bad plays: committee plays.

Davies has called Rogers a hero with a flaw and identified the flaw as his attempt to express his ideas in a play.[9] In *Pontiac and the Green Man* this is suggested when Rogers replies to his wife's anticipation that "you shall soon be free, Robert, and without a stain on your characters" with "perhaps our joint failure to write a play may be considered a stain." Certainly Rogers's effort at dramatic portrayal of his central concerns was a large part of what attracted Davies to him; he sympathized with the misunderstood playwright in Rogers. Yet Davies insists that in the play he was not just "whining about misunderstood playwrights"; he was interested in "misunderstood people — a much more common occurrence."[10] Davies's play does not in fact show Rogers brought down by his playwriting, but by the civilized world's inability to make room for one who does not march with the band. Rogers's own inability to make allowances for the views of the world is simply the dark side of the quality that is his greatest strength: his originality. Near the conclusion of the play, Rogers's talent for alienating those who might have been kindly disposed towards him is shown in his parting from Jones and also in his parting from his wife. When he declares his intention to return to the forest even though she will not accompany him, she wonders what he will do for "scenes of tenderness" and is disgusted by his callous reply: "Ah, Lizzie, you forget that I am a soldier. I shall live off the land."

That Rogers was unable finally to triumph over his opposition, "the world of the well-drilled military band," is an historical fact that the play does not state directly, but Davies implies his hero's downfall in a number of ways. The first comes in the pragmatical afterthought that follows Prevost's insistence that "no man who dreams as Major Rogers dreams is to be dealt with as a traitor or a felon," — "though it is a fact that dreamers often end their days in chains." The hints get stronger towards the end of the play, beginning with Rogers's account of the king's response to his hopes for the New World: "Major Rogers, you talk like an honest man, and I believe what you say. But where will you find men to heed you, eh? Still — a man must obey the promptings of his innermost heart. Go back to America, and I shall see that you are sent far west, and set in a command; do what you can with what you find, but I think, Major — and he spoke very solemnly here — I think that you will break your heart." Another indication of Rogers's ultimate fate is in his identification with Pontiac, whose brave hopes after his rebellion is defeated are shadowed by our recognition that his hopes will not be realized. Rogers weeps at Pontiac's concluding speech and explains, "I have written of the gulf that lies between hope and like[li]hood," and he knows that "the likelihood that follows hope is not [in] our power to control." When the court is ready to proceed to its decision, Rogers echoes a line from Pontiac's last speech: "Has Fate exhausted all her Stores of Wrath,/ Or has she other Vengeance in reserve?" The final lines and final image of the play reinforce our impression that Rogers's hope is not to be fulfilled, that his dream is not to be realized. The Court finds him innocent but has not the authority to free him; its report will be sent up the chain of command, and meanwhile Rogers, who longs to return to the forest, will be "confined to barrack." De Peyster states grimly, "If we cannot curb your mind, Major, we can at least restrain your person." The background has become leafy forest, and in it *"appears the figure of Ponteach, splendid and commanding: very slowly he gestures to Rogers to join him."* "Ponteach I am, and shall be Ponteach still!" Rogers declares, echoing Pontiac's last speech. *"He turns and moves decisively toward the figure of Ponteach, but as he is about to join him the sentries fall in and march him off the stage. The figure of Ponteach lingers for a moment, then fades."* The image effectively conveys the gelding of the hero.

Davies cut from the play lines which referred specifically to hero-gelding, as *Question Time* did, and which linked his historical play explicitly to the present. After Prevost's observation that Rogers is "an original," Davies once intended him to continue, "One might truly say, a hero. But heroes are out of fashion. . ." and to add that "the world is getting on as fast as it can with the task of gelding its heroes. It will take some time — a couple of centuries perhaps — but we shall see it done." Possibly he decided that the concluding image of the restraint which would prevent Rogers from pursuing his dream was strong enough without the words and that the gesture towards the twentieth century was too blatant. But possibly too he was uneasy about too much emphasis on Roger's heroism at the end of the play, because Davies does not show Rogers in heroic action, nor is his comedy an appropriate vehicle for a tragic hero. Davies had long been considering the fate of the hero in the modern world and in modern drama. Contemplating in 1962 some representatives of modern tragedy, he concluded that they were all about "doomed people brought low not by a single fault in a noble creature, but by circumstance working on spirits too feeble to resist." Davies felt certain that "heroism is not dead in our day," though it seemed to have vanished from the theatre. "Degradation, folly, and heroism are not banished from our world, but, in the mirror of that world which is our theatre, we do not want them to appear," he decided.[11] *Pontiac and the Green Man* is not a tragedy; for two-thirds of its length its tone is as light, its laughs as frequent as in any of Davies's comedies. But it becomes increasingly sombre in its final third as the play within the play draws to its conclusion and the gulf between Rogers's hopes and the likelihood of their fulfilment is emphasized. Rogers's spirit is not feeble, but neither the historical truth of his life after the trial nor the parameters of Davies's play encouraged him to portray Rogers in a climactic heroic action, either for comic triumph or tragic defeat. The Davies hero is in any case less a man of action than a man of soul, one who sees what others fail to see and whose integrity of mind and spirit allow him to maintain his vision unviolated.

The nature of Rogers's vision is what links *Pontiac and the Green Man* most clearly to *Question Time*, written two years earlier. Recognition of the connections between his public self, his inner self, and the land is what Peter Macadam possesses at the end of *Question Time*. This understanding Rogers possesses from the beginning; a sense of its importance is what he tries — for the most part unsuccessfully — to share with others. Rogers's reiteration of his report to the king contains phrases that are strongly reminiscent of *Question Time*: The English "are wonderful travellers in the body. . . but they do not take their souls with them. Their souls are forever English, and that is very fine in its way, but a new land has a soul as well — perhaps a very old soul — and those who would find what is best in the new land must find its soul, and humbly embrace that soul." He speaks of "the forests and plains, the rivers and mountains of ice, the great cataracts, so unlike anything in England or France. . . . So rich in meaning

for anyone who tries, even a little, to look and listen with the eyes and ears
of the New World." Davies de-emphasizes Rogers's historical fascination
with the potential wealth of the New World. His desire to find a Northwest
Passage to open a trade route to the Orient is not mentioned in *Pontiac and
the Green Man*. Davies's hero is less interested in material wealth than in
spiritual wealth: the new land is greater than the old, Rogers claims, "not
because of its richness — though it is rich as the Old World never was — but
because what hides here, to be discovered is a new spirit. . . . a spirit of
wisdom to infuse the life of man." Though Pontiac is a real, historical
figure, he becomes a symbol of the spirit of the land, of the vitality of the
natural world. In this he is equivalent to the purely symbolic figure of La
Sorcière in *Question Time*; he is identified with both Rogers and the land as
La Sorcière is identified with both Macadam's inner self and the land.
Rogers, with his ability to combine the best of the Old World and the New,
and his marked preference for the New, is comparable to the Shaman of
Question Time who learned the ways of civilization with his medical
training in Edinburgh but values more highly the primitive wisdom of the
Arctic. The techniques Davies uses in *Pontiac and the Green Man* are
vastly different from the Jungian fantasy of *Question Time*, but the thematic emphasis on the need to be attuned to both one's inner self and one's
natural surroundings is the same.

   Because the circumstances of *Pontiac and the Green Man*'s first production differed greatly from *Question Time*'s and because *Pontiac* has not
been published, it is not possible to make a valid comparison of critical
response to Davies's two plays of the seventies. *Pontiac*, staged in the
University of Toronto's MacMillan Theatre, was no more than a semi-
professional production, despite the presence in the cast of half a dozen
members of Actors' Equity, including David Gardner, who was working on
a Ph.D. at the University of Toronto, Rod Beattie, who had played Gloster
Ridley in Hunter's 1973 Hart House production of *Leaven of Malice*, and
Rex Southgate, who played Professor Vambrace in the same production.
Something of a family affair, the production featured Brenda Davies as Mrs.
Egerton and Hunter's wife Judith as Elizabeth Rogers, as well as giving old
friends Ronald Bryden and Laurier La Pierre a chance to act. The *Toronto
Sun* and *The Globe and Mail* both reviewed the production, but except for
praising Gardner and condemning amateurish performances by a number
of others, the two reviewers agreed on nothing. Bryan Johnson thought the
play was "rarely funny," a "muddle" that he concluded "Davies didn't
mean. . . to be taken seriously — but simply as a throw-away for the
amusement of his fellow academics."[12] Mackenzie Porter, however, found
the play "amusing, affecting and enthralling. . . a play full of Shavian
paradox, with wit, profundity and grief, a play evoking sudden gusts of

laughter, sudden chills of pity, a play rich in cutting satire. . . ." Maybe Johnson left early; Porter, who acknowledges "a few flat, superfluous passages in Act I," reports that "toward the end of Act I the audience becomes spellbound and remains so right through to the compelling climactic oration by Rogers in Act II and the beautifully staged final fadeout."[13]

Gina Mallet published a criticism of Hart House's sesquicentennial season in the *Toronto Star* after Pontiac's run was over that echoed Johnson's assessment of the play. Oddly, she saw in it "a chuckling, self-congratulatory commentary on colonist and colonialism that turns into a sort of pat-on-the-back for British imperialism" and complained that "the Indians are reduced to savages," and she concluded in Johnson's vein that maybe the play "was intended just for old grads."[14] This must have further exasperated Davies, who had registered a protest against Johnson's review. "There is a belief that authors and actors should not reply to criticism, though I have never discovered where this belief originated. Perhaps the critics thought of it," he muses in print. He was obviously taken aback by Johnson's conclusion that the play was meant as a simple-minded academic lark, and his comments point up ways in which *Pontiac*, though it contains no obvious references to the present, is nonetheless a play of the present: "Some of the circumstances that marked [Rogers'] trial — rigidity of mind, a refusal to examine long-standing grievances, and a lack of appreciation of realities that were plainly to be seen — have their counterparts in Canada today," he observed.[15] Certainly the close relationship between concerns of *Pontiac* and those of the very topical *Question Time*, as well as Pontiac's exploration of the relationship between the product of a writer's pen and the writer himself are indications that the subjects Davies treated in an eighteenth-century setting have enduring importance.

Davies, who was initially pleased at the prospect of co-operating to produce a musical entertainment, was disappointed in what he felt turned out to be a lack of co-operation: "The musical end of the production was not well integrated into the whole," he thought, and the play was "locked in" too early by the completed musical score.[16] *Pontiac* is very entertaining and not short of ideas worth pondering, but it is not among Davies's best plays, and he is himself less enthusiastic about it than about some of his others.[17] The conception suggested to Davies at the outset of including much of Rogers's play in a play about Rogers made for inevitable clumsiness. Inventive as always, he found ways of making the play within the play both entertaining and significant in relation to his own play. Yet his very success at finding a variety of devices that worked to integrate the performance of *Ponteach* into Rogers's trial worked against the possibility of creating a play that treats a particular focus of interest with much depth.

The discussion of drama in terms of the relationship between Rogers's plight and the content of his play works well, but all the attention to the acting troupe and their performance of the play seems to be massive diversion from the focus on Rogers's discovery of new values in the New World and his struggle against Old World prejudices. Hunter — and presumably Davies — found a connection in the idea that the acting troupe from the Old World that comes to bring ''art'' to Canada is doing it a disservice as much as the soldiers who come with their closed Old World minds.[18] However, this is not apparent in the play because of the circumstances of the troupe's production. Handed a script only the night before their performance, instructed to perform only selected scenes, interrupted and criticized in process, they could hardly be expected to produce great art. Their comical shortcomings seem amply accounted for by factors that have nothing to do with the Old World's failure to see with New World eyes.

Though an enthusiastic Porter thought that *Pontiac* might be a popular success in London and New York, it has not been staged again. Like *Question Time*, it requires a large cast, and though its setting is simple, a large number of people in period costume necessitates a large-budget production. Neither of Davies's plays of the seventies was written with economy in mind, and very few large-cast plays are widely produced.[19] *Pontiac*, less mystifying than *Question Time*, may have more popular appeal, yet *Question Time* is the greater play. Neither, however, has the economy (in either style or production costs) of Davies's plays of the fifties. Davies in his later years seems less willing to allow the fertility of his imagination to be bound by the practicalities of theatre economics and apparently resigned to achieving renown solely in the less restrictive form of the novel.

13

Conclusions

DAVIES thinks of his plays in terms of the stage rather than the page, and from the beginning he wrote his plays with production possibilities in mind. At first he wrote for London professional theatre; his experience at the Old Vic and his contacts with people there suggested plays designed to display the talents of a Gielgud or a Thorndike. They were romantic comedies in which the fullness of life in the central character is contrasted and brought into conflict with the sterility of others' narrow lives. This was to remain his central theme, though aspects of fullness and sterility vary, as do the settings, the relationships among characters, the nature of the conflicts, and the forms of the plays. Davies looked next to Canada's little theatres for productions, which resulted in ensemble plays that were easily staged, plays which focused specifically on Canadian life, though the themes that are expressed in terms of Canadian character are universal in implication. After 1948, all the plays were written with specific productions in mind: Davies wrote for the Peterborough Summer Theatre, for the Crest Theatre, for Upper Canada College, for the New York Theatre Guild, for CBC's drama hour, for the St. Lawrence Centre, for the University of Toronto. Rejection of a play, in the case of *General Confession*, or negative responses to performances of plays had obvious implications for further production possibilities, so criticism, as well as specific production requirements, had an impact on Davies's playwriting.

These factors had both good and bad effects. Writing to a set of specifications for production often fostered Davies's dramatic inventiveness. Fixing some of the dramatic parameters allowed him to work out the rest with more confidence, putting emphasis from the outset on what were

likely to be the strengths of a production. But sometimes such specifications worked against the creation of the best possible play, as when
Guthrie's extravaganza concept of *Leaven of Malice* resulted in a loss of
coherence or when the necessity to integrate large segments of *Ponteach*
entertainingly into *Pontiac and the Green Man* weakened the thematic
focus on Rogers's conflict with the Old World patterns of thought. Effects
of *General Confession*'s rejection — not only by the Crest, but by other
producers over the years — are difficult to assess, but there have been no
more plays without Canadian settings or without a good deal of business
that holds audience attention for the moment but sometimes detracts from a
sense of unified development of a central conflict. Davies seemed to feel
that he needed more action, more visual interest, more of a kaleidoscopic
effect for dramatic interest. The result was to diminish the impact of one of
his greatest strengths: the thoughtful, warm, and humorous revelation of
character. Even *Question Time*, which in fact never strays from its development of Macadam's inner struggle, seems to do so because of the
profusion of characters and centres of activity whose direct association
with Macadam's inner conflict can be forgotten. The central figure may be
eclipsed rather than revealed by the swirl of dramatic activity around him.

Though Davies wrote his plays with an eye to the views of people who
were in a position to produce them, his own standards for his plays
remained foremost in importance. Popular taste did not affect the basic
components of his playwriting. Nor did the success of a play such as
Overlaid or *Fortune, My Foe* mean that later plays were written on the
same lines. If anything, the success of one play freed Davies to exercise his
creative imagination along new lines with more assurance. Davies's best
plays are those which he wrote with most confidence in his ability to
entertain and illuminate his audience in his own way, with the least rancour
about his past "failures" or anxiety about finding a place for his plays in the
theatre. Thus, *Aesop* is a better play than *Punch*, which is burdened by
Davies's discouragement with the apparent lack of a place for his comedy in
contemporary theatre. *At My Heart's Core* improves on *Fortune, My Foe*
by displacing Davies's feeling of being among the oppressed minority who
value things of the mind in a materialistic society into another era when he
could sympathize with all of his characters instead of dividing them into
struggling victims and disagreeable oppressors. Apart from *Overlaid*, his
best plays, *At My Heart's Core*, *A Masque of Aesop*, *Hunting Stuart*, and
General Confession, were all written in the fifties when he was most
confident that he had made a place for himself in the world of theatre and
could freely offer his own best blend of entertainment and thoughtful
exploration of what is best in humanity.

General criticisms of Davies's style of playwriting and even his own ideas about why he may be considered "old-fashioned" are curiously at odds. There is the school that finds him too "talky." As in Shaw's plays, the dialogue carries the weight of the play, in contrast with a script by Pinter or Beckett in which stage directions are as prominent as dialogue and much of the play's point is read "between the lines." Some of those who object to the "talkiness" of Davies's plays simply prefer the more fashionable style of understatement; others are criticizing the plays as "idea plays," a label from which Davies recoils. In opposition to the school which finds Davies's plays too intellectual are those who find them too simplistic or too prone to "irrelevant" jokes and strokes of "unrealistic" theatrical effect. Simplified characters and conflicts and bold effects, of course, grow out of Davies's conviction that melodrama, designed to produce "emotion, the hottest and most violent that could be evoked,"[1] provided the kind of nourishment for the inner life that he values.

Are Davies's plays too intellectual or do they oversimplify? Do they depend too much on just plain talk or do they go in too much for theatrical effects? Certainly, individual tastes vary, which accounts for some conflict of opinion, and the fact is that Davies's plays encompass all these qualities. His characters' talk expresses both feelings and ideas, not one to the exclusion of the other. Melodramatic effects need not rule out more subtle and complex exploration of character and theme; Davies is a lifelong devotee of "that supreme melodramatist, Shakespeare."[2] Davies's plays do not appeal to those who have a more limited concept of theatre than his "total theatre" embraces. Davies enthusiasts are those who rejoice in his celebration of human totality. His conviction that the theatre of "discontent and underdoggery"[3] is not enough to feed the human spirit is surely justified. The positive, life-embracing quality of Davies's drama cannot be dismissed as old-fashioned; it is needed in all ages, most of all when it seems to be out of fashion. In addition, he writes for the whole human being, for both the mind and the heart. He often insists that his plays are strictly for entertainment, in part perhaps to persuade his public that he is not writing "idea plays," but as one admirer points out, when Davies says his play is "strictly for fun, for entertainment...it must be *his* idea of fun and entertainment. There is bound to be something more to it just because of the quality of mind which produces the fun."[4] Stimulating ideas *are* entertainment for those whose minds are a significant portion of their being; thought is one part of human totality. Emotion is another part, so the complete play for the complete person will offer both melodrama and ideas. Davies's view of human reality encompasses too what is usually called fantasy, as well as "ordinary" reality, so Gogmagog in *King Phoenix*, the spirits Casanova raises in *General Confession*, and the phantasms of

Question Time have a place in the plays along with more realistic characters. Magic is a metaphor for the mysterious, that part of our world which is
not understood by the intellect but is nonetheless true and meaningful.
Davies's fantasy may be nonsense to those whose conception of reality is
limited; his "low" comedy may not suit the intellectuals; his ideas may
bore those who just want some good laughs. His plays are for those who
want as much as possible of the whole range of theatre and the whole
experience of life in one package.

Though Davies seems to feel that his taste for melodrama makes him
old-fashioned, there is good reason to argue that his approach to melodrama
puts him ahead of the times rather than behind. His view of melodrama is
Jungian: the heroine "is not an autonomous human being; she is very
plainly a psychological appendage of the hero ... the External Image of His
Soul." "The Villain is also a portion of the Hero's composition — a
rejected and despised portion, a portion which is recognized in consciousness only on the rarest occasions, but a psychological fact none the less."[5]
Some of the characters in Davies's plays may be simplified portions of
humanity, but the whole picture of human reality presented in such a play is
not simple at all. Davies may simplify characterization by separating
Casanova or Macadam into component parts, but the inner world of man
that he portrays by so doing has considerable depth. If an ending seems to
oversimplify by implying that, for instance, Macadam can sail through life
with never a worry because he has embraced his anima, the oversimplification is in the mind of the beholder. The endings offer new hope for greater
joy and fulfilment but not a guaranteed solution to all of life's problems.

Davies is among those who are pushing back the frontiers of accepted
human truth, making "the heroic voyage of our times...the voyage into
man's spirit."[6] His cheerful outlook on life is the optimism of a man who
sees beyond the frontier not the terrors of the unknown but the promise of
unlimited human potential. In all his plays, from beginning to end, Davies
has combatted the waste of limited lives and championed the joys of the full
life for both the individual and society. The pain his characters experience
is the pain of limitations on their ability to live life fully; the joys are the joys
of self-realization, of embracing something in themselves or their world
that has formerly been distasteful or alien to them. Characters may not find
happiness, but they find the possibility of fulfilment. King Cole dies, but in
his acceptance of death as part of life he is fulfilled. Nicholas does not
marry Vanessa and begin a new life, but he finds the possibility for fulfilment in joining the battle against cultural poverty in mid-century Canada.
Casanova has little more time than King Cole in which to enjoy his new-
found sense of completion, but his whole life is transformed in retro-
spect by his acceptance of what he had formerly denied. The self-

discoveries of Ben Stuart and Peter Macadam do not define their future in terms of the usual happy ending. There is no sense of finality, but rather a greater potential — a wider world is before them; the frontiers of consciousness have been opened up.

Davies's use of magic and his conception of "real theatre" are both related to his image of man as, potentially at least, a fascinating and wonderful creature. However drab and small he may appear, there is a vast reservoir of enrichment and vitality available for him to draw on. Davies has always set himself the task of breaking down barriers to completeness, fostering the idea of wholeness. Perhaps the greatest change in Davies's treatment of this central theme over his career is in his perception of the nature of the reservoir of riches that fosters wholeness. The nature of the chief barriers to wholeness remains the same: Puritan morality, which labels some parts of human totality as undesirable, and materialism, which values the physical side of life at the expense of the spiritual side. In the early plays, the way to enrichment is culture, in particular, the arts; in general, any variety of experience that feeds the spirit instead of starving it in deference to morality and materialism. This enrichment comes largely from outside the individual, and contact with it can be cut off in the wrong set of conditions. Canadians needed Molière, opera, Don Quixote, Punch, Joey Grimaldi; lack of access to such enrichment or refusal to avail oneself of it because one "should" be doing "productive" things causes spiritual poverty in the early plays.

In his forties, assisted by Jung, Davies found another source of spiritual enrichment that is available to anyone who takes the trouble to reach it: the inner self. Developing parts of ourselves at the expense of other parts is the natural process of growth; renewing and strengthening the neglected parts, letting the conscious mind commune with the unconscious, is the natural way to self-enrichment for the mature person. This is done best in primitive societies that are close to nature, not in cultivated societies where lives are taken up with external activity. In the earliest one-act, *Hope Deferred*, the native Indian girl, Chimène, must leave Canada and live in France to find a fulfilling life in the theatre. In the latest play, *Pontiac and the Green Man*, the Indian chief Pontiac has a source of power in his unity with the natural world that is unknown to Europeans. Similarly, in *Question Time*, the Eskimo Shaman holds the key to fulfilment, which he finds in the primitive Eskimo way of life, not in the sophisticated culture of Edinburgh. Now Canada, the land with vast expanses of natural wilderness and a relatively underdeveloped culture is for Davies a centre of untapped potential, a place where spiritual wealth is more readily available than in the cultural centres he once felt must be the source of life's greatest riches.

Though most of his plays are set in Canada, to the more zealous Canadian nationalists Davies has often seemed not quite Canadian enough, from his earliest writing, when his cultured voice had in it something of Oxford and the Old Vic, to his latest, when the heroes of his Deptford trilogy find their souls in foreign settings. To those for whom current trends are all-important, he seems not quite modern enough; more than half of the plays have historical settings, and even the contemporary ones lack the style of understatement and the mood of disenchantment that characterizes much modern drama. But Davies, who has always assaulted barriers to wholeness, has never found the boundaries between present and past, or between Canada and the rest of the world, as important as the connections between them. The essence of humanity is universal; what is defined by temporal and national boundaries is trivial by comparison. Though all his novels are contemporary, in his playwriting he has a habit of gaining complete perspective on a theme by writing a pair of plays, one historical and one contemporary, on the same theme. *Hope Deferred* and *Overlaid* both show the forces of morality and materialism "overlaying" the characters who yearn towards food for the spirit. *King Phoenix* and *A Jig for the Gypsy* might be considered such a pair, though *A Jig for the Gypsy* is only relatively contemporary; King Phoenix and Benoni, with their openness to the whole of life, are pitted against the narrow and joyless views embodied in Cadno and the politicians. *Fortune, My Foe* and *At My Heart's Core* both treat the individual's own struggle to reconcile his desire for things of the mind and spirit with his need to make a home in Canada, where such things are undervalued. *Hunting Stuart* and *General Confession* both treat the individual's discovery within himself of ingredients of his character he had never recognized. *Question Time* and *Pontiac and the Green Man* both show the need for people to attune themselves to the voices of the natural world within and around them. Davies's basic themes trace his own inner growth, but they apply to people of all times, not just to those of modern Canada. Even in the contemporary plays, Davies insists on the importance of our connections with the past and with other nations: Nicholas gains strength and hope from Szabo's puppetry, a centuries-old European art; Ben Stuart finds Bonnie Prince Charlie within himself; in *Question Time* the Herald, who represents Canadian heritage, is given more credence than the Beaver, modern Canada's unfortunate choice of a totem animal.

At mid-century, when Davies was beginning to write, Canada was accustomed to losing her artists to other countries. In 1947 a writer for *Saturday Night*, praising Davies's work as an editor, predicted that his real future might be as a playwright and concluded his article with the fear that Davies might choose to live in Wales, where he said he felt most at home.

The writer, Graham McInnes, expressed regret at the thought, but regret was overridden by the conviction that "Davies should develop his skill as a writer in whatever place is most congenial: for his work overrides nationalist standards, and whatever he does will reflect credit upon Canada."[7] McInnes's fears proved unfounded, but his prophecy about Davies's future work was astute. Davies's work does reach beyond the limitations of national standards, but his commitment to Canada has increased: he stayed, like Nicholas in *Fortune, My Foe*, and he no longer feels drawn to live elsewhere. His plays, written in the decades during which Canadian drama grew to maturity, give dramatic expression to a wise and witty man's search, through history and his contemporary world, through nature and art, through mind and spirit, for himself.

NOTES

NOTES TO CHAPTER ONE: A PASSION FOR THE THEATRE

1. Robertson Davies, *Samuel March-banks' Almanack* (Toronto: McClelland and Stewart 1967), pp. 70-71. First published in *Peterborough Examiner* (4 March 1950).

2. Robertson Davies, *The Table Talk of Samuel Marchbanks* (Toronto: Clarke, Irwin 1949), p. 153.

3. *Tempest-Tost* was begun in summer 1949. (Davies to Stone-Blackburn [June 1979], n.d.) Davies's *Fortune, My Foe* was performed in the Dominion Drama Festival in May 1949.

4. Tyrone Guthrie, Introduction, *Eros at Breakfast and Other Plays* (Toronto: Clarke, Irwin 1949), p. ix.

5. Except where noted otherwise, the biographical information in this chapter is drawn from Samuel Marchbanks, [Robertson Davies], "The Double Life of Robertson Davies," *Liberty*, April 1954, pp. 18-19, 53-58. Gordon Roper, "A Davies Log," *Journal of Canadian Studies* 12:1 (February 1977), pp. 4-19; "The Myth and the Master," *Time* (Canada) 106:18 (3 November 1975), pp. 8-12; and Davies to Stone-Blackburn, 16 August 1977.

6. Robertson Davies, "Shakespeare over the Port," *The Enthusiasms of Robertson Davies*, ed. Judith Skelton Grant (Toronto: McClelland and Stewart 1979), pp 260-61.

7. Davies to Stone-Blackburn, 14 October 1982.

8. Davies, "Shakespeare over the Port," 261.

9. Robertson Davies, "Fifty Years of Theatre in Canada," *University of Toronto Quarterly* 50:1 (Fall 1980), pp. 70-71.

10. Davies, "Shakespeare over the Port," p. 262.

11. Davies to Stone-Blackburn, 6 April 1981.

12. Davies to Stone-Blackburn, 17 February 1981 and 4 March 1981. This play was not an early draft of *A Jig for the Gypsy*. It was never produced, and apparently no script survives.

13. Robertson Davies, *Shakespeare's Boy Actors* (London: Dent 1939).

14. Davies to Stone-Blackburn, 6 April 1981.

15. Elspeth Buitenhuis [Cameron], *Robertson Davies* (Toronto: Forum House 1972), p. 10.

16. Guthrie, Introduction, *Eros at Breakfast*, p. x.

17. James Forsyth, *Tyrone Guthrie* (London: Hamish Hamilton 1976), p. 196.

18. Martin Knelman, "The Masterful Actor Who Plays Robertson Davies," *Saturday Night* 90:2 (June 1975), p. 34.

19. Robertson Davies quoted by Renee Hetherington and Gabriel Kampf, "*Acta* Interviews Robertson Davies," *Acta Victoriana* 97:2 (April 1973), p. 72.
20. An examination of letters written by Davies in the forties shows that *The King Who Could Not Dream* was completed by the summer of 1944 and that *Benoni* was underway by the

fall of 1944, completed by February 1945. Judith Skelton Grant to Stone-Blackburn, 16 April 1984.
21. Graham McInnes, "An Editor from Skunk's Misery Is Winning Fame for Peterboro," *Saturday Night* (26 April 1947), p. 15.
22. Judith Roberts-Moore, Archivist, Public Archives of Canada, to Stone-Blackburn, 10 April 1981.

NOTES TO CHAPTER TWO: THE ONE-ACT PLAYS

1. In conversation with Judith Skelton Grant, Davies decided that *The King Who Could Not Dream* was written first, and sent to Gielgud some time before the end of 1945. (Grant to Stone-Blackburn, 6 June 1983).
2. Gordon Roper, "A Davies Log," *Journal of Canadian Studies* 12:1 (February 1977), p. 5.
3. Betty Lee, *Love and Whisky* (Toronto: McClelland and Stewart 1973), p. 292.
4. Davies to Stone-Blackburn, 6 April 1981.
5. An examination of letters written by Davies in the forties shows that *Hope Deferred*, like *Benoni*, was underway in the fall of 1944 and completed by February 1945. (Judith Skelton Grant to Stone-Blackburn, 16 April 1984.)
6. William D. LeSueur, *Count Frontenac* (Toronto: Morang 1910), pp. 336-37. This is certainly Davies's source, since his play includes whole phrases identical to LeSueur's, and *Hope Deferred* contains every particular of LeSueur's account except the claim that Frontenac never really intended to produce *Tartuffe*.
7. Gustave Lanctot, *A History of Canada*, transl. M. M. Cameron (Cambridge, Mass.: Harvard University Press 1964), p. 60.
8. LeSueur, *Count Frontenac*, p. 360.
9. *Eros at Breakfast and Other Plays* (Toronto: Clarke, Irwin 1949), p. 60. All quotations from the five one-act plays are from this text.
10. Robertson Davies, "Introduction to

Hope Deferred," Canada's Lost Plays, III, ed. Anton Wagner (Toronto: CTR Publications 1980), p. 176.
11. Guthrie, Introduction, *Eros at Breakfast*, p. xiv.
12. Davies, "Introduction to *Hope Deferred*," p. 176.
13. Guthrie, Introduction, *Eros at Breakfast*, p. xii.
14. Michael Tait, "Drama and Theatre," *The Literary History of Canada*, 2nd ed., ed. Carl F. Klinck (Toronto: University of Toronto Press 1976), Vol. 2, p. 152.
15. Robertson Davies, Epilogue, *At My Heart's Core & Overlaid* (Toronto: Clarke, Irwin 1966), p. 115.
16. *Ibid.*
17. Robertson Davies, "Robertson Davies," *Stage Voices*, ed. Geraldine Anthony (Toronto: Doubleday 1978), p. 66.
18. Davies, *The Table Talk of Samuel Marchbanks* (Toronto: Clarke, Irwin 1949), p. 242.
19. Emily Herbert, "A 'Capital' Story: The Workshop of the Ottawa Drama League," *CUE* 18:4 (February 1948), p. 10.
20. Davies to Stone-Blackburn, 17 February 1981.
21. *Ibid.*
22. Public Archives of Canada, Charles Rittenhouse, Ottawa Little Theatre Papers, M.G 28 I 30.
23. Lee, *Love and Whisky*, p. 293; Roper, "A Davies Log," p. 6.
24. Davies to Stone-Blackburn, February 1976.
25. Robertson Davies, Preface, *Four*

Favourite Plays (Toronto: Clarke, Irwin 1949), p. v.
26. *Ibid.*
27. Guthrie, Introduction, *Eros at Breakfast*, p. xiv.
28. An examination of letters written by Davies in the forties establishes that *At the Gates of the Righteous* was completed in May or June 1948 and *The Voice of the People* in June 1948. (Judith Skelton Grant to Stone-Blackburn, 16 April 1984.)
29. Davies, Preface, *Four Favourite Plays*, p. vi.
30. *Ibid.*
31. Robertson Davies, *Leaven of Malice* (Toronto: Clarke, Irwin 1954), p. 9.
32. Robertson Davies, *The Diary of Samuel Marchbanks* (Toronto: Clarke, Irwin 1947), p. 130.
33. Edward Mullaly, "Robertson Davies's 'Other' Plays," *Fiddlehead* 97 (Spring 1973), pp. 111-12; Geoffrey James, "Native Shaw,"

Time (Canada) 105:10 (10 March 1975), pp. 10-11; Herbert Whittaker, "*Question Time* Complex and Glittering," *Globe and Mail* (26 February 1975), p. 14; James Noonan, "Review of *Hunting Stuart and Other Plays,*" *Queen's Quarterly* 80 (Autumn 1973), p. 466.
34. Davies, "Robertson Davies," *Stage Voices*, p. 63.
35. Davies to Stone-Blackburn, February 1976.
36. Davies, Preface, *Four Favourite Plays*, p. vi.
37. Davies to Stone-Blackburn, February 1976.
38. Guthrie, Introduction, *Eros at Breakfast*, p. xiv.
39. Davies to Stone-Blackburn, February 1976.
40. Robertson Davies quoted by Donald Cameron in *Conversations with Canadian Novelists* (Toronto: Macmillan 1973), I, p. 42.

NOTES TO CHAPTER THREE:
THEATRE OF WHOLENESS AND CANADIAN LITTLE THEATRE

1. Davies, "Robertson Davies," *Stage Voices*, ed. Geraldine Anthony (Toronto: Doubleday 1978), p. 79.
2. *Ibid.*
3. Davies, "The Double Life of Robertson Davies," *Liberty*, (April 1954), p. 56.
4. Robertson Davies, *A Voice from the Attic* (New York: Alfred A. Knopf 1960), p. 158.
5. Davies to Stone-Blackburn, 16 August 1977.
6. Robertson Davies, *At My Heart's Core* (Toronto: Clarke, Irwin 1950), p. v.
7. Robertson Davies, "A Dialogue on the State of Theatre in Canada," *Canadian Theatre Review* 5 (Winter 1975), pp. 18-19.
8. Robertson Davies, *One Half of Robertson Davies* (Toronto: Macmillan 1977), p. 80.
9. Robertson Davies, "Through Ritual to Romance," *Saturday Night* 68:43 (1 August 1953), p. 8.
10. Robertson Davies, "Jung and the

Theatre" and "The Devil's Burning Throne," *One Half of Robertson Davies*, pp. 143-60, 179-200.
11. Davies to Stone-Blackburn, February 1976.
12. Davies, "A Dialogue on the State of Theatre in Canada," p. 25.
13. Davies, *At My Heart's Core*, p. vii.
14. Davies, "Robertson Davies," *Stage Voices*, p. 79.
15. Davies, *A Voice from the Attic*, p. 167.
16. Davies, *A Voice from the Attic*, p. 176.
17. Davies, *One Half of Robertson Davies*, p. 145.
18. Davies to Stone-Blackburn, February 1976.
19. I except *Three Gypsies* (1937) about which I know only that it was a modern comedy set in a Welsh country house about a love affair, and that the title comes from the song, "There Were Three Gypsies Came to My Door..." (Davies to Stone-Blackburn, 17 February 1981

and 3 March 1981). It was written before Davies began to work with Guthrie, who no doubt influenced his ideas about Real Theatre.

20. Davies, *One Half of Robertson Davies*, p. 146.

21. *Ibid.*, p. 131.

22. Davies to Stone-Blackburn, [June 1979] n.d. Michael Peterman provides a more detailed description of the play, taken from notes by Gordon Roper, in "Bewitchments of Simplification," *Canadian Drama* 7:2 (1981), pp. 103-4.

23. Davies to Stone-Blackburn, [June 1979], n.d.

24. Robertson Davies, *Hunting Stuart & Other Plays* (Toronto: New Press 1972), p. 105. All quotations from the play are from this text. Davies's note also says that he wrote *King Phoenix* in 1948, but an examination of letters he wrote in the forties shows that it was completed by February 1947. (Judith Skelton Grant to Stone-Blackburn, 16 April 1984.)

25. Geoffrey of Monmouth, *The History of the Kings of Britain*, transl. Lewis Thorpe (Baltimore, Md.: Penguin 1966), pp. 131-32.

26. Davies, *One Half of Robertson Davies*, p. 256.

27. Patricia Morley, *Robertson Davies* (Toronto: Gage 1977), p. 31.

28. Lug's observation, "He died as all men do; for a score of reasons" (192), is a thought that Davies explores in novels later, in connection with Revelstoke's death in *A Mixture of Frailties* and Staunton's in the Deptford Trilogy, as Frederick Radford notes in "Padre Blazon or Old King Cole — Robertson Davies: Novelist or Playwright?" *Canadian Drama* 7:2 (1981), p. 22.

29. Davies to Stone-Blackburn, 1 June 1977.

30. Davies, "A Dialogue on the State of Theatre in Canada," p. 33.

31. Dora Mavor Moore's New Play Society performed a number of Canadian plays between 1947 and 1950; among them were Lister Sinclair's *The Man in the Blue Moon*, Morley Callaghan's *To Tell the Truth* and *Going Home*, and John Coulter's *Riel* (Bill Tepper, "The New Play Society," *Canadian Theatre Review* 28 (Fall 1980): 18-33), but after some earlier acrimony between them, Davies did not see her group as a likely bet for production of his plays: "The New Play Society never showed any interest in my work except on one occasion when they asked me for a script of a one-act play in 1945 .... They decided not to do it because the end of the war made some alteration in their plans and I had the uttermost difficulty in recovering my manuscript from them and finally had to write Mrs. Moore a letter which she described, in her reply, as 'distasteful.' However, as it was fourteen months since I had sent it to them, and as nothing short of a distasteful letter would stir Dora, I have no regrets in this matter. They always seemed to me to be a Toronto group, interested in drama which they thought of as innovative" (Davies to Stone-Blackburn, 14 October 1982).

32. Davies, "A Dialogue on the State of Theatre in Canada," p. 23.

33. *Ibid.*

34. Davies to Earle Birney, 14 July 1948 (Thomas Fisher Collection, University of Toronto, Robarts Library).

35. Sydney Johnson, "Canadiana at MRT Studio," *Montreal Daily Star* (22 March 1948), p. 30.

36. Davies still recalls with horror one production of *Fortune, My Foe* for which the play had been substantially rewritten. "A character appeared on stage I didn't even recognize. It was painful to be judged on an end result which was not what I had intended" (Davies to Stone-Blackburn, 16 August 1977).

37. Davies, "A Dialogue on the State of Theatre in Canada," p. 24.

38. Davies, "The Double Life of Robertson Davies," p. 399.

39. Robertson Davies, "Directors for Canadian Theatres," *Robertson Davies, the Well-Tempered Critic*, ed. Judith Skelton Grant (Toronto:

McClelland and Stewart 1981), p.
37.
40. Robertson Davies, *Tempest-Tost*
(Toronto: Clarke, Irwin 1951), p. 29.
41. Davies, "A Dialogue on the State of
Theatre in Canada," pp. 33-34.
42. Davies, "Through Ritual to
Romance," pp. 7-8.
43. Davies to Stone-Blackburn, 17
February 1981.
44. Herbert Whittaker to Stone-
Blackburn, 15 August 1977.
45. Public Archives of Canada,
Theatre Canada Records, Vol. xix.

46. Betty Lee, *Love and Whisky*
(Toronto: McClelland and Stewart
1973), p. 237.
47. "*King Phoenix* Fascinates Little
Theatre Audience," *Peterborough
Examiner* (9 January 1953), p. 9.
48. "*King Phoenix* Wins Canadian
Drama Award," *Peterborough
Examiner* (19 January 1953), p. 9.
49. Davies to Stone-Blackburn, February
1976.
50. Davies, "Robertson Davies," *Stage
Voices*, p. 75.

NOTES TO CHAPTER FOUR: CULTURAL POVERTY IN MODERN CANADA

1. Davies, "The Double Life of
Robertson Davies," *Liberty* (April
1954), p. 56.
2. Davies to Stone-Blackburn, 17
February 1981.
3. "Invite Ottawa Players to Edinburgh
Festival," *Toronto Daily Star* (29
April 1949), p. 12.
4. Betty Lee, *Love and Whisky*
(Toronto: McClelland and Stewart
1973), p. 293.
5. Robertson Davies, *Four Favourite
Plays* (Toronto: Clarke, Irwin 1949),
p. 75. All quotations from the play are
from this text.
6. Davies to Stone-Blackburn, February
1976.
7. *Ibid.*
8. According to *A Voice from the
Attic*, Davies possesses a copy of
this joke book, *Nugae Venales,
or a Complaisant Companion;
Being New Jests, Domestic and
Foreign, Bulls, Rhodomontadoes,
Pleasant Novels, Lyes and
Improbabilities collected by John
Head* (London 1686). Perhaps he
himself contemplated something
like Nicholas's plan for it and
rejected the idea.
9. Nathan Cohen, "An Uninterrupted
Encounter with Torpidity,"
Toronto Daily Star (4 December
1967), p. 23.
10. Lucy Van Gogh (B. K. Sandwell),
"Foes to Fortune," *Saturday Night*
(13 December 1949), p. 23.

11. Judith Skelton Grant, "The Rich
Texture of Robertson Davies's
Fortune, My Foe," *Canadian
Drama* 7:2 (1981), p. 28.
12. Grant discusses some interesting
resemblances between this play
within a play and the rustics'
performance of "Pyramus and
Thisbe" in *A Midsummer Night's
Dream*, one of Davies's two
favourite Shakespearian comedies,
in "The Rich Texture of Robertson
Davies's *Fortune, My Foe*," pp.
31-32.
13. M.E.N., "Fortunate Foe," *Saturday Night* (13 December 1949), p. 23.
14. One adjudicator found the play
"wordy" and in need of cutting
(Richard Burbage, quoted in
"*Fortune, My Foe* Difficult Play,"
The Kitchener-Waterloo Record
(8 December 1948), p. 19), and B.
K. Sandwell called it "talky to an
almost Shavian degree": Lucy Van
Gogh, "Foes to Fortune," p. 23.
15. Davies, "A Dialogue on the State of
Theatre in Canada," *Canadian
Theatre Review* 5 (Winter 1975), p.
30.
16. A confession made by Davies in
"Robertson Davies," *Stage Voices*,
ed. Geraldine Anthony (Toronto:
Doubleday 1978), p. 69, though I
think there are few laughs in Davies's
plays that are not in keeping with
character and theme.

234   ROBERTSON DAVIES, PLAYWRIGHT

17. Charles Rittenhouse, "Canadian
Drama at Kingston," *CUE* 19:1
(October 1948), p. 15.
18. M.E.N., "Fortunate Foe," p. 23.
19. Margaret Ness, "Two Davies Plays
Score Drama Festival Wins," *Globe
and Mail* (21 February 1949), p.
12.
20. "Invite Ottawa Players to Festivals," p. 12.
21. Public Archives of Canada, Theatre
Canada Records, Vol. xix.
22. Van Gogh [B. K. Sandwell], "Foes
to Fortune," p. 23.

23 *Ibid.*
24. Nathan Cohen, "An Uninterrupted
Encounter with Torpidity," p. 23.
No other Canadian play in English,
perhaps; Gratien Gélinas' *Tit-Coq*
(also 1948) was equally successful.
25. Davies agrees that it must now be
done as a period piece in an
interview with Ann Saddlemyer,
"A Conversation with Robertson
Davies," *Canadian Drama* 7:2
(1981), p. 115.
26. Lucy Van Gogh [B. K. Sandwell],
"Foes to Fortune," p. 23.

NOTES TO CHAPTER FIVE: CULTURAL POVERTY IN COLONIAL CANADA

1. Davies, *At My Heart's Core &
Overlaid* (Toronto: Clarke, Irwin
1966), p. 112. All quotations from
the play and from Davies's epilogue
to it are from this text.
2. Frances Stewart, *Our Forest Home*,
ed. E. S. Dunlop, 2nd ed.
(Montreal: Gazette 1902), p. 125.
3. *Ibid*, p. 185. Another such passage
appears on p. 132.
4. Susanna Moodie, Chapter 5. "Our
First Settlement and the Borrowing
System," *Roughing It in the Bush*
(Toronto: McClelland and Stewart
1962).
5. Patricia Morley, *Robertson Davies*
(Toronto: Gage 1977), p. 23.
6. Davies to Stone-Blackburn, February
1976.
7. Moodie, *Roughing It in the Bush*, p.
213.
8. *Ibid*, p. 210.
9. Cantwell "is certainly a villain,"
Davies says in *Stage Voices*, ed.
Geraldine Anthony (Toronto:
Doubleday 1978), p.78.
10. Neil Carson, in "Canadian Historical Drama: Playwrights in Search of a
Myth," *Studies in Canadian
Literature* 2:2 (Summer 1977), pp.
213-25, is mistaken when he says
that "Mrs. Stewart's regret for having
left the social life of Ireland, Mrs.
Moodie's ambition to be a successful
writer, and Mrs. Traill's desire to
excel as a naturalist are all regarded
as evil," but he is right in discerning
balance as the ideal (219). The desire

to excel is not in itself evil; it
becomes so only if it unbalances the
personality.
11. Elspeth Buitenhuis [Cameron],
Robertson Davies (Toronto: Forum
House 1972), pp. 69-70.
12. Davies, *One Half of Robertson
Davies* (Toronto: Macmillan 1977),
p. 194.
13. This distinction is elaborated in the
contrast between Giles Revelstoke
and Benedict Domdaniel in *A Mixture
of Frailties*.
14. Herbert Whittaker quite rightly
protested the omission of the horn
in a 1974 production of the play in
Peterborough. "*At My Heart's Core*
Survives Well after 25 Years." *Globe
and Mail* (8 July 1974), p. 16.
15. Stewart, *Our Forest Home*, pp. 88,
153-54.
16. Theo and Eileen Dombrowski discuss
the theme of judgments of fellow
men and self-judgment in Davies's
work in "Every Man's Judgement:
Robertson Davies' Courtroom,"
Studies in Canadian Literature 3:1
(Winter 1978), pp. 47-61.
17. Davies, *At My Heart's Core*
(Toronto: Clarke, Irwin 1950), p. 80.
18. Davies to Stone-Blackburn, [June
1979], n.d.
19. Gordon Roper, "A Davies Log,"
Journal of Canadian Studies 12:1
(February 1977), p. 7.
20. Davies, *One Half of Robertson
Davies*, p. 143.

21. Vincent Tovell, review of *At My Heart's Core, University of Toronto Quarterly* 20:3 (April 1951), p. 275.
22. Michael Tait, "Drama and Theatre," *The Literary History of Canada*, ed. Carl F. Klinck (Toronto: University of Toronto Press 1976), vol. 2, p. 153.

23. Davies to Stone-Blackburn, [June 1979], n.d.
24. Comments on the critical response to the play are based on abstracts of reviews in John Ryrie, *Robertson Davies: An Annotated Bibliography* (Toronto: ECW Press 1981), pp. 236-38, 262-64.

NOTES TO CHAPTER SIX: *A MASQUE* FOR U.C.C. AND *A JIG* FOR THE CREST

1. Robertson Davies, *A Masque of Aesop*, annotated ed. (Toronto: Clarke, Irwin 1955), p. v. All quotations from the play and from Davies's introduction and notes are from this text.
2. Review of *A Masque of Aesop, Canadian Library Association Bulletin* 9:4 (January 1953), p. 110.
3. Vincent Tovell, review of *A Masque of Aesop, University of Toronto Quarterly* 22 (April 1953), p. 292.
4. Rota Lister, "Masques for Boy Actors: Aesop and Punch Restored," *Canadian Drama* 7:2 (1981), pp. 63-79, discusses *A Masque of Aesop* as a celebration of the ideals of humane education, ideals to which U.C.C. and Davies himself subscribe.
5. "College Boys Produce a Masque," *Globe and Mail*, final ed. (3 May 1952), p. 8.
6. Herbert Whittaker, "Show Business," *Globe and Mail* (6 December 1954), p. 29.
7. Richard Howard, U.C.C. Headmaster, to Stone-Blackburn, 8 December and 22 December 1981.
8. V.H., "One-Act Play," *Globe and Mail*, final ed. (6 December 1952), p. 10, and H. T. K[irkwood], "A Masque of Aesop," *Canadian Forum* (January 1953), p. 237.
9. *Canadian Library Association Bulletin*, p. 110; Lucy Van Gogh [B. K. Sandwell] "Light Satire," *Saturday Night* (20 December 1952), p. 31; Tovell, review of *A Masque of Aesop*, pp. 292-93.
10. Michael Tait makes this point in his assessment of Davies's plays published before 1960, among which he judged *Aesop* most successful. "Drama and Theatre,"

The Literary History of Canada, ed. Carl F. Klinck, 2nd ed. (Toronto: University of Toronto Press, 1965), vol. 2, p. 153.
11. Davies to Stone-Blackburn, 6 April 1981.
12. *Renown at Stratford, Twice Have the Trumpets Sounded*, and *Thrice the Brinded Cat Hath Mew'd*.
13. Herbert Whittaker, "Premiere of a New Play, *A Jig for the Gypsy*," *Globe and Mail* (11 September 1954), p. 12.
14. Donald Davis to Stone-Blackburn, January 1982.
15. Robertson Davies, *A Jig for the Gypsy* (Toronto: Clarke, Irwin 1954), pp. v-vi. All quotations from the play and from Davies's introduction are taken from this text.
16. Patricia Morley, *Robertson Davies* (Toronto: Gage 1977), p. 1.
17. Mavor Moore, *4 Canadian Playwrights: Robertson Davies: Gratien Gélinas; James Reaney; George Ryga* (Toronto: Holt, Rinehart and Winston 1973), p. 16.
18. Elspeth Buitenhuis [Cameron], *Robertson Davies* (Toronto: Forum House 1972), p. 67.
19. Davies, *A Jig for the Gypsy*, p. vi.
20. Robertson Davies, "Ben Jonson and Alchemy," *Stratford Papers 1968-69*, ed. B. A. W. Jackson (Hamilton: McMaster University Library Press 1973), p. 42.
21. Robertson Davies quoted by Alan Twigg, *For Openers: Conversations with 24 Canadian Writers* (Madeira Park, B.C.: Harbour Publishing 1981), p. 42.
22. Robertson Davies quoted by Donald Cameron, *Conversations with*

Canadian Novelists (Toronto: Macmillan 1973), I, p. 39.

23. Robertson Davies quoted by Renee Hetherington and Gabriel Kampf, "*Acta* Interviews Robertson Davies," *Acta Victoriana* 97:2 (April 1973), p. 78.
24. Robertson Davies, "I'm Not Superstitious (Touch Wood)," *Reader's Digest* (August 1979), p. 36.
25. Davies to Stone-Blackburn, February 1976.
26. Bronwen's involvement in politics was simply part of her youthful, romantic desire to share the enthusiasms of those she admires — first her father and then Vaughan.
27. M. W. Steinberg, "Don Quixote and the Puppets: Theme and Structure in Robertson Davies' Drama," *Canadian Literature* 7 (Winter 1961), p. 52.
28. E. G. Wanger, "The Gypsy in Barbara Shines in Davies' Play," *Globe and Mail*, final ed. (15 September 1954), p. 13.
29. Jack Karr, "Showplace," *Toronto Daily Star* (15 September 1954), p. 19.

30. Steinberg, "Don Quixote and the Puppets," p. 53.
31. Davies, *One Half of Robertson Davies* (Toronto: Macmillan 1977), p. 153.
32. Petermann, "Bewitchments of Simplification," *Canadian Drama* 7:2 (1981), p. 101.
33. Karr, "Showplace," p. 19.
34. Herbert Whittaker to Stone-Blackburn, 15 August 1977.
35. Nathan Cohen, "Theatre Today: English Canada," *Tamarack Review* 13 (1959), p. 13.
36. Donald Davis, "The Davis View," *Canadian Theatre Review* 7 (Summer 1975), p. 39.
37. Davies, "Fifty Years of Theatre in Canada," *University of Toronto Quarterly* 50:1 (Fall 1980), p. 77.
38. Karr, "Showplace," p. 19.
39. Barbara Chilcott to Stone-Blackburn, 8 November 1981.
40. Karr, "Showplace," p. 19; Wanger, "The Gypsy in Barbara Shines in Davies Play," p. 13.
41. *Plays and Players* 1:4 (January 1954), p. 20.

NOTES TO CHAPTER SEVEN:
THE MAGIC OF SELF-DISCOVERY IN *HUNTING STUART*

1. Davies, *A Voice from the Attic* (New York: Alfred A. Knopf 1960), pp. 225-27.
2. "About 1950" is the earliest date Davies has reported for beginning his reading of Jung (Davies to Stone-Blackburn, 6 April 1981), though he may not have begun a serious study of Jung until a few years later: 1954 or 1955, he has told Judith Skelton Grant (Grant to Stone-Blackburn, 6 June 1983).
3. Davies, *One Half of Robertson Davies* (Toronto: Macmillan 1977), p. 143.
4. Patricia Monk discusses this natural affinity of Davies for Jungian thought in the first chapter of *The Smaller Infinity: The Jungian Self in the Novels of Robertson Davies* (Toronto: University of Toronto Press 1982).

5. C. G. Jung, "Archetypes of the Collective Unconscious," *The Collected Works of C. G. Jung*, ed. Sir Herbert Read, Michael Fordham, and Gerhard Adler, Bollingen Series XX, vol 9(i) (Princeton, N.J.: Princeton University Press, 2nd ed. 1968), p. 31, .(65).
6. Deduced from a comparison of *A Jig for the Gypsy* with a typescript of *Benoni* in Davies's possession.
7. Robertson Davies, *Hunting Stuart & Other Plays* (Toronto: New Press 1972), p. 52. All quotations from the play are from this text.
8. Bad Bill Balmer in *At the Gates of the Righteous* is captivated by the same two-bit book on phrenology.
9. Cadno in *King Phoenix* might be considered a scientist, but his magic and his religious role as Archdruid

make him difficult to identify with modern scientists.

10. Davies, "Robertson Davies," *Stage Voices*, ed. Geraldine Anthony (Toronto: Doubleday 1978), pp. 77-78.

11. Donald Cameron, *Conversations with Canadian Novelists* (Toronto: Macmillan 1973), I, pp. 35-36.

12. Davies, "Robertson Davies," *Stage Voices*, p. 69.

13. *Ibid.*

14. Davies quoted in Cameron, *Conversations with Canadian Novelists* (pp. 37-38).

15. Davies to Stone-Blackburn, February 1976.

16. Donald Davis to Stone-Blackburn, January 1982.

17. "Showbusiness: Mr. Davies Replies," *Globe and Mail* (5 December 1955), p. 15.

18. Graham Whitehead, review of *Hunting Stuart and Other Plays*,

Dalhousie Review 53 (Spring 1973), p. 165.

19. Herbert Whittaker, "Showbusiness," *Globe and Mail*, final ed. (23 November 1955), p. 26.

20. Davies, "Robertson Davies," *Stage Voices*, p. 77.

21. Edward Mullaly, "Robertson Davies' 'Other' Plays," *Fiddlehead* (Spring 1973), p. 111; Jamie Portman, "Davies' *Hunting Stuart* a Quaint but Amiable Anachronism," *Calgary Herald* (8 August 1975), p. 37.

22. Portman, "Davies' *Hunting Stuart...*" p. 37.

23. Whittaker, "Showbusiness," (23 November 1955), p. 26.

24. Herbert Whittaker, "Showbusiness: Please, Mr. Davies!" *Globe and Mail* (1 December 1955), p. 10.

25. Whittaker, "Showbusiness" (23 November 1955), p. 26.

26. William New, "Lives of Ghosts and Lovers," *Canadian Literature* 59 (Winter 1974), pp. 105-6.

NOTES TO CHAPTER EIGHT: JUNG AND CASANOVA

1. Robertson Davies, *Hunting Stuart & Other Plays* (Toronto: New Press 1972), p 197. All quotations from *General Confession* are from this text.

2. Davies, *Hunting Stuart & Other Plays*, p. 197.

3. Davies uses the spelling "Charpillion." I have retained Casanova's spelling in references to *The Memoirs* and Davies's in references to *General Confession*.

4. *The Memoirs of Jacques Casanova de Seingalt*, 12 vols., transl. Arthur Machen (Aventuros 1925), X, p. 14. Davies recommends Machen's translation in his Writer's Diary review, "Casanova de Seingalt," *Peterborough Examiner* (12 December 1959), p. 5; rpt., *The Enthusiasms of Robertson Davies*, ed. Judith Skelton Grant (Toronto: McClelland and Stewart 1979), pp. 77-79.

5. Davies to Stone-Blackburn, 16 August 1977.

6. C.G. Jung, *Collected Works* 9(i), p. 27, (52).

7. *Ibid.*, p. 37, (77).

8. *Ibid.*, p. 20, (44).

9. *Ibid.*, p. 37, (80).

10. *Ibid.*, p. 20, (44).

11. *Ibid.*, p. 19, (41).

12. Davies, *One Half of Robertson Davies*, p. 123. Davies is actually talking about people who feel compelled to write throughout their lives, which Casanova did not, though he treats Casanova's urge to write his memoirs as an instance of "writer's conscience."

13. Davies quoted by Ann Saddlemyer, "A Conversation with Robertson Davies," p. 113.

14. Paraphrased in *a Voice from the Attic*, quoted in *The Manticore* and in *One Half of Robertson Davies*.

15. Davies, "Robertson Davies," *Stage Voices*, p. 76.

16. Jung, "The Stages in Life," *The Collected Works*, pp. 387-403.

17. Colin Wilson, *The Occult* (New York: Vintage 1971), p. 285.
18. Wilson, *The Occult*, pp. 289-90.
19. Casanova, *The Memoirs*, VI, p. 186.
20. E. W. Dupee, Introduction, *The Memoirs of Casanova*, transl. Lowell Bair (New York: Bantam 1968), p. xiv.
21. Jung, "The Phenomenology of the Spirit in Fairy Tales," *The Collected Works*, 9(i), p. 222, (406).
22. Jung, "Archetypes of the Collective Unconscious," *The Collected Works*, 9(i), p. 28, (59).
23. Jung, "The Stages of Life," *The Collected Works*, 8, p. 400, (789).
24. Jung, "Phenomenology of the Spirit," *The Collected Works*, 9(i), p. 231, (421).
25. Davies to Stone-Blackburn, February 1976.
26. *Ibid*.
27. My account of the Crest's failure to produce *General Confession* is based on interviews with Barbara Chilcott, 8 November 1981, Donald Davis, January 1982, and Davies, February 1976.
28. Ross Stuart, "The Crest Controversy," *Canadian Theatre Review* 7 (Summer 1975), p. 10.

29. Davies brought the play to the attention of various directors over the years, but none took it up. It was considered by the Stratford Festival in 1982 but rejected (Davies to Stone-Blackburn, 14 July 1982, 14 October 1982).
30. Davies to Stone-Blackburn, February 1976.
31. My comments are partly based on abstracts of four reviews in John Ryrie, *Robertson Davies: An Annotated Bibliography* (Toronto: ECW Press 1981), pp. 242-43.
32. Graham Whitehead, review of *Hunting Stuart & Other Plays*, *Dalhousie Review* 53, (Spring 1973), p. 167.
33. Patricia Morley, *Robertson Davies* (Toronto: Gage 1977), p. 54.
34. Patricia Monk, "Quike Bookis: The Morality Plays of Robertson Davies," *Canadian Drama* 7:2 (1981), p. 89.
35. James Noonan, review of *Hunting Stuart & Other Plays*, *Queen's Quarterly* 80 (Autumn 1973), p. 467.
36. Davies quoted by Ann Saddlemyer, "A Conversation with Robertson Davies," *Canadian Drama* 7:2 (1981), p. 113.

NOTES TO CHAPTER NINE: A NOVEL FOR BROADWAY

1. Davies to Stone-Blackburn, 20 July 1982.
2. Claude T. Bissell, review of *A Mixture of Frailties*, *University of Toronto Quarterly*, 28 (July 1959), pp. 370-1; Mary Dunnett, "Human Foibles and Frailties,' *Globe and Mail* (23 August 1958), p. 9; Arnold Edinborough, "Enriched with Humanity," *Saturday Night* 13 (13 September 1958), pp. 29-31.
3. Robertson Davies, preface to *Question Time* (Toronto: Macmillan 1975), p. vii. An apparent change of mind is reflected in Ann Saddlemyer's "A Conversation with Robertson Davies," *Canadian Drama* 7:2 (1981), p. 111, where Davies, "dancing a jig at the

success of the dramatization of *Nicholas Nickleby*," says he does not distinguish between material for the novel and that for drama, but even there he acknowledges that "a play is conditioned by the time it takes to perform it....the concentration is different."
4. Davies to Stone-Blackburn, February 1976.
5. Arthur Bryden, "New Yorkers Scout Love and Libel," *Globe and Mail* (7 October 1960), p. 28.
6. *Theatre Arts* (February 1961), p. 71.
7. Herbert Whittaker, "Davies Play Dazzling with Familiar Setting but Needs Sorting Out," *Globe and Mail*, final ed. (3 November 1960), p. 46.

8. Nathan Cohen, "Book into Play," *Toronto Daily Star* (3 November 1960).
9. John Gardiner, *Windsor Daily Star* (9 November 1960).
10. Davies to Stone-Blackburn, 16 August 1977.
11. James Forsyth, *Tyrone Guthrie* (London: Hamish Hamilton 1976), p. 270.
12. Tony Van Bridge to Stone-Blackburn, August 1977.
13. "Leaven of Malice," *Canadian Drama* 7:2 (1981), p. 166. All quotations from the play are from this text.
14. Davies to Stone-Blackburn, 3 March 1981.
15. Davies to Stone-Blackburn, February 1976.
16. *Leaven of Malice* (Toronto: Clarke, Irwin 1964), p. 207. All quotations from the novel are from this text.
17. Davies, preface to *Question Time* (Toronto: Macmillan 1975), pp. xi-xii.
18. Urjo Kareda, "*Leaven of Malice* an 'Ingeniously Sprung Trick-Box' on Stage," *Toronto Star* (13 October 1973), p. F3.
19. Urjo Kareda, "*Leaven of Malice* Earns Its Place," *Toronto Star* (30 May 1975), p. E4.
20. Herbert Whittaker, "*Leaven of Malice* Still Troubled," *Globe and Mail* (12 October 1973), p. 15.
21. Davies to Stone-Blackburn, February 1976.
22. Robertson Davies, "A Writer's Diary," *Calgary Herald* (5 November 1960), p. 7.
23. *Ibid*, (3 December 1960), p. 7.
24. Davies quoted by Herbert Whittaker, "Those Theatre Perils Are Tempting Robertson Davies Again," *Globe and Mail* (12 May 1973), p. 27.
25. Walter Kerr, "First Night Report: *Love and Libel*," "*New York Herald Tribune* (8 December 1960), p. 18.
26. Howard Taubman, "Theatre: Literary Humor," *New York Times* (8 December 1960), p. 44.
27. Harold Clurman, "Theatre," *The Nation* (24 December 1960), pp. 510-11.
28. Donald Davis says that he and Davies were "in touch" as Davies wrote *Hunting Stuart*, but they did not discuss *General Confession* (Davis to Stone-Blackburn, January 1982).
29. Herbert Whittaker, "Guthrie Opens *Love and Libel* Rehearsals," *Globe and Mail* (7 October 1960), p. 28.
30. Whittaker, "Those Theatre Perils ...," p. 27.

NOTES TO CHAPTER TEN:
PUNCH, DEMONIC HUMOUR, AND *THE BLACK ART*

1. The following account of Davies's activities is based on Gordon Roper's "A Davies Log," *Journal of Canadian Studies* 12:1 (February 1977) and John Ryrie's *Robertson Davies: An Annotated Bibliography* (Toronto: ECW Press 1981).
2. Richard B. Howard, U.C.C. Headmaster, to Stone-Blackburn, 8 December 1981.
3. *A Masque of Mr. Punch* (Toronto: Oxford University Press 1963), p. 5. All quotations from the play are from this text.
4. Davies to Stone-Blackburn, February 1976.
5. Davies's use of and variations from John Payne Collier's *Punch and Judy* (1828) are discussed by Judith Skelton Grant in *Robertson Davies* (Toronto: McClelland and Stewart 1978), p. 14, and by Rota Lister in "Masques for Boy Actors: Aesop and Punch Restored," *Canadian Drama* 7:2 (1981), p. 76.
6. Davies, *A Masque of Mr. Punch*, p. xi.
7. Davies, *A Voice from the Attic* (New York: Alfred A. Knopf 1960), p. 202.
8. *Ibid*, 249. Also *Stephen Leacock* (Toronto: McClelland and Stewart 1970), p. 51 and *Samuel March-*

banks' Almanack (Toronto: McClelland and Stewart 1967), p. 249.
9. Davies, *A Voice from the Attic*, p. 229.
10. *Ibid.*, pp. 228-29.
11. Davies quoted by Alan Twigg, *For Openers: Conversations with 24 Canadian Writers* (Madeira Park, B.C.: Harbour Publishing 1980), p. 33.
12. Davies, *A Voice from the Attic*, p. 217.
13. Davies, *Stephen Leacock*, pp. 26, 54.
14. Davies quoted by Donald Cameron, *Conversations with Canadian Novelists* (Toronto: Macmillan 1973), I, pp. 42-43.
15. Davies, *Stephen Leacock*, pp. 51, 26.
16. Robertson Davies, *World of Wonders* (Toronto: Macmillan 1975), p. 92.
17. Elspeth Buitenhuis [Cameron], *Robertson Davies* (Toronto: Forum House 1972), p. 34.
18. Lister, "Masques for Boy Actors," p. 77.
19. From a typescript of *The Centennial Play* in the Metropolitan Toronto Library.

20. Davies to Stone-Blackburn, 13 October 1981.
21. General notes to 14-page typescript in Davies's possession.
22. Davies to Stone-Blackburn, February 1976.
23. Davies to Stone-Blackburn, 13 October 1981.
24. Herbert Whittaker, "Those Theatre Perils Are Tempting Robertson Davies Again," *Globe and Mail* (12 May 1973), p. 27.
25. Accepted by Methuen in 1968 (Roper, "A Davies Log," p. 12) but not published until 1975 as part of *The Revels History of Drama in English*, Vol. VI, 1750-1880.
26. Published in *Stratford Papers 1968-1969*, ed. B.A.W. Jackson (Hamilton: McMaster University Library Press 1972).
27. Whittaker, "Those Theatre Perils...," p. 27.
28. *Ibid.*
29. Robertson Davies, *Brothers in the Black Art* (Vancouver: Alcuin Society 1981), p. 27. All quotations from the play are from this text.
30. Davies to Stone-Blackburn, 13 October 1981.

NOTES TO CHAPTER ELEVEN:
THE POLITICIAN IN SEARCH OF HIMSELF

1. Herbert Whittaker, "Those Theatre Perils Are Tempting Robertson Davies Again," *Globe and Mail* (12 May 1973), p. 27.
2. Davies, *One Half of Robertson Davies* (Toronto: Macmillan 1977), pp. 71-74.
3. Davies, "The Undiscovered Self," *Saturday Night* (24 May 1958); rpt. in *The Enthusiasms of Robertson Davies*, ed. Judith Skelton Grant (Toronto: McClelland and Stewart 1979), p. 177.
4. *Question Time* (Toronto: Macmillan 1975), p. 5. All quotations from the play are from this text.
5. Richard Plant, "Cultural Redemption in the Work of Robertson Davies," *Canadian Drama* 7:2 (1981), p. 46.

6. Scott Young, "Hero Gelding," *Globe and Mail* (28 February 1975), p. 27.
7. Bernard Shaw, *Complete Plays with Prefaces*, II (New York: Dodd, Mead 1965), pp. lxxxviii-lxxxix.
8. Davies, "Robertson Davies," *Stage Voices*, ed. Geraldine Anthony (Toronto: Doubleday 1978), pp. 68-69.
9. Davies, *One Half of Robertson Davies*, pp. 285-86.
10. Patricia Morley, *Robertson Davies* (Toronto: Gage 1977), pp. 56-57; Plant, "Cultural Redemption in the Work of Robertson Davies," p. 45; Michael Peterman, "Bewitchments of Simplification," *Canadian Drama* 7:2 (1981), p. 107; also reviewers of the St. Lawrence production.

11. Peterman, "Bewitchments of Simplification," p. 106.
12. Young, "Hero Gelding," p. 27.
13. Urjo Kareda, *"Question Time* Is a Grand Disaster," *Toronto Star* (26 February 1975), p. E20.
14. An exception is Patricia Monk, *"Question Time," Dalhousie Review* 55 (Winter 1975-76), p. 770.
15. William Lane, *"Question Time," Quill and Quire* 41:12 (3 November 1975), p. 24.
16. Though I consider these criticisms invalid, there is a perceptive criticism in a review by Ann P. Messenger ("Words and Images," *Canadian Literature*, 73 [Summer 1977], pp. 110-12), with which I concur. Messenger observes that the rational language of sequential thought that Davies uses is inconsistent with the play's visual presentation (and central premise) of a wandering mind, the mental space and time of the central character.
17. Kareda, *"Question Time* Is a Grand Disaster," p. E20.
18. Patricia Monk, "Quike Bookis: The Morality Plays of Robertson Davies," *Canadian Drama* 7:2 (1981), p. 88.
19. Davies to Stone-Blackburn, February 1976.
20. Davies quoted by Ann Saddlemyer, "A Conversation with Robertson Davies," *Canadian Drama* 7:2 (1981), p. 113.
21. Leon Major to Stone-Blackburn, 23 February 1976.

NOTES TO CHAPTER TWELVE: THE INNERMOST HEART

1. Davies to Stone-Blackburn, February 1976.
2. Martin Hunter and Ronald Bryden to Stone-Blackburn, 27 October 1977.
3. Davies, "Robertson Davies," *Stage Voices*, ed. Geraldine Anthony (Toronto: Doubleday 1978), p. 79.
4. *Pontiac and the Green Man* has not been published. My source is a 75-page acting copy used by Ronald Bryden in the role of Prevost, sent to me by Davies. There are a few changes in the typescript, written in by Bryden during rehearsals, which were approved by Davies (Davies to Stone-Blackburn, 20 July 1982). Before the first scene from *Ponteach* in the typescript, which is *Ponteach* I, ii, Bryden has written "Insert." Since I saw *Ponteach* I, i performed, I assume this was the substance of the insert. There may well have been other changes made which had no bearing on Bryden's role and which he did not record.
5. Bryden said they "all" used Cuneo and mentioned *Northwest Passage* as the source of the trial records, but Davies said he read only Parkman and the *D.N.B.* Because they consulted during the time Davies wrote the script, indirect influence from what Bryden and Hunter read is possible.
6. Davies to Stone-Blackburn, 27 October 1977. Davies made extensive cuts in the scenes from *Ponteach* he included, but he reproduced Rogers's lines verbatim. The rare and minor deviations from this practice were necessitated by the cuts.
7. Davies to Stone-Blackburn, 27 October 1977.
8. Davies, Epilogue, *At My Heart's Core & Overlaid*, (Toronto: Clarke, Irwin 1966), p. 112.
9. Davies to Stone-Blackburn, 27 Otober 1977.
10. *Ibid.*
11. Robertson Davies, "The Theatre," *The Arts as Communication*, ed. D. C. Williams (Toronto: University of Toronto Press 1962), pp. 27-29.
12. Bryan Johnson, "Pontiac Gets Lost in a Hopeless Muddle," *Globe and Mail* (27 October 1977), p. 15.
13. Mackenzie Porter, "Green Man Enthralling Colonial History,"

Toronto Sun (28 October 1977), p. 70.

14. Gina Mallet, "The Letdowns at Hart House Are Hurting," *Toronto Star* (7 November 1977), p. D6.
15. Robertson Davies, "Drama Criticism," *Globe and Mail* (29 October 1977).
16. Davies to Stone-Blackburn, 17 February 1981 and 27 October 1977. This disappointment did not prevent Davies from again teaming up with Holman in 1981, when Holman wrote the music and Davies the libretto for a children's opera.

17. Davies to Stone-Blackburn, 2 December 1981.
18. Martin Hunter to Stone-Blackburn, 27 October 1977.
19. A look through the *Canadian Theatre Review Yearbooks* for 1974-79 shows that Alden Nowlan and Walter Learning's Sherlock Holmes play *The Incredible Murder of Cardinal Tosca* is the single exception, with nine productions in the two years following its première; even the Chalmers Award-winning plays of James Reaney's Donnellys trilogy are neglected.

NOTES TO CHAPTER THIRTEEN: CONCLUSIONS

1. Davies, *One Half of Robertson Davies* (Toronto: Macmillan 1977), p. 185.
2. *Ibid.*, p. 181.
3. Davies quoted by Alan Twigg, *For Openers: Conversations with 24 Canadian Writers* (Madeira Park, B.C.: Harbour Publishing 1981), p. 40.

4. Tony Van Bridge to Stone-Blackburn, August 1977.
5. Davies, *One Half of Robertson Davies*, pp. 190, 194.
6. *Ibid.*, pp. 285-86.
7. Graham McInnes, "An Editor from Skunk's Misery Is Winning Fame for Peterboro," *Saturday Night* (26 April 1947), p. 15.

BIBLIOGRAPHICAL NOTE

Indispensable to any study of Davies's work is *Robertson Davies, an Annotated Bibliography*, ed. John Ryrie (ECW Press, 1981). Primary entries include published plays, of course; they also allow one to trace Davies's journalism, his reading (nearly a thousand book reveiws are included), and his public addresses. Secondary entries include theses and interviews as well as articles and books and selected reviews of Davies's books and performances of his plays. I found the play reviews especially helpful though I wished for a still more complete listing. My notes include some additional play reviews.

Two monographs, Elspeth Buitenhuis [Cameron]'s *Robertson Davies* (Forum House, 1972) in the Canadian Writers & Their Works series and Judith Skelton Grant's *Robertson Davies* (McClelland and Stewart, 1978) in the New Canadian Library's Canadian Writers series, devote

a few pages to the plays. Specifically focused on the plays is Patricia Morley's monograph, *Robertson Davies* (Gage, 1977) in The Profiles in Canadian Drama series. A full-length book by Patricia Monk, *The Smaller Infinity: The Jungian Self in the Novels of Robertson Davies* (University of Toronto Press, 1982) provides a useful exploration of Davies's affinity for Jungian thought, though it does not deal with the plays directly.

There are a number of books that record Davies's views on literature and theatre. In *A Voice from the Attic* (Alfred A. Knopf, 1960) Davies the reader writes about reading, and there is a chapter on plays as literature and one on humour. *One Half of Robertson Davies* (Macmillan, 1977) is a collection of Davies's speeches that includes a provocative series of lectures on evil in literature and a section, "Thoughts about

Writing," in which "The Conscience of the Writer" and "Jung and the Theatre" are particularly valuable. Judith Skelton Grant has edited two collections of Davies's articles, *The Enthusiasms of Robertson Davies* (McClelland and Stewart, 1979) which includes Davies's commentaries on favourite characters, books, and such life-long enthusiasms as Shakespeare, and *Robertson Davies, The Well-Tempered Critic: One Man's View of Theatre and Letters in Canada* (McClelland and Stewart, 1981), which includes Davies's "A Dialogue on the State of Theatre in Canada" among other articles on Canadian theatre throughout Davies's lifetime. *Stage Voices*, edited by Geraldine Anthony (Doubleday, 1978) is a collection of twelve Canadian playwrights's comments on their lives and plays that includes explicit commentary by Davies on his own plays.

A biography of Davies is not yet available, though Judith Skelton Grant has undertaken the project. Useful in this respect are journalistic profiles "The Myth and the Master," *Time* (Canada) (3 November 1975), pp. 8-12 and "The Masterful Actor who Plays Robertson Davies," *Saturday Night*, Vol. 90, No. 2 (June 1975), pp. 30-35, Gordon Roper's "A Davies Log" in *Journal of Canadian Studies'* special Davies issue, Vol. 12, No. 1 (February 1977), pp. 4-19,

and Davies's "Shakespeare over the Port" in *The Enthusiasms of Robertson Davies* and (as Samuel Marchbanks) "The Double Life of Robertson Davies," *Liberty* (April 1954), pp. 18-19, 53-58.

Studies of Canadian theatre history that bear directly on Davies's playwriting career are Betty Lee's *Love and Whisky* (McClelland and Stewart, 1973) about the Dominion Drama Festival and *Canadian Theatre Review*'s special issue on The Crest Theatre, *CTR* 7 (Summer 1975), as well as Davies's "A Dialogue on the State of Theatre in Canada," which appears in *CTR* 5 (Winter 1975), pp. 16-36 and in *Robertson Davies, The Well-Tempered Critic*. Davies describes twentieth-century theatre in English Canada in "Fifty Years of Theatre in Canada," *The University of Toronto Quarterly*, Vol. 50, No. 1 (Fall 1980), pp. 69-80. *Cue*, Montreal Repertory Theatre Magazine (1930-1961) is of interest for its chatty commentary on Little Theatre activities.

A generally valuable source of information on Davies's drama is *Canadian Drama*, Vol. 7, No. 2 (1981), a special Davies issue which includes a chronology and checklist, seven critical articles on the plays, an interview of Davies, and the script of *Leaven of Malice*.

INDEX

Acting, 33, 35
Actors, 4, 35, 46
Allegory, 21
Allen, John, 49
Amateur theatre, 11, 232n36; effect on plays, 31, 44; limitations of, 3-4, 35, 44-47, 51. *See also* Dominion Drama Festival; London Little Theatre; Montreal Repertory Theatre; North Toronto Theatre Guild; Ottawa Drama League; Peterborough Little Theatre
Androcles and the Lion, 40
Apollo, 93-94
The Apple Cart, 7
Applebaum, Louis, 182
Art: and life, 146-47; and message, 145-46; and heroism, 210, 215; truth in, 209; vs. virtue, 13-15, 88-89. *See also At My Heart's Core; Fortune, My Foe*
Arthur Sutherland International Players, 51, 69
As You Like It, 8
At My Heart's Core, 35, 71-91, 110, 116; art in, 78-80, 86-88, 89; and *Fortune, My Foe*, 71-72, 79, 81, 88, 89, 90, 226; and other plays, 51, 110, 131, 204, 222; cultural deprivation in, 77-79, 83-84, 181; history play, 29, 72, 89-90, 117, 133, 212; judgment in, 81-82; productions of, 90-91, 98; rebellion in, 71, 82, 85-86; subplot, 84-88, 89, 113, 120
At the Gates of the Righteous, 24-27, 237n7; composition of, 22, 231n28; conclusion of, 26-27; dialogue in, 26, 29; rebellion in, 30, 143; Shavian, 24-25
Atack, H.E., 94
Atkinson, W.A., 69

Bartholomew Fair, 153
Beattie, Rod, 218
Beckett, Samuel, 174, 175, 178, 223
Benoni, 9, 11, 36, 51, 98, 230n5. *See also A Jig for the Gypsy*
Bible, 23, 26
Birney, Earle, 45
Brantford Expositor, 5
Brothers in the Black Art, 183-87
Bryden, Ronald, 205, 218, 241n4

Cagliostro, 144
Callaghan, Morley, 232n31
Cameron, Elspeth Buitenhuis, 80, 98, 181
Canada Council, 46, 175
Canadian Repertory Theatre, 90
Carson, Neil, 234n10
Casanova: Memoirs, 132, 133, 140-41, 143, 144
CBC, 183, 221
The Centennial Play, 181-82, 197
The Centennial Spectacle, 182-83, 194
Chambers, Sir Edmund, 7
Characterization, 28
Chekhov, 33, 34, 44, 80
Chilcott, Barbara, 98, 113, 116, 131, 133, 149
Chorus, 42, 61, 63, 160, 161
Cicerci, Leo, 46
Clurman, Harold, 171
Coghill, Neville, 7
Cohen, Nathan, 70, 155
Colburne, Maurice, 7
Collier, John Payne, *Punch and Judy*, 176, 239n5
Comedy, 40-41
Corsican Brothers, The, 7
Coulter, John, 10; *Riel*, 232n31
Crest Theatre, 10, 132, 221; and *General*

Confession, 150, 222; and *Hunting Stuart*, 131; and *A Jig for the Gypsy*, 98, 110, 113
Critics, 80, 210
Cuneo, John R., *Robert Rogers of the Rangers*, 207-8

Davies, Brenda Mathews, 8-9, 11, 49, 69, 90, 218
Davies, Florence Sheppard McKay, 5-6
Davies, Jennifer, 9
Davies, Miranda, 9
Davies, Rosamond, 9
Davies, William Robertson: actor, 6, 8, 49; birth and childhood, 5-7; identified with characters, 35, 58, 227; director, 7, 10, 33, 49, 69, 89, 97; editor, 9, 22, 160; education, 6-8; humorist, 82, 88; journalist, 6, 7, 9; interest in music, 7; Marchbanks persona, 3-4, 4-5, 46-47, 49, 197; plays in youth, 6-7; reviewer, 9, 48, 90, 97-98, 172; stage-manager, 8; teacher, 8, 172-73
Davies, William Robertson: works of:
"Ben Jonson and Alchemy," 183
"The Canada of Myth and Reality," 198
"Casanova de Seingalt," 237n4
"Dialogue on the State of Theatre in Canada," 33-34, 35, 46-48, 68
The Diary of Samuel Marchbanks, 9, 23
"The Double Life of Robertson Davies," 6-9, 46-47, 51
Fifth Business, 106, 128, 151, 180, 183, 187, 188, 226, 232n28
Hunting Stuart and Other Plays, 183, 202
Introduction to *Love and Whisky*, 49
"Jung and the Theatre," 89
Leaven of Malice (novel), 9, 21, 22-23, 81, 98, 154, 156-59, 162-63, 164, 166, 168, 169
"Lost Scene from the Merry Wives of Windsor," 153
The Manticore, 115, 151, 183, 187, 188, 199, 200, 226, 232n28
"Masks of Satan," 80
A Mixture of Frailties, 21, 117, 154, 232n28, 234n13
The Rebel Angels, 107, 203
Samuel Marchbanks' Almanack, 9
Shakespeare's Boy Actors, 7-8, 11, 92
Shakespeare for Young Players, 9, 92
The Table Talk of Samuel Marchbanks, 9, 18
Tempest Tost, 5, 46, 47, 92, 229n3

A Voice from the Attic, 35, 115, 172, 179-80
World of Wonders, 180, 188, 194, 226, 232n28
"A Writer's Diary," 170, 172
See also play titles: *At My Heart's Core; At the Gates of the Righteous; Brothers in the Black Art; The Centennial Play; The Centennial Spectacle; Eros at Breakfast; Fortune, My Foe; General Confession; Hope Deferred; Hunting Stuart; King Phoenix; The King Who Could Not Dream; A Jig for the Gypsy; Leaven of Malice; A Masque of Aesop; A Masque of Mr. Punch; Overlaid; Pontiac and the Green Man; Question Time; Three Gypsies; The Voice of the People*
Davies, William Rupert, 5-6, 184, 186
Davis, Donald, 69, 98, 112, 113, 116, 131, 133, 149, 239n28
Davis, Murray, 98, 113, 116, 133, 149
Dawson, J.A., 94
Day, Marie, 182
Democracy, 95, 197
Denison, Merrill, 10; *Brothers in Arms*, 11
Devil, 74-77, 79-80
Dialogue, 22, 26, 29, 35-36, 120, 133
Dickens, Charles, *Great Expectations*, 6
Directors, 4, 47
Dominion Drama Festival, 4, 9, 10, 11; productions of Davies's plays, 19, 45, 48-49, 52, 69, 174, 176. *See also* Amateur theatre
Don Quixote, 54, 66-67, 175, 225
Doubling, 194
Dreams, 35-36, 143, 149; in plays, 38, 142, 149, 212-13
Dupee, E.W., 144

Edinburgh Festival, 19
Education, 46, 65-66, 68, 92-93, 173, 235n4
Emotion, 33, 34, 57-59, 175, 177-78; vs. intellect, 20-21, 30, 41
Endings, 26-27, 110-11, 130-31, 198
Eros at Breakfast, 19-22, 27, 28; criticism of, 19, 21; emotion vs intellect in, 20-21, 30, 41; Jungian theme in, 30, 116; prizes and productions of, 19, 31, 32, 45, 69; satire of Canadian dullness in, 21, source of, 19-20

Fairbairn, A.M.D., *Ebbtide*, 11
Fairy tale, 74, 71. *See also* Myth; Romance

Fantasy, 28, 233-24. *See also* Dream; Romance; Supernatural

Forsyth, James, 155-56

Fortune, My Foe, 29, 51-72, 112, 224, 226, 233n8, 233n12; art in, 60-66, 68, 83; Canadian theme of, 52, 69; and *Aesop*, 93-97; and *General Confession*, 145, 148; and *Heart's Core*, 87, 226; and *Hunting Stuart*, 120, 123; and *Jig*, 103, 107; and *Punch*, 175; and *Question Time*, 197, 204; and other plays, 94, 117; Don Quixote in, 66-67; double plot of, 53; education in, 65-67, 68; emotion in, 57-59; immigrants in, 53-63; productions of, 51-52, 69-70, 98, 232n36; scholars' struggle in, 54-57, 58, 60. *See also At My Heart's Core*

Freeman, David, 151

French, David, 151

Freud, Sigmund, 123, 132; *Wit and Its Relation to the Unconscious*, 179

Frontenac, Louis de Buade, 12-13

Gardner, David, 205, 206, 218

Gélinas, Gratien: *Tit-Coq*, 234n24

General Confession, 29, 115, 132-52, 222, 224; art and life in, 146-47; art and message in, 145-46; Casanova's *Memoirs* in, 133, 140-42; and *A Mixture of Frailties*, 154; and other plays, 116-17, 175, 194, 199, 204, 226; conception of, 132-33; criticism of, 150-52; dream in, 143, 149; judgment in, 148-49; Jungian plot of, 137-39; magic in, 142-43, 223; minor characters in 147-48; reason vs. intuition in, 144-45; unproduced, 149-50, 153, 171, 221, 222; writing as psychoanalysis in, 149-40

Geoffrey of Monmouth, *The History of the Kings of Britain*, 36, 38

Gielgud, Sir John, 8, 11, 48, 49, 221

Gilbert and Sullivan, 7

Gill, Robert, 69, 113

Glen, Donald, 90

Goldsmith, Oliver: *She Stoops to Conquer*, 8; *The Good Natured Man*, 8

Gray, John: *Bright Sun at Midnight*, 150; *Ride a Pink Horse*, 150

Grimaldi, Joey, 83-84, 91, 225

Guthrie, Tyrone: Davies's admiration for, 34, 48; director of *Love and Libel*, 154-55, 158, 171, 222; friend of family, 5-6, 8-9, 11; hired Davies at Old Vic, 8; influence on Davies, 194,

231-32n19; introduction to Davies's one-acts, 14, 15, 21, 27; shared projects, 97, 153, 182

Hamlet, 7

Hart House Theatre, 7, 69, 113, 156, 183, 205, 219

Hartman, Ron, 48

Helpmann, Max, 113, 131

Hero, 197, 210, 214-17

History in contemporary plays, 226. *See also Hunting Stuart*

History plays, 14-15, 29, 36, 51, 226. *See also At My Heart's Core; Hope Deferred; Pontiac and the Green Man*

Holman, Derek, 205, 242n16

Hope Deferred, 12-15, 28, 31, 45, 230n5; art vs. virtue in, 13-15, 88-89; and other plays, 18, 29, 52, 149, 225, 226; historical source and dramatic licence, 12-13, 230n5

Hope-Wallace, Philip, 52

Humour: Davies's, 5, 40, 115-16, 149; subject of study in *Fortune*, 56, 233n8; theory of in *A Voice from the Attic*; evident in *Punch*, 178-80

Hunt, Hugh, 8

Hunter, Judith, 218

Hunter, Martin, 156, 183, 205, 206, 220

Hunting Stuart, 115, 116-31, 222, 239n28; and other plays, 116-17, 120, 176, 194, 204; criticism of, 129, 131; heredity vs. environment in, 126-27; Jungian theme of, 115-117, 127-28, 225; magic in, 125-26; and *General Confession*, 29, 132, 137, 142, 145, 226; satire of scientists in, 120, 123-25; satire of the narrow-minded in, 120-22; structure of, 117, 130

Ibsen, Henrick, 8, 33, 34, 139-40

The Importance of Being Earnest, 18

Indians, 13-14, 84, 225. *See also Pontiac and the Green Man*

Individuality, 107-8, 112-13

Intellect, 190-91, 200-201. *See also* Emotion

Jarvis, Kenneth, 69-70

Jig for the Gypsy, A, 98-114, 115, 116, 120, and *Aesop*, 95; and *General Confession*, 143, 148; and *Hunting Stuart*, 116, 226, and *King Phoenix*, 116, 226; and *Punch*, 176; and *Question Time*, 195, 197, 204; individuality in, 107-8, 112-13; love in, 99, 101, 108-10; magic and intuition in,

100, 101, 104-7, 111; natural and supernatural in, 110, 111-12; politics in, 99, 101-2, 103, 107, 108; realism and romance in, 107, 110; satire and romance in, 98-99, 103, 110
Johnson, Bryan, 218-19
Johnson, Sydney, 45, 94
Jonson, Ben, 94, 103, 183; *Bartholomew Fair*, 153
Judgment, 81-82, 148-49, 208, 210-11
Jung, C.G., 123, 133, 236n2; in Davies's works, 30, 115-16, 125, 188, 224; in *General Confession*, 137-39, 144-45, 146, 148, in *Hunting Stuart*, 125, 128; in *Pontiac*, 212-13; in *Question Time*, 188, 199, 204; "Archetypes of the Unconscious," 137-39, 145; "Phenomenology of the Spirit in Fairy Tales," 145; *The Undiscovered Self*, 189. *See also* Dreams

Kareda, Urjo, 169, 202
Kerr, Walter, 171
King, Dennis, 155, 171
King Phoenix, 36-44, 48-50, 51, 116, 223, 224, 232n24, 236-37n9; and *Fortune* and *Heart's Core*, 51, 52, 61, 90; and *General Confession*, 148; and *Jig*, 107, 111, 116, 226; and *Question Time*, 204; and novels, 232n28; comedy and regeneration in, 40-41, 43; passion and intellect in, 41-42, 133; productions and criticism of, 48-50; ritual and myth in, 39-40, 44; theatrically of, 38-39; villain in, 42-43
The King Who Could Not Dream, 9, 11, 36, 51, 194, 230n1, 232n22
Kingston, Ont., 6, 51, 67

Lanctôt, Gustave, *A History of Canada*, 12
Langham, Michael, 153
LaPierre, Laurier, 218
Laufer, Murray, 182
Laval, François de Montmorency, 12
Leacock, Stephen, 154, 173, 179, 183
Learning, Walter, *The Incredible Murder of Cardinal Tosca*, 242n19
Leaven of Malice (play), 154-71, 176; adaptation considerations, 156-59; character development in, 167-69; criticism of, 155, 156, 169; Guthrie production tour, 154-56, 170-71; memory scenes in, 164-65; revivals of, 183, 205, 218; scenes that condense novel, 159-61; scenes translat-
ed directly to stage, 162-64; structure of, 167, 222; visual element of, 166-67
Le Cid, 13
Lee, Betty, *Love and Whisky*, 48-49
Leigh, Vivian, 8
Lennoxville Festival, 183
LePan, Douglas, "Coureurs de Bois," 198
LeSueur, William D., *Count Frontenac*, 12-13, 230n6
Lister, Rota, 181
Little Theatres. *See* Amateur theatre
London Little Theatre, 91
Love. *See Eros at Breakfast; King Phoenix; A Jig for the Gypsy; Hunting Stuart; General Confession*
Love and Libel, 154-56. *See also Leaven of Malice* (play)
Lyons Mail, The, 7

Macbeth, 8
Macdonald, Grant, 69, 97
McInnes, Graham, 226-27
Mackenzie, William Lyon, 71; Rebellion, 81, 85, 86
MacVannel, Earla, 28
Magic, 26, 38, 39, 111, 125-26, 142-43, 223-24, 225. *See also A Jig for the Gypsy*
Major, Leon, 203
Major Barbara, 40
Mallet, Gina, 219
Man and Superman, 7, 195
Marchbanks. *See* Davies, Marchbanks persona; Davies, works, *The Diary of Samuel Marchbanks*, "The Double Life of Robertson Davies," *Samuel Marchbanks' Almanack, The Table Talk of Samuel Marchbanks*
Martin-Harvey, John, 7, 34
Masque, 94
Masque of Aesop, A, 92-97, 157; and *Punch*, 173, 175, 180, 222; criticism of, 92-93, 96-97; education in, 92-93, 235n4; mob opinion vs. truth in, 94-95
Masque of Mr. Punch, A, 172-81, 222; criticism of, 180-81; Davies on humour in, 178-80; Punch as elemental man in, 175, 177-78; satire on modern taste in, 175-78
Massey College, 172-73
Melodrama, 34, 80, 223, 224
Merchant of Venice, The, 7
Merry Wives of Windsor, The, 7
Messenger, Ann P., 241n16
Midsummer Night's Dream, A, 7, 89, 233n12
Miller, Arthur, *Death of a Salesman*, 164

Mitchell, W.O., 181
Molière, 225; *Tartuffe*, 12
Montreal Repertory Theatre, 45
Moodie, Susanna, 72, 79, 181; *Roughing It in the Bush*, 78, 79
Moore, Dora Mavor, 7, 232n31
Moore, Mavor, 98; *The Ottawa Man*, 150
Monk, Patricia, 151
Morley, Patricia, 78-79, 98, 131, 151
Murphy, Arthur L., 181
Music, 35, 187, 225, 242n16; in plays, 16, 67, 94, 208, 211
Myth: and history, 90; Davies's fondness for, 5, 32, 36; in *At My Heart's Core*, 71; in *King Phoenix*, 36, 38, 40
Mythical era, 49, 50

Nature: and magic, 111-13; and man, 197-98, 225
Needles, William, 52
New, William, 131
New Play Society, 232n31
New York Theatre Guild, 154, 221
Nicholas Nickleby, 238n3
Nicol, Eric, 181
North Toronto Theatre Guild, 48
Nowlan, Alden, *The Incredible Murder of Cardinal Tosca*, 242n19; *Nugae Venales, or a Complaisant Complaint*, 233n8

O'Casey, Sean, 44
Oedipus Rex, 7
Old Vic Repertory Theatre, 8-9, 221, 226
One-act form, 32
O'Neill, Eugene, 7, 44
Opera. *See* Music
Ottawa Drama League, 18-19, 45, 69
Ottawa Little Theatre, 182
Overlaid, 15-19, 116; and *Hope Deferred*, 15, 18, 29, 226; and other plays, 22, 52, 67, 176; characterization in, 28; criticism of, 15, 18-19, 27, 31, 222; Pop lover of life in, 16-17, 18, 132; productions of, 19, 32, 45, 98; style of, 27-28; spiritual poverty in, 16, 18, 29
Oxford University, 7-8, 58, 226

Palmer, George A., *Madame Verite at Bath*, 11
Parkman, Francis, *The Conspiracy of Pontiac*, 207
Pearson, Lester, 175
Peterman, Michael, 112
Peterborough, Ont., 71

Peterborough Examiner, 9, 90, 172. *See also* Davies, editor
Peterborough Little Theatre, 10, 11, 49, 69, 89
Peterborough Summer Theatre, 90, 221
Phipps, Jennifer, 202
Pickthall, Marjorie, *The Woodcarver's Wife*, 11
Pinter, Harold, 223
Pirandello, Luigi, 7, 34
Plant, Richard, 194
Playwrights, Canadian, 3-5
Pogue, Kenneth, 195, 202
Politics. *See A Jig for the Gypsy; Question Time*
Pontiac, 205, 213
Pontiac and the Green Man, 205-20, 222; and *Question Time*, 29, 217-18, 225, 226; court and theatre alternate routes to truth in, 208, 210-11; criticism of, 218-20; Davies's hero, 212, 214-17; Davies's views of drama in, 209; heroism and art in, 210, 215; historical sources for, 205, 207-8, 241n5; production of, 205-6, 218; relationship between author and hero in, 212-13
Porter, Mackenzie, 218-19, 220
Priestley, J.B., *The Glass Cage*, 150
Primm, John, 90
Professional theatre, 10, 44, 46, 92, 97, 98, 115. *See also* Stratford; Crest

Queen's University, 7, 51
Question Time, 108, 188-204, 205, 222, 223, 225; and *Pontiac*, 129, 206, 216-18, 219, 220, 226; the beaver as national totem in, 195-97; Canadian physicians satirized in, 200; criticism of, 202-4, 241n16; hero vs. democratic leader in, 197; political satire in, 195; self smothered by professionalism in, 188-89; shaman as Jungian analyst in, 199-200; value of the irrational in, 200-202
Questors, 113

Realism, 27-28, 33-35; and romance, 107, 110. *See also* Theatricality
Reaney, James, 242n19
Reason, 144; and the irrational, 200-202. *See also* Emotion vs. intellect
Rebellion, 30, 71, 82, 85-86, 143
Religion, 13-15, 40, 62
Renfrew, Ont., 6
Richard II, 8
Ridley, Rev. Roy, 7

Ringwood, Gwen Pharis, *Still Stands the House,* 11
Ritual, 34-36, 38-39, 44, 112
Rittenhouse, Charles, 18-19, 69
Roberts, Kenneth, *Northwest Passage,* 207-8
Rogers, Robert, 205, 206, 213, *Ponteach,* 205, 206, 222, 241n6
Romance, 34, 36, 98-99, 107, 110, 116, 124-25. *See also* Fairy tale; Fantasy; Myth
Romanticism, Davies's, 5, 31, 32, 36
Romeo and Juliet, 8
Royal Society of Canada, 183
Ryga, George, 151

St. Lawrence Centre, 183, 188, 203, 204, 221
Saint-Vallier, Jean Baptiste, 12
Sandwell, B.K., 9, 70
Satire, 21, 22, 31, 94, 98-99, 103. *See also Hunting Stuart; A Jig for the Gypsy; A Masque of Mr. Punch; Question Time*
Saturday Night, 9, 48, 172
Science, 73, 78, 125-26
Scientists, 120, 123-25, 236-37n9
Scott, James, 52
Settings, 27-28, 33, 51
Shakespeare, 223, 233n12; Davies acts in or directs, 7, 8, 69; in Davies's education, 6, 7; in Davies's plays, 61, 174, 178. *See also* Stratford Shakespeare Festival
Shaw, G.B., 7, 34; Davies compared with, 24-25, 40, 195, 223
Shaw Festival, 156, 183
Simpson, Percy, 7
Sinclair, Lister, *The Man in the Blue Moon,* 232n31
Southgate, Rex, 218
Speaight, Robert, 69
Steinberg, M.W., 110
Stewart, Frances, 72, 75; *Our Forest Home,* 81
Stewart, Thomas, 72
Stratford Shakespeare Festival, 113, 238n29; Davies's enthusiasm for, 34,

48; Davies's work for, 4, 10, 97-98, 153; in *Mr. Punch,* 174-175
Straw Hat Players, 98, 113
Style, 27, 34-35
Supernatural, 37, 38, 110, 111-12
Sutherland, Arthur, 51, 69
Synge, J.M., 44

Tait, Michael, 15, 90
Taubman, Howard, 171
Thamesville, Ont., 5
Taming of the Shrew, The, 7-8, 69
Theatre design, 34
Theatricality, 5, 32, 33, 38. *See also* Realism
Thériault, Yves, 181
Thorndike, Sybil, 11, 221
Three Gypsies, 8, 229n12, 231-32n19
Tovell, Vincent, 90
Traill, Catharine Parr, 72
Traitor's Gate, 8
Trudeau, Margaret, 194
Trudeau, Pierre, 194-95
Twelfth Night, 7, 89

University of Toronto, 4, 172, 206, 218, 221. *See also* Hart House Theatre
Upper Canada College, 6-7, 92, 94, 96, 173, 180, 221

Van Bridge, Tony, 155, 156, 183, 223
Villains, 42-43
Voltaire, 144
Voice of the People, The, 22-24, 27, 30, 31, 94, 231n38

Wales, 5, 9, 58, 98, 227
Webster, John, *The Duchess of Malfi,* 201
Whittaker, Herbert, 112, 170, 183; director, 48-49, 98; reviewer, 129, 131, 155, 234n14
Williams, Tennessee, 174, 175, 178
Wilson, Colin, 143
Wilson, John, 110
World War II, 8-9
Wray, Maxwell, 48-49
Writing, as psychoanalysis, 139-40

Young, Scott, 202, 203